The Biblical Seminar
74

CIPHERS IN THE SAND

CIPHERS
IN THE SAND

Interpretations of the Woman
Taken in Adultery (John 7.53–8.11)

edited by
**Larry J. Kreitzer and
Deborah W. Rooke**

Sheffield Academic Press

Copyright © 2000 Sheffield Academic Press

Published by
Sheffield Academic Press Ltd
Mansion House
19 Kingfield Road
Sheffield S11 9AS
England

Typeset by Sheffield Academic Press
and
Printed on acid-free paper in Great Britain
by Biddles Ltd
Guildford, Surrey

British Library Cataloguing in Publication Data

A catalogue record for this book is available
from the British Library

ISBN 1-84127-141-1

CONTENTS

ABBREVIATIONS

AB	Anchor Bible
AL	*American Literature*
ANET	James B. Pritchard (ed.), *Ancient Near Eastern Texts Relating to the Old Testament* (Princeton: Princeton University Press, 3rd edn, 1969)
AQ	*The American Quarterly*
ASE	*Anglo-Saxon England*
ATQ	*American Translation Quarterly*
AV	Authorized Version
Bib	*Biblica*
BSac	*Bibliotheca Sacra*
BTB	*Biblical Theology Bulletin*
BZ	*Biblische Zeitschrift*
BZAW	Beihefte zur *ZAW*
BZNW	Beihefte zur *ZNW*
CBC	Cambridge Bible Commentary
CChr	Corpus Christianorum
CHR	*Catholic Historical Review*
EETS	Early English Text Society
ELH	*English Literary History*
ICC	International Critical Commentary
JAS	*Journal of American Studies*
JBL	*Journal of Biblical Literature*
JETS	*Journal of the Evangelical Theological Society*
JSNTSup	*Journal for the Study of the New Testament*, Supplement Series
JSOT	*Journal for the Study of the Old Testament*
JSOTSup	*Journal for the Study of the Old Testament*, Supplement Series
JTS	*Journal of Theological Studies*
LFQ	*Literature/Film Quarterly*
LP	*Literature and Psychology*
LSE	*Leeds Studies in English*
MFS	*Modern Fiction Studies*
MGH	Monumenta Germaniae Historica
MLN	*Modern Language Notes*
MLS	Modern Language Studies

NCBC	New Century Bible Commentary
NCF	*Nineteenth-Century Fiction*
NEB	*New English Bible*
NEQ	*New England Quarterly*
NHR	*The Nathaniel Hawthorne Review*
NRSV	New Revised Standard Version
NovT	*Novum Testamentum*
NTS	*New Testament Studies*
ÖTBK	Ökumenische Taschenbuch-Kommentar zum Neuen Testament
PL	J.-P. Migne (ed.), *Patrologia cursus completus…* *Series prima [latina]* (221 vols.; Paris: J.-P. Migne, 1844–65)
PMLA	*Proceedings of the Modern Language Association*
PQ	*Philological Quarterly*
RB	*Revue biblique*
REB	Revised English Bible
RSV	Revised Standard Version
RV	Revised Version
SAF	*Studies in American Fiction*
SBLDS	Society of Biblical Literature Dissertation Series
SN	*Studies in the Novel*
SEÅ	*Svensk exegetisk årsbok*
SL	*The Scarlet Letter*
SR	*The Sewanee Review*
TBC	Torch Bible Commentary
TLS	*Times Literary Supplement*
TOTC	Tyndale Old Testament Commentaries
TRHS	*Transactions of the Royal Historical Society*
VT	*Vetus Testamentum*
WBC	Word Biblical Commentary
ZAW	*Zeitschrift für die alttestamentliche Wissenschaft*
ZNW	*Zeitschrift für die neutestamentliche Wissenschaft*

LIST OF CONTRIBUTORS

Mark Atherton, Regents Park College, Oxford

Elizabeth Green, Bari, Italy

Larry Kreitzer, Regents Park College, Oxford

Tom O'Loughlin, University of Wales, Lampeter

Deborah Rooke, Regents Park College, Oxford

Jayne Scott, Scottish Churches Open College

Martin Scott, Edinburgh

Jane Shaw, Regents Park College, Oxford

INTRODUCTION: THE CULTURAL RECEPTION OF JOHN 7.53–8.11

Jane Shaw

Literary critics and cultural historians have, in the past few decades, increasingly emphasized the cultural circulation and reception of texts. Many literary critics have therefore privileged an analysis of the reader's (or readers') response to a text over a reading of the text's form or consideration of the author's intentions. This literary-critical impulse has had widespread influence within biblical hermeneutics in recent years.[1] In turn, cultural historians have emphasized the contexts in which texts or stories have been interpreted, tracing the history of a story's or text's reception and thus its impact in a given community. In any society, some texts hold particular cultural power and are therefore regarded as having some manifestation of 'truth' to pass on to every generation. Hans-Georg Gadamer (1984) calls such a text a 'classic', and the interpretations of such a text its 'effective history'. The pre-eminent example of such a classic text in the West is, of course, the Bible.[2] Within the Bible there are particular stories which capture the imagination of many generations, and therefore come to be invested with a particular power. The literary critic Mieke Bal has named such texts 'ideo-stories'.

About four years ago, Larry Kreitzer and I were at an inter-disciplinary conference on religion in Prague, and we began discussing the ways in which certain biblical stories have especially powerful and interesting histories. This was in a city where the power of story and the significance of cultural and communal memory are richly illustrated by

---

1. For the literary-critical approach, see, e.g., Tompkins (1980) and Fish (1980). For an example of the influence on biblical hermeneutics, see Schüssler Fiorenza (1984).

2. Non-religious myths and stories also hold enormous cultural power in our Western society. For a historical and literary approach to this subject, see, e.g., the work of Marina Warner (1996, 1995).

the continuing importance to Czech identity of Jan Hus, the proto-Protestant martyr of 600 hundred years ago. As colleagues from different academic disciplines, we thought how exciting it would be to track the reception or 'effective history' of one particularly potent biblical text (or 'ideo-story') from its writing to the present day, drawing on the work of scholars in the fields of biblical studies, systematic and pastoral theology, and historical and literary studies. The result is this book.

The story of the woman taken in adultery (Jn. 7.53–8.11) was selected because its themes about gender and sexuality, and judgment and forgiveness, touch on issues which are at the heart of any discussion about the place of marriage in the structures and arrangement of society, and have therefore been echoed throughout the centuries in many cultural forms. As Larry Kreitzer expresses it in his own article: 'Within the great literature of the world there are many tales of fallen women, sad and heart-breaking women who have been caught in the snare of an illicit relationship and are made to bear the social consequences of it. The theme is an enduring one and seems to capture the imagination of every age and every culture'.

Deborah Rooke's article, which opens this collection, underscores how deep and long are the societal origins of such a theme. Setting the scene for the context in which the story of the woman taken in adultery would have been received in Jesus' and early Christian times, Rooke points to the ways in which the primary characteristics of the Israelite marriage relationship was the fundamental inequality of the man and woman. Because authority was based in the male head of the household, and the household was (as in so many other societies since) the basic unit of the State, that authority had to be maintained. The problem of a women committing adultery was not one of purity, but rather that such an act brought with it the potential that she might bear another man's children, and too, brought shame on her husband whose authority was thereby threatened.

The world of Nathaniel Hawthorne's novel *The Scarlet Letter*—seventeenth-century Puritan New England—was not so differently structured from ancient Israel or first-century Palestine in terms of marriage and the household. The household was still, for Puritans, 'a little commonweal' or a miniature state (this was not yet the time of the private family of modernity). If order was to be maintained in the State, then order must be maintained in the household: male authority had to remain intact. Kreitzer, in his exploration of this classic novel and subsequent film adaptations of the story, illustrates the ways in which the themes of adultery and transgression are explored in similar ways in the story from John of the woman taken in adultery and in Hawthorne's novel. A religious society such as the Massachusetts Bay Colony of the seventeenth century, which was consciously built on biblical models of society, took up not only the structures, but also the attitudes of those models. We should not be surprised, then, that Hawthorne has many themes in his novel that parallel themes in the biblical story. Kreitzer explores these parallel themes, such as the place of accusation in both texts. He demonstrates the ways in which both stories rely upon a hostile crowd; the absent or hidden male adulterous partner; secret signs (Jesus scribbling ciphers in the sand, or Hester Prynne's scarlet 'A') and the space of the temple or church for the accusation itself. The message of compassion and grace in the face of a hostile and condemning crowd is therefore of central theological concern to both texts in their exploration of the effects of transgression and judgment on both the transgressors and the judges in any patriarchal society.

The endurance of these themes in our own day is investigated by Jayne Scott in her essay on the violence shown towards women in contemporary society, and the responsibility which Christianity must bear for perpetuating the attitudes that have promoted such violence. Scott outlines the prevailing assumptions which allow violence against women to continue in many places unchallenged: men in authority have a right to be there; women should be blamed for their so-called complicity with the violence; women who accept violence to protect others (e.g. children) are weak. She illustrates some of the ways in which such attitudes have been perpetuated by Christian thinkers, ranging from Tertullian in the second and early third centuries to the Dominican authors of the witch-hunting document in the fifteenth century, *Mallaeus Maleficarum*, and then contrasts such attitudes with those of Jesus in the story of the woman taken in adultery. For Jesus both refused to accept the validity of violence as a means of maintaining male authority, and questioned the societal structures which required that male authority. In taking that stance, Jesus exposed the sin of the judgmental accusers and, if we are to take a lesson for our own context, illustrated how important it is for a man, who has voice and power, to speak out against violence and male authority.

The emancipatory potential of the story is explored by Elizabeth Green, who examines the (surprisingly few) feminist readings of the text in John. She notes that Jesus, his ability to sidestep the trap set for him by the Pharisees, and his subsequent compassion for the women have been the focus of feminist attention. Thus the figure of Jesus in this story 'overturns hierarchies of sin and status...restoring honour to that which is marginalized', as one feminist commentator considered by Green puts it. While sympathetic to the feminist scholars who, noting the woman's silence in this story, have tried to reconstruct her experience, Green nevertheless places her emphasis on the theological significance of the story. If one of the dilemmas faced by feminists within Christianity is to make sense of female suffering vis-à-vis the crucified and suffering Christ, then a story such as this may enable us 'to see in the woman caught in adultery an icon of the Christ'. As Green concludes, 'if Christ becomes symbolically female to redeem the victims of patriarchy, then the women taken in adultery becomes an icon of the risen Christ'.

This is a radical and innovative theological reading of the story, and it may point to the ways in which the story's emancipatory possibilities have led to its unstable history within the Christian canon and tradition. For, as Martin Scott explains, the text's inclusion in the New Testament canon was not in any way simple. While the story clearly had a life in the early Christian churches, its status was not secure: it was initially excluded from the canonical Gospels and was only included in the fourth Gospel later. One of the ironies of the story of the woman taken in adultery is that 'Jesus' opponents, who seek to condemn another of adultery, themselves come under such suspicion and innuendo within a matter of a few years!' This twist in the story, coupled with the early Church's strict disciplinary codes about sexual sin, suggest reasons why the story may have been viewed with suspicion and anxiety by many early Christians. Scott suggests that by the fourth century the Church's disciplinary codes about sexuality were well established, at which point the text could be allowed into the canon; the climate was such that its 'theologically explosive content' has been tamed and could be handled by the Church's male power structures. Scott ends, like Green, with an innovative interpretation of the text: namely, that the woman was *not* guilty, as so many commentators over the centuries have presumed, but was in fact innocent and was released from injustice by Jesus. Scott therefore looks forward to the ways in which 'this unjustly treated woman, along with her parallel sister figure Susanna, (can) finally begin to celebrate her true liberation from male oppression'.

Thomas O'Loughlin echoes some of Martin Scott's themes of inclusion and exclusion in his analysis of the treatment of the text by the Latin fathers, noting that only four of them give it more than cursory treatment: Ambrose, Jerome, Augustine and Cassidorus. The story's inconvenience to husbands and its challenge to deep-seated male fears about female sexuality may account for its lack of prominence in the writings and preaching of the Latin fathers. As Augustine himself noted, this was a text which many found sensitive and which went against the norms of his society.

Mark Atherton likewise points to the relatively few treatments of the story of the woman taken in adultery in Anglo-Saxon literature. Nevertheless, the Anglo-Saxon texts which do explore this story illustrate an interesting point: the ways in which the writers recast the biblical story to fit their own environment and literary genres allow it to resonate with other literary works of the period, and thus 'speak' to a newly converted people.

The essays gathered in this book provide a rich survey of the ways in which this evocative story from John's Gospel about the woman taken in adultery has resonated in myriad ways in many times and places. They afford a glimpse of the history of the reception of the text in an exemplary inter-disciplinary manner. But they do something more: they each provide exciting new insights into the text for our own day, adding to its 'effective history'. If we are to draw a conclusion from the book it is that the emancipatory potential of this story from John has been repeatedly ignored, tamed and side-stepped. In this, they are surely providing a particular instance of a larger theological theme which runs throughout the history of Christianity: that is, the gap between the liberating potential of Jesus' words and actions as presented by the Gospel writers, and the largely conservative agenda of the churches down the centuries. Therefore, this history of the reception of Jn 7.53–8.11 provides a challenging illustration of the ways in which the Christian churches, when faced with the egalitarian promise of the early Jesus movement, have repeatedly capitulated to the world's patriarchal values.

BIBLIOGRAPHY

Fish, Stanley
 1980 *Is There a Text in This Class? The Authority of Interpretative Commu-
     nities* (Cambridge, MA: Harvard University Press).
Gadamer, Hans-Georg
 1984 *Truth and Method* (New York: Crossroad).
Schüssler Fiorenza, Elisabeth
 1984 *Bread Not Stone: The Challenge of Biblical Feminist Interpretation*
     (Boston: Beacon Press).
Tompkins, Jane P. (ed.)
 1980 *Reader-Response Criticism: From Formalism to Post-Structuralism*
     (Baltimore: The Johns Hopkins University Press).
Warner, Marina
 1976 *Alone of All Her Sex: The Myth and Cult of the Virgin Mary* (London:
     Weidenfeld & Nicholson, 1976).
 1995 *From the Beast to the Blonde: On Fairy Tales and their Tellers* (London:
     Vintage, 1995).

WAYWARD WOMEN AND BROKEN PROMISES: MARRIAGE, ADULTERY AND MERCY IN OLD AND NEW TESTAMENTS[*]

Deborah W. Rooke

At the beginning of a collection of essays based around the New Testament story of the woman taken in adultery (Jn 7.53–8.11), it might seem rather strange to have a piece that is as much to do with Old Testament themes as it is with the New Testament episode just mentioned. However, justification for this is not difficult to provide, and indeed, seems almost superfluous, since it is universally agreed that the New Testament's dependence upon the Old makes an understanding of the Old Testament an essential tool in the equipment of those who are looking for a better understanding of the New. It is this desire that has led to the inclusion of the present piece in the current collection. The intention here is to examine Old Testament material that deals with the area of marital relationships, especially material in which the issue of adultery arises, in the hope of being able to shed fresh light on the story of the woman taken in adultery. The task will be pursued under three main headings: (1) Old Testament legislation concerning marriage and adultery; (2) the use of marriage as a metaphor for the relationship between Israel and Yahweh; and (3) Jesus and the woman taken in adultery. The three sections are interconnected in that the first section will discuss the Old Testament laws about marriage and the principles behind them, while the second and third sections will be examples of Old and New Testament texts that can profitably be read in the light of the conclusions drawn from that discussion.

* I am grateful to the members of the Old and New Testament Seminar at King's College London for their helpful and encouraging comments in response to a pre-publication presentation of this essay.

1. *Old Testament Legislation Concerning Marriage and Adultery*

It is easy to assume that because of surface similarities between mar-riage as it appears in the Old Testament context and marriage as it appears in present-day Western society, the understanding of the insti-tution in the two contexts is also similar. However, this is not the case. Certainly in both contexts marriage can be defined as the legally recognized joining of a man and a woman as lifelong partners; but the rationale and the conceptual framework behind such joining in the ancient context differ in several significant respects from their modern counterparts. Modern-day Western ideas about marriage are increas-ingly influenced by the concept of equal rights for all that is a hallmark of our society, and although it would be foolish and blatantly untrue to say that in the light of this every modern Western marriage is conceived and run as a partnership of equals, it is generally true to say that, at least in the eyes of the law, adult men and women are regarded as equal in that they have equal rights to self-determination and to recourse to the law for protection and justice.

However, this is a very different scenario from that formed by the principles governing marriage in the society that framed the Old Testament laws about marriage. It is by now a commonplace in biblical scholarship, particularly in anthropological and feminist circles, that the Old Testament reflects a society in which female sexuality was under the control of and at the disposal of males;[1] and one of the places where this can be seen most clearly is in the legal material relating to mar-riage, adultery and divorce. The most extensive set of provisions con-cerning these matters is found in the book of Deuteronomy, where there are three relevant blocks of legislation: 22.13-29, 24.1-4 and 25.5-10. In 22.13-29 are what might be called laws on sexual conduct, and these certainly reflect the concept of male dominance in matters of sexuality. Their most notable feature is that whenever an irregular sexual union occurs, its severity is assessed and damages are awarded according to the male party who has been offended. This is evidenced by two facts: first, nowhere is the marital status of the offending male referred to, whereas in every case the marital status of the woman is what deter-mines the punishment; and secondly, even when an unmarried woman is violated there is a male party to be compensated, namely her father.

---

1.   Mace 1953: 227; Pressler 1994: 103.

Thus, the man who slanders his bride by falsely claiming that she was not a virgin has to compensate her father for the slander (22.13-19), and a bride who (presumably by choice) is not a virgin is to be stoned on her father's doorstep in order to emphasize how she has shamed him (22.20-21).[2] Once a woman is married (or betrothed, which was as binding as marriage), she is bound to her husband in all matters of sexual activity, and if a married or betrothed woman is discovered with another man then both she and her partner are to be put to death (Deut. 22.22-24; cf. Lev. 20.10). Once again, the rationale for the punishment includes a reference to the offended male party (22.23); the man is to be put to death not because he has violated the woman as such, but because he has appropriated another man's wife. However, where a man seizes upon an unattached virgin and is discovered, the punishment is not death for either of them; rather, the man must marry the woman with no possibility of divorce (Deut. 22.28-29; cf. Exod. 22.16-17 [Heb. 14-15]). The point of this stipulation is that a deflowered virgin was

2.   Phillips (1981: 10) views this as the community's expression of disapproval against the father for allowing his daughter to become pregnant while in his care. But the main point to note is the very tangible link between bride and father: she is not just put to death on her own account, but because of the shame incurred by another male through her actions.

Wenham (1972: 330-36) argues that this provision is not concerned with a bride's suspected lack of virginity at the time of her marriage, but with the case of a bride who has committed post-betrothal adultery and as a result may already be pregnant with another man's child by the time she consummates the marriage with her husband. Wenham claims (330) that the seduction of an unbetrothed girl was a fairly minor offence (Deut. 22.28-29), and that because unbetrothed girls who were caught in intercourse escaped 'scotfree' (332), the death penalty for the guilty bride in this case therefore suggests that the crime being punished was effectively adultery (332-33). However, the scenario pictured in Deut. 22.20-21 is one where neither the father nor the prospective husband had prior knowledge of the woman's condition, so the case of the unbetrothed girl *caught* in an illicit liaison is not relevant, and the restriction of the supposed offence to post-betrothal adultery becomes arbitrary. If the father is genuinely unaware of his daughter's condition, rather than knowingly trying to marry off a violated girl to an unsuspecting husband, then there will be no way of telling whether the illicit act took place before or after betrothal. Also, Wenham's claim that the law focuses on a subsequent suspicion of pregnancy rather than on an initial absence of virginity seems unlikely, since surely the lack of virginity would be discovered before any other signs of pregnancy became apparent. See also n. 27 below for Wenham's argument that the term *bᵉtûlâ*, usually translated 'virgin', is more appropriately translated 'girl of marriageable age'.

extremely unlikely ever to find a husband, and this situation represented one of financial loss for her father who would receive no bride price for her and would have to continue to support her.[3] Hence, marrying her to the man who had violated her was a way of mitigating the effects of such loss, however undesirable the match might be.[4] The fact that the man might already be married was immaterial, since male polygamy was permissible, if rare outside the upper classes (cf. Deut. 21.15-17; 1 Sam. 1.1-2).

Further Deuteronomic examples of the control claimed by males over female sexuality are in the law of divorce (Deut. 24.1-4) and the so-called levirate marriage (Deut. 25.5-10). As far as divorce is concerned, it is apparently a male prerogative; there is no equivalent law enabling a woman to divorce her husband. Indeed, the very concept of a female right to initiate divorce seems nonsensical in a society where lone women would often have found it extremely difficult to subsist. No indication is given of the grounds on which divorce was deemed legitimate, beyond the fact that the husband finds 'some indecency' in his wife.[5] It is unlikely that this would have referred to lack of sexual purity, because the penalty for that would be death rather than divorce; beyond that, however, it could have been something extremely trivial to which the husband simply took exception.[6] The custom of levirate marriage is more about preservation of the male line and a man's property than it is about control of female sexuality,[7] but it engages the female sexuality

3. Pressler 1994: 104-105.
4. The law in Exod. 22.16-17 [Heb. 14-15] allows the woman's father the right to refuse permission for the marriage, but this right is not mentioned in Deut. 22.28-29. It is difficult to say which is the more humane scenario from the woman's point of view; in both cases the interests served are primarily those of the woman's father instead of those of the woman herself.
5. Stienstra (1993: 85-87) argues that childlessness and adultery were probably the main reasons for divorce, although she notes that there is no direct indication in the Old Testament of divorce because of childlessness and all the examples of divorce on the grounds of adultery are provided by the marriage metaphor (Hos. 2.2; Isa. 50.1; Jer. 3.8). See also Mace (1953: 250-51).
6. Mace 1953: 255-56; Phillips 1973: 159-60; Mayes 1979: 322. Thompson (1974: 243) conjectures that 'some immodest exposure or unwomanly conduct is meant'.
7. Frick disagrees with this, suggesting that the levirate custom was 'concerned just as much, if not more, with the support and protection of the widow as it is with the perpetuation of family property within the immediate family' (1994: 147).

for its own ends, and illustrates the male right of disposal over female sexuality. The widow of a son-less man must be prepared to marry her dead husband's brother, who will then attempt to father a son with her; this son will be deemed the son of the dead man and will bear his name, thereby protecting the family's property rights.[8] Although this arrangement would certainly provide some kind of security for the widow by giving her a new husband, the primary aim is the perpetuation of the dead man's name via the begetting of a son to inherit his property, as is evidenced by the procedure for when a man refuses to take his brother's wife in this way. There is a public ceremony of shaming for the unwilling suitor, not on the grounds of his failure to provide for the woman's welfare, but on the grounds of his failure to build up his brother's house in Israel (Deut. 25.9-10). The whole levirate concept also means that the childless widow is not free to marry the man of her own choice until she has been formally released from her obligation to marry her brother-in-law.

The Priestly legislation is less comprehensive in its coverage of marital matters, dealing only with the questions of adultery and suspected adultery within established marriages.[9] However, its coverage in these areas displays the same kind of attitudes towards female sexuality as are found in Deuteronomy. As in Deuteronomy, adultery consists of sexual intercourse between a married woman and a man apart from her husband, and is punishable by death for both parties (Lev. 20.10); and like the Deuteronomic provisions for divorce, the trial by ordeal for suspected adultery (Num. 5.11-31) is a 'men only' prerogative. A man who suspects his wife of unfaithfulness is entitled to bring her before the priest and subject her to a ritual which will determine by its results whether or not his suspicions were groundless.[10] If they were—that is, if the outcome of the ritual is favourable, whatever that might mean in

---

8. Davies (1981: 141-42) argues that the concept of 'name' is bound up with that of 'inheritance', and that the way to preserve a man's name was to keep his property in the family. He cites the example of the daughters of Zelophehad who claim an inheritance among their father's brothers so that the name of their father should not be taken away from his family (Num. 27.4).

9. Lev. 18.6-23 and 20.11-21 cover the question of forbidden and incestuous sexual/marital relationships, but the only matters of conduct in licit marriage relationships that are covered in P are adultery and the trial of the suspected adulteress.

10. Phillips (1981: 8) regards Num. 5.11-31 as 'an ancient paternity rite designed to determine the legitimacy of the husband's children'.

reality—there is no comeback for the wife, no redressing of the balance; and there is no equivalent ritual for a woman who may suspect her husband of adultery, since the concept of a wife being damaged by her husband's adultery is largely meaningless. Men who engaged in extra-marital sexual relations could not transgress against their own marriage, but only against the marriage of another man if the other woman was another man's wife.

In the light of this summary, therefore, it is abundantly clear that a primary characteristic of the Israelite marriage relationship was the fundamental inequality of the male and female parties involved in it. The rights of males over female sexuality meant that women were in a position of subordination and dependence, and although wives were certainly not slaves, neither were they free to be self-determining in the way that their husbands were, since rights over another person's sexuality can only be exercised at the cost of that individual's personal autonomy.[11] The result of this is that it is possible to speak of a double standard which shows itself most particularly in the area of sexual mores. What was acceptable sexual behaviour for men was subject to severe condemnation when it was practised by women. This is illustrated particularly clearly by the story of Judah and Tamar (Gen. 38). Both Judah and his daughter-in-law Tamar are widowed, but whereas Judah's status means that he has no immediate sexual loyalty to anyone, and is free to bestow his sexual favours on whomsoever he pleases, Tamar is supposedly to keep herself in readiness for the time when Judah decides to allow his surviving son to marry her in accordance with the levirate custom, despite the fact that as time goes on it becomes increasingly unlikely that this will ever happen. When Judah sleeps with a woman he regards as a prostitute, even though others find out about it there is no evil consequence for him to fear other than loss of dignity when he is unable to find the woman in order to deliver the promised payment (Gen. 38.20-23).[12] However, once Judah hears that Tamar has

---

11. In commenting on Deut. 22.13-29, Cunliffe-Jones (1951: 129) observes, 'While these laws bring the main offender sternly to task, they do not treat women fully as persons having an adequate status which must be taken fully into account. They helped rather than hindered that goal, but in themselves they do not embody it.'

12. Mace (1953: 235) argues that the reason for Judah's embarrassment is because he is afraid of it getting around that he had been with a religious prostitute; but contemporary scholarship has thrown considerable doubt on the existence of

been involved in prostitution, he orders her to be burned (Gen. 38.24), and it is only the revelation that she is the 'prostitute' with whom Judah himself had slept that saves her. No matter how much genuine affection and love there may in fact have been between husbands and wives in ancient Israel, at bottom the inequality remained, and a husband (or male for whom a woman was destined, whether actually or potentially)[13] was entitled to the exclusive sexual loyalty of his wife even though the wife was not entitled to expect the same from her husband.[14]

This desire to control female sexuality is rooted in the patriarchal structures of Israelite society, which were based on the principle that authority was vested in the male head of the household. Hence, because men were the ruling class, their needs and desires were what determined societal structures and mores. Three factors in particular can be cited as lying behind the attitude towards women. First, Israel was what

religious prostitution as such in Israel. For further discussion of supposed religious prostitution in Israel, see n. 42 below. Hugenberger (1998: 325) argues that Judah fears intense social stigma for having consorted with a prostitute; but it seems more likely that he fears the loss of face involved in having been taken advantage of by a woman.

13. Cf. Pressler (1994: 107 n. 10): '...according to Deuteronomy 22:20-21, a woman who enters into a first marriage as a non-virgin violates her husband's claims to her sexuality, claims that are retroactive'. The example of Judah and Tamar implies that the same is true for a levirate-obligated widow who engages in extra-marital sexual activity. Although she is not a virgin and has already been married, she nevertheless retroactively violates the claim to her sexuality of her potential husband. See also Bird (1989: 77). Hence, Hugenberger's citation of Tamar as an example of a *single* woman whose extra-marital sexual activity is a matter of grave concern is incorrect (1998: 319, 326). Because Tamar is under the levirate obligation she is regarded as being in the same position as a betrothed woman, even though she is a widow without a husband.

14. Hugenberger (1998: 313-38) disputes the existence of the double standard, and argues that sexual fidelity was expected from husbands as much as from wives. However, the very fact that polygamy (more precisely, polygyny) was permissible, as already noted, means that the understanding of what constituted 'sexual fidelity' must have been different from the present-day Western understanding. Also, as remarked above, nowhere in the Deuteronomic legislation is the adulterous man's marital status even mentioned, let alone used as a factor in determining the seriousness of the offence committed; and the status of the violated woman determines which *male* party on *her* side (i.e. husband or father) has been offended (Deut. 22.22, 24, 29). There is no sense there that a man's adultery can hurt his own wife. See also n. 16 below.

is known as a 'male seed' society; in other words, there was no concept of a child being the product of both male and female gametes. Rather, in the Israelite world-view men provided the seed and women the soil for the nurture of a new life, so that women were viewed as carriers of sown seed rather than as contributing partners in the creative process, and to that extent secondary to men. Secondly, in a society where the only concept of life after death was an earthly one—that is, the survival of the family line rather than of the individual—the overwhelming need was for a man to beget sons in order that they, as seed-bearers, could continue his family line.[15] To do this, he obviously needed a wife or wives who could incubate his own seed, as it were, and so nurture his sons. If a wife committed adultery, she could end up nurturing another man's sons, which was a threat to the purity of the line and therefore to the continuance of her husband's family. Finally, in a patriarchal society, an important element of being a man was having control over the women for whom one was responsible, both to protect them from other harmful influences and to engender obedience in them. Hence, a wife's adultery was not merely an emotionally damaging crime against her husband or a threat to his line of descent, it was a crime which brought shame upon him as a man, since it indicated either that he was unable to protect his women against other men, or that he was unable to engender obedience in his women, or both.[16] Such a slight had of course to be made good.

15. Phillips 1981: 7.

16. For a discussion of these issues, see White (1995: 16-18); Stone (1996: 41-46). This seems to be the light in which to interpret the stories of Shechem and Dinah (Gen. 34) and Tamar, Amnon and Absalom (2 Sam. 13). Hugenberger (1998: 326-27) uses these two stories, along with that of Judah and Tamar (Gen. 38), to support his contention that there was no 'double standard' in Israelite marriage and men were just as obliged to be faithful to their wives as wives were to their husbands (313). As part of this argument he claims that the three stories demonstrate that sexual activity on the part of unmarried women was a matter of great concern, and so the idea that men could sleep with other unattached women with impunity is incorrect. However, there are several points to be made against his interpretation. In the first place, the whole point of a double standard is that one group is condemned for doing what another group can do with impunity; just because single women were condemned for extra-marital sexual activity does not necessarily mean that men were under an obligation to refrain from the same activity. In the second place, as already noted, Tamar (Gen. 38) is not an example of an unattached woman; rather, she is effectively betrothed because of her obligation under the levirate mar-

In the light of such societal structures and attitudes, it is possible to suggest an explanation for the significance of the words, 'So you shall purge the evil from among you/from Israel', which appear at intervals throughout the Deuteronomic legislation. The phrase usually follows a declaration that the death penalty is due for a given crime, and in the context of the marriage and adultery laws, it appears in the laws describing sexual offences committed by women for which the punishment is the death of the woman. This is true in the case of a woman who is found not to be a virgin on her wedding night (Deut. 22.21), and where a married or betrothed woman is found with a man other than her lawful husband (Deut. 22.22, 24). However, the same is not true in the case of a man deemed guilty of violating a betrothed woman where the woman herself is deemed innocent (Deut. 22.25-27). Even though the man is to be put to death for his act, there is no statement that his death is

---

riage provision (see n. 13 above). In the third place, both Dinah (arguably) and David's daughter Tamar (definitely) are represented as being coerced into sexual union with their respective partners (Gen. 34.1-2; 2 Sam. 13.1-14). This hardly constitutes 'sexual activity on the part of unmarried women' but is more correctly termed rape. Hugenberger's treatment is therefore a classic example of what van Dijk-Hemmes calls the misnaming of female experience (see n. 53 below for further details). Finally, in terms of the 'honour–shame' paradigm just outlined, the real concern in Gen. 34 and 2 Sam. 13 is with the men whose honour has been violated by the fact that another man has appropriated a woman under their care without their permission. This is especially clear in Gen. 34.31, where far from arising out of 'a negative view of "pre-marital sex"' (Hugenberger 1998: 327), Dinah's brothers' fearsome response is to avenge their own honour. Their sister has been treated like a harlot (34.31)—that is, no permission has been sought from her male guardians prior to intercourse. Their authority has therefore been flouted and so they have to re-establish it. Dinah does not speak once during the whole course of events, and her wishes and feelings are never given expression; she is a passive catalyst for a male battle, being first raped and then taken to live with foreigners before being snatched back again to her father's house. The real story is about masculine pride rather than female pre-marital sexual 'activity'. Similarly, Amnon's sin is in not asking permission for Tamar to be with him (2 Sam. 13.13), which flouts the established guidelines of male authority over her, and Absalom's vicious response can be seen as avenging his own honour for his failure to protect his full sister Tamar from their half-brother Amnon's evil designs. When, too, the whole incident is set against the backdrop of implicit struggles between David's offspring for eventual succession to his throne (according to 2 Sam. 3.2-3 Amnon is David's eldest son and Absalom is Amnon's younger half-brother), to regard it as merely stigmatizing female extra-marital sexual activity is extremely naïve. For discussion of the Amnon–Tamar–Absalom incident, see Stone (1996: 106-119).

intended to 'purge the evil from Israel'. The other crimes for which Deuteronomy prescribes the death penalty in order to 'purge the evil from Israel' are worshipping false gods (13.5 [Heb. 13.6]; 17.2-7), disobeying the legal ruling of a priest or a judge at the central sanctuary (17.12), murder (19.13), rebelling against one's parents (21.18-21), and kidnapping and selling into slavery a fellow-Israelite (24.7).[17] Commentators who have offered an explanation of the 'purging' phrase attached to all of these crimes have tended to view it as indicating that the community as a whole must cleanse itself from the guilt of the specified crime by means of the death of the offender;[18] but they have not ventured to suggest precisely what it might have been about these particular crimes that made them so horrendously polluting. In fact, Mayes goes so far as to deny any link at all between the various circumstances of the phrase's use,[19] thereby effectively rejecting the possibility of using it as an interpretative key. However, a link between the cases where the phrase appears can be identified. Apart from the death penalty for murder, which the text states is intended to purge blood guilt from Israel (19.13), all of the crimes punishable by death which also have the 'purging' phrase are characterized by the refusal to respect those who are in positions of (God-given) authority and thereby to maintain the proper (hierarchical) ordering of society.[20] In other words, they are

17. The phrase also appears in the law concerning a man who brings a false charge against another Israelite; if the charge is false, then the false witness shall suffer the punishment he intended should have been inflicted upon the accused, so as to purge the evil from the people's midst (Deut. 19.19). This may mean putting the false accuser to death, but it may not, so the case has not been included with the above examples. If it is to be considered along with them, the rationale behind appending the 'purging' phrase would be the same as for illegitimate capture and sale of a fellow-Israelite, that is, usurping the right of disposal over one's fellow. See the discussion below.

18. Driver 1895: 152; Phillips 1973: 95; McKeating 1979: 64; Dion 1980: 329-30, 349.

19. Mayes states that the origin and background of use of the phrase are obscure, and says that 'there is no clear unity either of form or content in these laws apart from the formula' (1979: 233).

20. See Stulman (1992: 48-49, 53, 55, 56, 62). The main focus of Stulman's article is on the treatment of sex and familial crimes in the Deuteronomic law. He argues that in the case of sexual and familial crimes, Deuteronomy's demand for communal stoning of the guilty party witnesses to a period of transition, in which the responsibility for justice in such cases was removed from the paterfamilias and vested in the community via local and regional judicial tribunals. Taking Stulman's

basically crimes of rebellion. Worshipping false gods is specifically de-scribed as rebellion against God (13.5 [Heb. 13.6]), and disobeying the sanctuary officials or one's parents is similarly a form of rebellion against those whom God has placed in authority.[21] Kidnapping a fel-low-Israelite and selling him as a slave is to claim an illegitimate power of disposal over him,[22] thereby exalting oneself in an illegitimate fash-ion and flouting the rules governing the ordering of society. Hence, when the command to stone an adulterous or promiscuous woman in order to purge the evil from Israel is viewed in the light of these other examples and of the generally acknowledged subordinate position of women in Israelite society, it seems that the primary reason for stoning her is not because she has incurred some kind of moral or ritual impu-rity via the sexual act itself. Rather, it is because in sleeping with a man of her own choice she has disregarded the authority of the men to whom she is viewed as being subject (cf. Num. 5.19).[23] The 'evil' which must be purged is therefore her rebellion, which poses a threat to the very fabric of Israel's patriarchal society and so must be stamped out before it has a chance to spread.

For a woman, then, adultery is fundamentally a crime of rebellion; but this is not its only vice. As already noted, it is also a crime which threatens a man's claim to paternity of the children born in his house,[24] and a close examination of the Deuteronomic laws shows that this aspect of the crime is also catered for in the stipulations laid down there about illicit sexual unions. When interpreting the Deuteronomic provi-sions, it is not unknown for betrothal, inasmuch as it is virtually mar-riage, to be equated with marriage, and for the provisions which apply to the betrothed woman to be read back into the provisions which apply

point of view, the injunction to stone those who refuse to obey the stipulations laid down by judicial authorities (17.12) can be seen as a measure intended to enforce the new provisions and to claim divine sanction for the role of the judges as part of the proper ordering of the community.

21. For further discussion of this idea, see Bellefontaine (1979), especially pp. 19-20.

22. Mayes 1979: 324, 303-304.

23. So also Pressler (1993: 42).

24. See Mayes (1979: 311); Pressler (1993: 42). Sirach 23.22-23 gives this as one of three lamentable consequences of a woman's adultery, the other two being her disobedience of the law of God and her offence against her husband. The wife's conception of a child by a strange man is mentioned twice in these two verses; obviously it was something that Sirach found particularly distasteful.

to the married woman.[25] The result is that some commentators assume that a distinction was made between the married woman who commits adultery in the town (guilty) and the married woman who was attacked in open country (not guilty), because that distinction is made in the case of betrothed women who are discovered in illicit sexual unions. However, the fact that betrothal was as legally binding as marriage should not be allowed to obscure the fact that there *is* a difference in the provisions for the married woman and for the betrothed woman. The text is quite clear that for a married woman who is found with a man other than her husband the penalty is death, and there are no mitigating circumstances (Deut. 22.22). Bearing in mind the threat to a husband's paternity which would be posed by his wife's involvement in an irregular union of any kind, this makes sense. By putting to death a wife proven guilty of sex with another man, the insoluble question of paternity of any potential offspring of the irregular union was avoided before it arose. Obviously if the woman had been in a normal marital relationship prior to the extra-marital act, paternity of a child which arrived approximately nine months later would be impossible to determine.[26] Hence, all married women who were found in illicit unions had to be disposed of, because that was the only sure way to protect the purity of a husband's blood-line as well as punishing the woman for her rebellion. The same considerations would apply to the bride who was found not to be a virgin on her wedding night: if she was subsequently found to be pregnant there would be no guarantee that the child was her husband's. Once again, therefore, stoning serves not only to punish rebellion but to protect the purity of the husband's blood-line. However, the specific use of the term 'betrothed' in the rather more nuanced provisions of Deut. 22.23-27 implies that the case of a betrothed woman who was violated was viewed differently from a case of illicit sex in the context of an established marriage, and this is borne out by the contents of the regulations themselves. The different, in some ways more lenient,

25. Thus Phillips (1981: 11); Pressler (1993: 32, 39 n. 51; 1994: 107). Similarly, Stulman (1992: 59) cites Deut. 22.23-27 which deal specifically with the violation of a betrothed woman rather than a married woman, and then comments, 'Illicit sex with *a married or engaged woman (vv. 23-24)* is an offense perceived to endanger the state and cosmic order' (emphasis added).

26. This, of course, is the logic in the story of David and Bathsheba, where David tries unsuccessfully to persuade Uriah to sleep with Bathsheba in order to hide the fact that she is pregnant with David's child (2 Sam. 11.1-13).

treatment for betrothed women implies recognition of a crucial difference in their status: betrothed women were (or were expected to be)
virgins.[27] On the assumption that the betrothed woman was a virgin
when the illicit liaison took place, if she did subsequently conceive it
would be possible to determine the paternity of the child—or at least to
know that it definitely was not the husband's child.[28] It is therefore possible to show mercy to a betrothed woman who has lost her virginity to
an attacker, since not only has she not rebelled against her husband,
neither has the purity of his line of descent been irretrievably compromised. True, he has been deprived of the right to a virgin bride; but the
extent of the damage is limited by the fact that if she does turn out to be
pregnant as a result of her ordeal this will soon be established, the child
will be known to be the attacker's, and, assuming the marriage goes
ahead and she remains faithful to her husband, all subsequent children
of their marital union will definitely be his. However, the betrothed
woman who has consented to sleep with a man other than her future
husband must, like the married woman, be stoned along with her lover,
because even if the question of compromising the purity of her husband's blood-line does not arise, her action constitutes a deliberate
rejection of her husband's authority and is therefore a threat to the stability of society.

   In all of these laws, it should be noted that there is no provision for

   27. Wenham (1972) argues that the term $b^e t\hat{u}l\hat{a}$ in these provisions which has
traditionally been rendered 'virgin' does not necessarily signify 'virgin', but 'young
woman of marriageable age'. If Wenham is correct, the provisions would be more
wide-ranging, in that they could then also cover the case of a woman betrothed for a
second marriage who was not (and could not legitimately be expected to be) a virgin—although the woman would still have to be 'young', which would limit the
number of cases to which that particular provision could be applied. However,
Pressler (1993: 25-28) points out that words often acquire specialized meanings
when they are used in legal contexts, and that the use of the term $b^e t\hat{u}l\hat{a}$ elsewhere
in the laws requires the sense of 'virgin'. Certainly it does seem more natural to
interpret the term here as 'virgin', given that it is used in 22.28-29 which speak of
giving the woman's father payment for her violation, and if she were widowed or
divorced and therefore eligible for a second marriage she would presumably be
independent of her father.
   28. Phillips (1981: 22 n. 27) refers to the Talmudic law whereby an unmarried
woman who has taken part in sexual intercourse either voluntarily or involuntarily
must wait for three months before being married (*b. Yeb.* 35a). This is obviously
addressed to just such a situation as the one being described.

what modern legal processes would recognize as rape—that is, forcible
sexual intercourse with a woman against the woman's will which therefore constitutes an offence against the woman.[29] As remarked above,
all extra-marital intercourse which involves a married woman is condemned as adultery deserving the death penalty, with no mitigating circumstances. The nearest that the Deuteronomic laws come to making
provision for rape is in the laws concerning the betrothed woman who
is set upon in the countryside (22.25-27), and the unbetrothed virgin
who is seized (22.28-29). In the first case, the woman is spared death as
an adulteress because she is presumed innocent, and in the second case
she is spared death but given to the man who violated her until he dies.
However, even though these are merciful treatments according to the
standards of the time, they are a long way from what modern Western
society would find acceptable. As noted above, the case of the violated
unbetrothed virgin is treated from the point of view of her father; it is
not her rights that have been infringed but his, because he is now highly
unlikely to be able to find her a husband and must continue to support
her. Hence, the prescribed 'penalty' for the violator is intended to compensate the father for damaging his goods as much as to provide for the
woman who through no fault of her own has been rendered virtually
ineligible for marriage. As for betrothed women, it seems that the location of any illicit act is what determines their guilt or innocence, and
therefore their right to life or condemnation to death; but again, this is
far from satisfactory. Certainly, the woman assaulted in the open country is spared death, unlike her paramour; but this is cold comfort. After
all, a prosecution against the man could only be brought if the pair were
discovered by at least two witnesses (Deut. 19.15), and the whole point
of the stipulation not to kill the woman attacked in the countryside was
that no one would be there to hear her cries for help. Hence, the
likelihood of there being any witnesses, and therefore of the offended
husband being able to bring a successful prosecution against the rapist
in such a case, was correspondingly small. The woman who is assaulted
in the town is in an even worse position. If she does not cry out, she is
assumed to have consented to the assault; but if she does cry out, she
may well be discovered, and if she is discovered with another man in
the town then she is guilty by definition. This is what might be called
the Deuteronomic double-bind: crying out leads to discovery, but

29. Pressler 1993: 37 n. 46.

discovery in the town is a sure sign of guilt; so whether she cries out or remains silent she is liable to be condemned.[30] There is no recognition that silence might be a woman's way of saving her life from the man who is bent on violating her; it seems that she is expected to preserve her husband's honour even at the cost of her own life. And if she manages to conceal her violation from her husband-to-be, on the grounds that this is by far the safest course of action for her own survival, she is then liable to be stoned when on her wedding night he finds that she is not a virgin as expected (22.13-21). From this it appears that although the laws appear to deal even-handedly with men and women who commit what is regarded as adultery, in actual fact the woman is more likely to pay the penalty for illicit sexual activity, however that activity came about, because she is the one who is liable to discovery when it becomes evident that she has lost her virginity or is pregnant.

The picture of how women were treated in the society to which the laws were directed therefore seems quite a bleak one. However, as McKeating points out, there is a need for interpretative caution when dealing with legal material, because the laws may be prescribing ideal standards of behaviour rather than describing actual practice. For this reason, McKeating argues that it is inappropriate to make legal material the starting point for an assessment of a society's actual ethical stance. Instead, he regards narratives as a more suitable starting point, because they provide information about what actually happened rather than about what certain groups of people thought ought to happen, and often contain unselfconscious material about the ethical standards and behaviours of a given society.[31] It is certainly true that, as McKeating points out, there are no actual examples in the Old Testament of adulterous women or men being put to death,[32] so to that extent the regulations about adultery in Leviticus and Deuteronomy must be classed as 'ideal'. Nonetheless, this may be due at least in part to the difficulty of implementing the recommendations, rather than because they were not

30. No doubt the harsher penalty for the woman caught in the city reflects the greater shame brought on her husband by his inability to protect or control his wife in his own back yard, so to speak. Compare the provision of law 197 in the Hittite law code, which reads, 'If a man seizes a woman in the mountains, it is the man's crime and he will be killed. But if he seizes her in [her] house, it is the woman's crime and the woman shall be killed' (Goetze 1969: 196).

31. McKeating 1979.

32. McKeating 1979: 58.

regarded as worthwhile or binding. The very fact, as already noted, that it is necessary to have two witnesses to a crime in order to sustain a charge (Deut. 19.15) would in itself account for the non-legal evidence McKeating cites to the effect that, rather than being stoned, adulterers were just as likely to buy their way out of trouble if they were men or to be shamed or divorced by their husbands if they were women.[33] Discovery of an adulterous pair by an aggrieved husband is conceivable, but discovery by two or more people would be quite unlikely—especially where adultery took place in the open countryside. It is also true that there are sufficient narratives showing women's sexuality at men's disposal in order to make the general ethos of the legislation credible as a true reflection of the attitudes of the time.[34] Women may not regularly have been executed for adultery, but they were nevertheless in a position of subservience in the eyes of those who drafted Israel's legal tradition, as is underlined by the fact that the laws about adultery with its concomitant punishments are there at all.

In summary, then, an analysis of the law regarding marriage and adultery gives the following picture. In the patriarchal and patrilineal structure of Israelite society, marriage was characterized by the woman being bound to her husband in a legal relationship that gave him the sole and absolute right of use of her sexual capacity. Adultery consisted of a woman who was married or betrothed having sex with a man other than her husband, and was a grave sin for three reasons. First, it was an act of rebellion against the proper social and cosmic order, because it was a flouting of the husband's claim to his wife's sexuality and there-fore of his authority; secondly, it jeopardized the purity of the hus-band's blood-line; and thirdly, it challenged the husband's manhood because it implied that he was unable either to engender respectful obedience in his wife or to protect her from the designs of another man.

2. The Use of Marriage as a Metaphor for the Relationship between Yahweh and Israel

What effect, then, does such an understanding of marriage and adultery have on an understanding of the way in which the concept of marriage

---

33. E.g. Prov. 6.27-35; Ezek. 16.37-39. See McKeating (1979: 59-62).
34. See, e.g., Gen. 29.15-30; 38; Judg. 15.1-2; 1 Sam. 18.17-19; 25.44; 2 Sam. 3.14-15; Est. 1.10–2.4.

is used as a metaphor for the relationship between Yahweh and Israel?[35] This idea of Yahweh as husband to his people Israel is surely one of the most emotive metaphors in the Old Testament. It would seem at first glance to imply a sense of completeness, a finding of true identity, and mutuality of loving care—images no doubt reinforced by the New Testament metaphor of the Church as the bride of Christ, bought with his blood, cleansed and presented in faultless splendour (Eph. 5.25-27). However, in the light of the discussion above concerning the principles underlying the marriage laws, this impression is at the very least open to question. Indeed, a closer examination of the way in which the marriage metaphor is used in the Old Testament reveals quite a different tone from the idyllic ideal of the New Testament image, and far from being a positive figure the Old Testament marriage metaphor is almost wholly negative in its application. The most fully developed examples of the metaphor, which account for all but 10 of the 171 verses in which the metaphor can be clearly identified, appear in prophetic writings which not only castigate their audiences for wanton sin, but also warn of impending doom, interpreted as divine punishment for that sin.[36] These major instances of the metaphor depict a highly dysfunctional marriage, and they are used to underline not the faithfulness of Yahweh but the faithlessness of Israel. This they do by either implicitly or explicitly invoking the existence of a legal bond between Yahweh and Israel comparable to that between husband and wife, and then declaring that Israel is the unfaithful wife who has violated the bond by her actions and who must therefore be punished with due severity.

The earliest identifiable consistent exposition of the marriage metaphor is in the work of Hosea, whose prophecies date from the final decades of the northern kingdom Israel prior to its obliteration in

35. There is no space here to examine general theories of how metaphors work. For a discussion of the theory of metaphor in relation to the marriage metaphor, see Galambush (1992: 4-10); Stienstra (1993: 17-40) and Weems (1995: 23-25).

36. The major instances consist of Hos. 1.2; 2.2 (Heb. 2.4)–3.3; Jer. 2.2, 20, 23-25, 33; 3.1-3, 6-13, 20; 4.30-31; 13.22, 26-27; Ezek. 16.1-63; 23.1-49. The remaining verses which make explicit use of the metaphor come in Deutero- and Trito-Isaiah (Isa. 50.1; 54.4-8; 57.7-8; 62.4-5). Of these passages, 54.4-8 and 62.4-5 are indisputably positive, speaking of Yahweh's love for and commitment to the people; 50.1 admits that there has been a separation between Yahweh and people, but insists that the separation was not a divorce (that is, a permanent irrevocable separation); and 57.7-8 uses sexual imagery to refer to idolatrous worship, and so is once again negative in its impact.

722 BCE by the ever-encroaching Assyrian forces. As is well known, Hosea 1–3 is a kind of 'marriage sandwich', consisting of what are apparently biographical (autobiographical?) reminiscences concerning Hosea's own relationship with an unfaithful wife (or wives) (1.2-9; 3.1-3), on either side of a chapter of poetic diatribe in which Israel's apostasy away from Yahweh is expressed in terms of a marriage devastated by the wife's infidelity (2.2-13 [Heb. 2.4-15]). The metaphors of adultery and harlotry are used quite freely in these opening chapters to describe Israel's shameless and blatant abandonment of God for the worship of Baal.[37] Indeed, the opening words of God's message to Hosea are, 'Go, take to yourself a wife of harlotry and have children of harlotry, for the land commits great harlotry by forsaking the Lord' (1.2). Additionally, the poetic diatribe of ch. 2 speaks several times of Israel running after her lovers (2.5, 7, 13 [Heb. 2.7, 9, 15]).[38] The overall message is that because of this abandonment of God the people are risking great punishment (2.2-3, 9-13 [Heb. 2.4-5, 11-15]), although there is also the hope of restoration following the punishment (2.14-23 [Heb. 2.16-25]). When seen in the light of the rest of Hosea's message, these three chapters are programmatic for that message, inasmuch as they summarize in a concise metaphor what is communicated in more detail in the subsequent chapters. The later chapters in their turn put flesh on the bones of the metaphor, describing in more specific terms the sins hinted at in the metaphor (4.1–5.4; 8.1-6, 11-14; 9.1; 10.1-3; 13.1-2). They make it quite clear that the people are heading for great suffering at the hands of their God if they fail to mend their ways (5.8-

37. Galambush (1992: 49) suggests that the woman in the metaphor of Hos. 2 should be regarded as a personification not of the land or the people but of Israel's capital city Samaria, because this gives the most consistent reading of the metaphor.

38. It is interesting to note that the Targum to Hos. 1–3 removes virtually all the references to adultery and harlotry by allegorizing the narrative portions in chs. 1 and 3 and by decoding the metaphor in ch. 2. The result is that the message of all three chapters is expressed in terms of Israel's apostasy instead of in terms of a wife's unfaithfulness. Thus, the Lord's initial command to Hosea in 1.2 is rendered, ' "Go [and] speak a prophecy against the inhabitants of the idolatrous city, who continue to sin. For the inhabitants of the land surely go astray from the worship of the Lord" ' (Cathcart and Gordon 1989: 29). In the same spirit of censorship, the indictment of 2.2 (Heb. 2.4) is rendered, 'Reprove the congregation of Israel and say to her that, because she does not humble herself in my worship, my Memra will not hear her prayer, until she removes her evil deeds from before her face and the worship of her idols from among her towns' (Cathcart and Gordon 1989: 31).

14; 7.11-16; 9.11-17; 10.13-15; 13.7-11), although as before there is also a promise of restoration (14.1-9 [Heb. 14.2-10]).

A century or so later Jeremiah, with a sense of an equivalent impending doom for the southern kingdom of Judah, picks up on the imagery used by Hosea, and sprinkles it throughout his initial indictment of his fellows. For Jeremiah, the people are not just a faithless wife (Jer. 3.20) but a brazen, insatiable harlot who sleeps with anyone and everyone (Jer. 2.23-25; 3.1-3, 6-13). As was the case with Hosea, there is also an appeal to repentance embodied within the metaphor (3.12-13), but the threat of punishment from the same hand as the one that could grant forgiveness is equally apparent (13.22, 26-27). This is perhaps the least coherent of the major occurrences of the metaphor; Jeremiah does not use it in a sustained, developed way, but rather as one weapon of indictment that is used alongside several others in order to give a general impression of the people's lawlessness and disobedience. However, the same is not true of the metaphor as it appears in Ezekiel. A decade or so after Jeremiah's warnings, the punishment he threatened has been realized: the Babylonians have launched their initial blistering onslaught against Judah and deported a large group of Jerusalemites to Babylon. In this situation, Ezekiel takes up the marriage metaphor and uses it in its most vicious form in an equally blistering and sustained verbal onslaught against the exiles. In Ezekiel 16, Jerusalem in her religious and political apostasy is compared to a shameless, ungrateful and reprobate woman, wantonly betraying the trust of the man who rescued her from her abandonment as an infant and later married her and provided richly for her.[39] This version of the marriage metaphor is probably based on Hosea 2,[40] but it is far more uncompromising. The metaphor in Hosea, coming as it does in a time of prosperity before there was evidence of

39. Galambush (1992: 81) comments that Ezekiel's depiction of Jerusalem's foreign origins deconstructs the 'givenness' of the relationship between deity and city, so that the 'marital' relationship between them is depicted as a reflection of Yahweh's kindness and the contingency of the city's position is emphasized.

40. Both passages incorporate the image of the adulterous woman as a child (Hos. 2.3 [Heb. 2.5]; Ezek. 16.1-7), both refer to the goods provided by Yahweh for the ungrateful spouse (Hos. 2.8-9 [Heb. 2.10-11]; Ezek. 16.9-13), and both refer to punishment for her infidelities (Hos. 2.9-13 [Heb. 2.11-15]; Ezek. 16.35-43) followed by restoration (Hos. 2.14-23 [Heb. 2.16-25]; Ezek. 16.53-54, 59-63). Galambush (1992: 52) views Ezekiel's version of the metaphor as the resolution to the problem posed by Hosea's use of the metaphor, which portrays the omnipotent Yahweh as vulnerable and impotent in respect of his wife's fidelity.

disaster, is used to urge the people to repentance as well as to condemn their sin (2.2 [Heb. 2.4]), but in Ezekiel the tone of the metaphor is much starker and much more strident. Addressed to a situation of disaster, it is basically a message of out-and-out condemnation, and even though there is the promise of restoration at the end of the chapter it is as much of a threat as a promise (16.53-63). Unlike Hosea 2, where restoration is to be a blissful re-creation of newly wedded bliss between husband and wife (2.16-23 [Heb. 2.18-25]), the restoration in Ezekiel is apparently going to be used as a further way of impressing upon the already downtrodden city both her unutterable depravity and the sovereign power of God; indeed, the whole idea of restoration is almost spiteful.

In Ezekiel 23 the metaphor is extended further, to include both Jerusalem and Samaria as adulterous, promiscuous women whom Yahweh originally claimed as his wives but whom he eventually repudiates. The descriptions of sins committed and punishments to be meted out are just as grotesque as those in Ezekiel 16, and the conclusion to the chapter is even more uncompromising. Here there is no restoration, not even the 'spiteful' restoration promised to Jerusalem in 16.53-63. There is only the promise that both Jerusalem and Samaria will be destroyed as a way of ending 'lewdness in the land' (23.48), so that all women should take note and avoid committing the same sins.[41] Here too the sinful cities will come to a knowledge of God, but this time instead of being via restoration it will be via destruction (23.46-49).

In each of these prophetic passages, then, the metaphor of an unfaithful wife or harlotrous woman is used in order to convey a message of deep disapproval concerning what the prophets regarded as Israel's religious and political apostasy.[42] Such usage belies the rather sentimental

41. On this verse, Darr (1992: 189) comments, 'one discerns a later editor's effort to admonish *women* (but not men) to refrain from illicit sexual behavior. The original imagery's inclusiveness has collapsed into a threat intended for women alone.'

42. It is a common assumption that the use of the metaphor of adultery or harlotry for Israel's apostasy was fuelled by the sexual nature of the rites undertaken as a part of Canaanite fertility religion, and that what was being attacked was the Israelites' involvement in sacred prostitution in the foreign cult. However, there is no need to make such an assumption, not least because the evidence for such rites in Israel at that time period is virtually non-existent. See Oden (1987: 131-53); Bird (1989); Keefe (1995: 78-79). Also, the metaphor works equally well, indeed better, without the assumption, which complicates the thrust of the metaphor. It makes no

conception of the marriage metaphor as one of sweetness and light and love and devotion. In fact, given the kind of invective towards the women Israel, Jerusalem and Samaria that characterizes the passages just described, it seems that in its major manifestations the main thrust of the marriage metaphor is not one of love and tenderness, but one of theodicy, and that the subsequent remaining instances of the metaphor which are used positively (Isa. 50.1; 54.4-8; 62.4-5) are cases of reversing the main thrust rather than defining it.[43] Indeed, the fact that the metaphor is so prominent in the book of Ezekiel in particular, for which theodicy is a major concern, is extremely telling in this respect. Given a theological world-view whereby a god's failure to avert from his people catastrophes of a political, economic or environmental nature pointed to either his powerlessness or his abandonment of his people, the prophets who claimed to speak in Yahweh's name had to have a way of interpreting the disasters they either promised or witnessed if Israel's God— and their faith in him—was to be vindicated; and the marriage metaphor was one of the tools they used in order to do this. They used the metaphor in contexts of threatened or actual disaster, not to reassure Israel of Yahweh's protection, but rather to warn Israel that the disaster was Yahweh's just and rightful punishment of a wayward and sinful people.

It may seem rather strange to the modern-day Western reader that what might reasonably be expected to be an image of devotion and commitment should be used in this harsh and uncompromising way. However, in the light of the legal material already examined, such a usage should come as no surprise. The discussion of the laws on marriage and adultery showed that they arise out of a society in which marriage is a binding pact between two unequal parties, in which the weaker (female) party is in a position of subordination to and dependence on the stronger (male) party. As is well known, the conviction that such a pact (or covenant) existed between Yahweh and Israel is evidenced throughout the Old Testament, with its clearest and most developed expressions in the account of the Sinai theophany (Exod. 19–24) and in the book of Deuteronomy. Hence, the marriage relationship becomes a suitable metaphor for the Yahweh–Israel relationship because both relationships are viewed as legally binding and both exist between unequal

sense, for example, to claim that the men of Israel are being likened to sacred prostitutes in Hos. 2.

43. Particularly striking in this respect is the implication of a *de facto* divorce between Yahweh and people in Jer. 3.1-3, which is refuted in Isa. 50.1-2.

parties; as a husband has authority over his wife, so Yahweh has authority over the people of Israel. But the element that really makes the marriage metaphor work as a theodicy is the fact that in the unequal structure of a marriage certain transgressions of the wife against her husband's authority render her liable for severe punishment. As the laws demonstrate, the primary area in which a husband has authority over his wife is that of her sexuality; indeed, what a husband acquires above all when he marries a woman is the sole right of use of her sexuality. She is not allowed to enter into sexual relations with other men but must give exclusive loyalty to her husband. If she does go in search of alternative sources of sexual gratification apart from her husband, she is guilty of adultery and is liable for severe punishment. Taking sexuality as the means whereby husband and wife share intimacy and through which a man ensures the continuation of his family name to subsequent generations, the equivalent in the Yahweh–Israel relationship is the people's religious devotion. Just as a wife's sexuality belongs to her husband and is not hers to bestow at will on whoever she chooses, Yahweh's acquisition of the people in covenant means that their devotion belongs to Yahweh and is not theirs to bestow at will on whichever deity they choose. They cannot legitimately go off in search of alternative sources of religious gratification apart from Yahweh, and if they do go after other gods, they are guilty of apostasy and are liable for severe punishment. The metaphorical association of adultery and apostasy is strengthened by the fact that the law as it appears in Deuteronomy presents both apostasy and female adultery as effectively versions of the same basic crime, in other words, as crimes of rebellion which merit the death penalty in order to purge the evil from Israel's midst (Deut. 13.5 [Heb. 13.6]; 22.21, 22, 24; cf. also Lev. 20.1-2, 10). Hence, when either adultery or apostasy actually occurs, punishment must be inflicted on the guilty parties, because their deeds constitute an act of rebellion which violates the proper ordering of society and cosmos and is therefore a grave threat to society's well-being (or, rather more cynically speaking, to those in positions of dominance).

Once the basic framework for the metaphor is established, then, it can be used to give very clear justification for the punishment inflicted upon the people, because it shows that Israel's religious unfaithfulness is as deeply damaging for Yahweh (and for a society based upon Yahwism) as a wife's sexual unfaithfulness is for her husband. This damage takes two major forms. First of all, there is the question of paternity, an issue expressed briefly but tellingly in Hosea's version of the metaphor, where Yahweh refuses to pity his wife's children because they are 'children of harlotry' (Hos. 2.4-5 [Heb. 2.6-7]). In this sense, adultery is not simply a one-off occurrence; it has permanent and irreversible consequences for the wronged husband, in that the purity of his blood-line is compromised. The same is true for apostasy: it is not just a case of rebellion in those who commit it, but it can have serious and lasting consequences for religious observance in subsequent generations of worshippers, who will be brought up to worship the new gods of their parents rather than the old God of their grandparents. Just as a human husband cannot afford to risk the pollution and potential destruction of his blood-line because of his wife's adultery, so Yahweh cannot tolerate the possibility of his 'name' dying out—that is, of his reputation and cult which should continue down through the generations being destroyed—because Israel has gone to worship at other shrines and therefore Israel's children are being dedicated to, and growing up to worship, other gods.

The second major damaging effect is linked with the first, and is concerned with Yahweh's identity as God. It would be no exaggeration to say that in the kind of society for which the Deuteronomic laws were framed and to which the prophetic marriage metaphors were addressed, a wife's adultery was a threat to her husband's very being, because it threatened not only his future existence via his descendants but also his present identity and status as a man. And just as a wife's adultery not only threatened her husband's line of descent but challenged his very manhood, so Israel's apostasy challenges Yahweh's very godhood.[44] In order to be worth worshipping—that is, in order to deserve the title of 'god'—a god must be seen to be active and powerful;[45] and a god who simply lets worshippers go off and worship another deity without doing anything about it, especially when there is supposed to be a binding covenant between that god and the worshippers, is no god. Hence, Yahweh is virtually bound to take strong, highly visible action against those who have committed apostasy in order to continue to merit the title of god and therefore the people's worship. [46]

44. See Galambush (1992: 34).

45. See, e.g., 1 Kgs 18.20-39; Isa. 41.21-29; 46.1.

46. This concern for the destruction of Yahweh's (true) cult and the resultant threat to his godhood seems to be particularly important in Ezekiel's version of the marriage metaphor. See Galambush (1992: 78, 81, 86-88), who remarks of Ezekiel,

The defence of Yahweh's godhood appears in both Hosea and Ezekiel as a rationale for the indignities suffered by the people, in that both prophets show that Yahweh's actions will lead to a restoration of the relationship between God and people and their acknowledgment of Yahweh's true divine status. At the end of Hosea 2, the result of the re-wooing of the metaphorical wife is that she will no longer call God 'my Baal' but 'my husband' (2.16 [Heb. 2.18]), and that she will 'know the LORD' (2.20 [Heb. 2.22]). Although the phrasing is rather allusive, this can be read as the people's acknowledgment of Yahweh's godhood which results from what they have experienced, both good and bad, at his hand. The punishments of deprivation (2.9-13 [Heb. 2.11-15]) followed by deliberate, demonstrative restoration (2.14-15 [Heb. 2.16-17]) show Yahweh's control over nature combined with his commitment to the people of Israel, so that in the light of these acts the woman's acknowledgment of him as 'my husband' (*'ishi*, 2.16 [Heb. 2.18]) is in effect Israel's newly enlightened re-confession of Yahweh as their true divine covenant-partner. The subsequent promise that Israel 'shall know the LORD' (2.20 [Heb. 2.22]) has overtones of marital intimacy and so can be seen as describing the nature of the newly restored relationship, but it also follows the promise that Yahweh will make a covenant for Israel with all creation (2.18 [Heb. 2.20]), and so needs to be read in the light of that promise. 'Knowing the LORD' thereby carries the double implication of knowledge gained by seeing the power of the covenant-maker in action and knowledge gained by intimate association with that same covenant-maker. Taken together, these two statements imply that as a result of Yahweh's actions Israel will know precisely who and what this Yahweh god is, and are therefore an affirmation that Yahweh's position as God in the eyes of Israel is restored. Similarly, in Ezekiel 16, Yahweh's act of undeserved restoration will result in the people of Jerusalem knowing that 'I am the LORD' (16.62), a thought which recurs throughout the book of Ezekiel and ties in with what might be called Ezekiel's 'name theology' whereby Yahweh restores the people not for their own sake but for the sake of his own name (Ezek. 36.22-23; 39.7, 25). In Ezekiel 23 it is not restoration but destruction of

---

'The marriage metaphor is especially suited to depict the defilement of Yahweh's temple. If the city is a woman, then the temple is her vagina, and the offense of Jerusalem's granting illicit "access" to foreign men and competing gods becomes plain, both as a legal transgression and as a personal injury to the husband' (87).

the cities of Jerusalem and Samaria that is promised, but the effect of vindicating Yahweh's godhood is the same: 'you shall know that I am the LORD' (Ezek. 23.49).

Hence, in its function as a theodicy, the metaphor addresses the question of God's identity and status. As a loving and powerful God, who is pictured in male terms (even though an explicit sexuality is denied 'him'),[47] it is inconceivable that God should allow certain things to happen to 'him' or to 'his' people. Because 'he' is loving and powerful, it is inconceivable that 'he' should allow 'his' people to come to serious harm at the hands of other nations or because of natural disasters such as famine or flood. On the other hand, because 'he' is 'male' (and therefore a member of the dominant class in society), it is inconceivable that 'he' should allow 'himself' to be brought into disrepute by the rebellious philanderings of 'his' subordinate people. The result is an impasse, which the marriage metaphor resolves very neatly. The pattern of the unfaithful wife who is severely chastised but who contrary to expectation is accepted back, chastened, by her husband, provides a framework within which God can be loving and all-powerful, while at the same time preserving 'his' honour. He can chastise his unruly people by allowing (or causing) them to suffer environmental disaster or military reversal; this underlines his power and vindicates his reputation. He can then restore them to their privileged position; this again underlines his power and vindicates his reputation, but in addition it can be seen to speak of his superhuman love and faithfulness. In this way, the interpretation of events which is offered by the marriage metaphor absolves God of the charge of being inconsistent or inconstant or impotent, because it provides the rationale for what Israel has suffered and is still to suffer.

When the underlying assumptions which allow the marriage metaphor to be read as theodicy are exposed, it is no longer possible to read the metaphor naïvely as Yahweh's legitimate expression of wounded

---

47. Despite the frequent denials of commentators, there is, however, metaphorical reference to Yahweh's sexuality in Hos. 2.20 (Heb. 2.22) where Israel is said to 'know the Lord' as a result of the restoration process, and in Ezek. 16.8, where Yahweh's covering the young girl and entering into a covenant with her can be taken as a reference to sexual intercourse. Ezek. 16.20 also refers to the children born to Yahweh by the woman-city, the implication being that they have been fathered by him with his 'wife'. See Eilberg-Schwartz (1994: 110-12); Hugenberger (1998: 273-75).

love when faced with the people's blatant rejection, as generations of exegetes have done. Certainly it was the intention of the prophets who framed it that the metaphor should be read in this way, and indeed, the social context for which it was composed guaranteed that that was how it would be received. But in any other circumstances the intensity of the threatened punishment, particularly in Ezekiel although to a lesser extent in Hosea, would be profoundly disturbing, raising the question of why it has appeared acceptable in these circumstances for so long. The reason for the beguiling nature of the marriage metaphor, and the reason that it works as theodicy, violence included, is precisely that it is a metaphor of a *broken* marriage, so that in the light of his wife's shameless behaviour it seems justifiable for the jilted husband to behave as he does towards her. After all, he does promise to take her back again (Hos. 2.14-20 [Heb. 2.16-22]; Jer. 3.11-13; Ezek. 16.59-63), which he surely ought not to have to do after the way she has treated him. And indeed, the wife's infidelity is a complicating factor. If the metaphor spoke of marital abuse for no apparent reason then there would be no hesitation in condemning the husband's behaviour; but the whole point is that it is in some sense *deserved* punishment that is meted out. This is what the metaphor is meant to convey to the people of Israel about their own misfortunes, and this is what makes it so readily acceptable. But as shown already, the underlying assumptions about the marriage relationship are that husband and wife are not equal; the relationship, and therefore the metaphor, is one of power, domination and control as much as it is one of love, a point made by many feminist scholars.[48] Even though it can be argued that the Israelite wife was not a chattel, she certainly did not have the right to self-determination. She owed her sexuality to the man who was legally responsible for her, and if she broke that obligation in any way the law demanded that she be put to death in order to 'purge the evil' of rebellion from the society of which she was a part. It is also rather disconcerting to realize that the metaphor is set in a context where what would today be regarded as rape is viewed as a property crime against a husband or father rather than a personal violation of the woman in question. Although the concept of forced illegitimate sexual relations with the woman does not appear in the metaphor—indeed, the very opposite is true, that the woman herself has apparently courted illegitimate liaisons—the same view of female

48. See Darr (1992: 188-89); Yee (1992: 199-200); Weems (1995: 16-18).

sexuality that makes rape into a property crime against the man responsible for her makes it justifiable for that man to beat and abuse her if
she demeans him by failing to submit to his authority and bestowing her
sexual favours elsewhere. It is this that is so disturbing.

The matter is confused further by the fact that the metaphor is a
metaphor about God. Even if humans do not or should not have the
right to abuse their fellow humans, surely God has the right to inflict
whatever punishment he sees fit? No one else is qualified to mediate
between him and his adulterous wife, and so like *Alice in Wonderland*'s
cunning old Fury he is judge and jury who tries the whole cause and
condemns her to death. Once again, the metaphor is plausible when it is
applied to the divine. But it is precisely this plausibility that makes it so
dangerous. It implies that it is acceptable for every husband to behave
in the same way towards his wife. By applying the metaphor to God,
the metaphor itself is deified; husbands become like gods, with the right
to treat their wives as they wish.

Neither can the metaphor's unpleasant implications be defused by
dismissing the threatened punishment of the unfaithful wife as 'only a
metaphor'. The way metaphors work is by tapping into commonly
accepted ideas about the topic which is being used as a metaphor, and
applying those ideas to the topic which is being expressed by means of
the metaphor.[49] It follows from this that if those who heard the
metaphor did not recognize in the pattern of punishment of unfaithful
wives an accepted and in their eyes legitimate way of proceeding, the
metaphor would have failed in its prime duty of theodicy. Inasmuch as
the metaphor has been chosen in order to illuminate what is going to
happen to Israel and why, it needs to make links with the experience of
those to whom it was initially addressed and to ring true with them. If
there were no such practice of punishing unfaithful wives in Israel, the
metaphor would seem harsh, cruel and indefensible, incomprehensible
even, and would fulfil no purpose except that of alienating the people to
whom it was addressed. As noted earlier, men and women may not
regularly have been executed for adultery in ancient Israel, but the
presence of the marriage metaphor implies that the alternative, at least
for adulterous women, would have been little better.

49.　Stienstra 1993: 22-23.

3. *Jesus and the Woman Taken in Adultery*

Given, then, that this study is meant somehow to illuminate the story of
the woman taken in adultery, what needs to be done now is to see how
some of these thoughts can apply to that situation. A woman caught in
the act of adultery is brought before Jesus by the scribes and Pharisees,
and Jesus is told that the law of Moses requires that they stone her. He
is then invited to offer his opinion on how they should treat her. When
he does not answer, they persist in their questioning until he tells them
that the one of their number who is without sin is to open the stoning.
Faced with this demand, they leave one by one until only the woman is
left before Jesus. He dismisses her without condemning her, but with
the exhortation not to sin again.

There are three parties involved in the situation as it is presented to
Jesus, and as the role of each is examined more closely it becomes clear
that, contrary to initial impressions, this is far from being the cut-and-
dried case that the accusers are presenting it as to Jesus. Perhaps the
most obvious difficulty is that only two of the parties involved are actually present, namely, the woman and her accusers. The third party—that
is, the man with whom the woman is supposed to have slept—is not
present, and indeed, he is never even mentioned. As commentators have
noted, if this truly was a case of adultery, and the woman had indeed
been caught in the very act, then not only she but also her partner should
have been stoned.[50] Indeed, according to the law there are no circumstances where a woman alone is to be stoned for sexual transgression
except in the case of the non-virgin bride (Deut. 22.13-21), and this is
not the scenario which is being presented to Jesus. This naturally raises
the question of why the man was not brought to justice as well, and the
response that comes most readily to mind is that it is an example of the
double standard described earlier, whereby men's extra-marital pecca-
dilloes could be overlooked but not women's, despite the fact that the
law specifies death for both parties in proven cases of adultery. However, the injustice is deeper than that. The double standard is made considerably more offensive when it is remembered that the Ten Commandments, including the commandment not to commit adultery (Exod.
20.14; Deut. 5.18), are framed in the second-person masculine singular

---

50. Lindars 1972: 309; McKeating 1979: 58-59; Sloyan 1988: 97; Carson 1991:
334.

(Heb. ‫לֹא תִנְאָף‬; Gk οὐ μοιχεύσεις).[51] In other words, it is the male who has the responsibility under the law to refrain from adultery, and although that does not exonerate adulterous women from blame (adultery is, after all, a team game) it certainly multiplies the injustice in this case to realize that the woman brought to Jesus is due to take all the punishment for something that the absent man was commanded not to do. The law does not even address her directly, and yet she is being made to bear the full weight of its fury.

Turning to the woman herself, it is pertinent to ask whether she was guilty at all in a way that would be recognizable to modern notions of sexual misdemeanour. As noted above, rape in the sense of violation of a woman against her will which therefore constituted an offence against the woman herself was simply not recognized by the ancient law, and a woman's presumed resistance to a would-be lover's advances could only be used to mitigate her punishment if she was a betrothed virgin rather than in a consummated marriage relationship. If a married woman was found with a man other than her husband, then the very fact that she had been sexually involved with another man was enough to secure her condemnation, regardless of how that involvement came about. If the woman brought to Jesus was married rather than simply being betrothed, as seems most probable,[52] there would have been no question

---

51. It is worth noting that the use of the verb μοιχεύω, which designates adultery in the LXX of Exod. 20.14; Deut. 5.18; Lev. 20.10 and in the New Testament, including Jn 8.4, generally follows the convention of classical Greek whereby the active form denotes the male partner and the passive form the female partner. Although the LXX does not maintain this distinction in every instance where the verb is used, the New Testament does, so that the woman brought to Jesus is described as μοιχευομένη (Jn 8.4). Given the formulaic and conventional character of linguistic usage in general, which means that derivation is not always a reliable guide to later significance, this fact in itself cannot necessarily be regarded as implying the woman's passive violation rather than her active participation in an adulterous act. Nonetheless, it is interesting that the idiom testifies to the perception of adultery as something that men do in which women are involved, rather than as something that women do that also involves men. The use of this form of the verb in Jn 8.4 is doubly interesting, given that there is a variant μοιχάομαι which is used of both men and women without distinction in form. However, this variant does not occur in the LXX in the legal provisions concerning adultery. Presumably the use of the passive of μοιχεύω in Jn 8.4 was to stress the connection with the legal language of the LXX, but it also serves to cast doubt on precisely how guilty the woman was, or could be regarded as being in the eyes of the law.

52. For the arguments in favour of the woman being married rather than simply

of asking whether or not the man she was found with had forced himself upon her. She would have been deemed guilty regardless of the circumstances of the illicit union.[53]

Given the ambiguity of the situation, then, it is no surprise that Jesus
refuses to give a snap judgment. Rather, when he finally does respond,
it is to underline the ambiguity by turning the focus from the woman
onto her accusers. Thus far, in the absence of the woman's partner in
adultery, all the negativity has been focused on the woman herself, in
an attempt to arouse righteous indignation and revulsion at her crime.
But Jesus' eventual reply turns the spotlight away from her and throws
it squarely onto the Pharisees and scribes: the one among them who is
without sin may throw the first stone. As is commonly observed, Jesus'
words are a variation on the Deuteronomic law of stoning, according
to which it is the witnesses to a capital crime who are to throw the
first stones (Deut. 17.7). The law was presumably meant to protect the
accused from wrongful execution; Thompson comments that the witnesses who began the stoning would be exposing themselves to blood
revenge should their testimony prove false,[54] and so laying on them the
responsibility of initiating the execution was a way of testing the
validity of their testimony. When Jesus' response is viewed against this
background, it too can be seen as a test of the accusers' testimony. It is
unclear from the text of Jn 8.4 whether or not the scribes and Pharisees
themselves had caught the woman; although a few late manuscripts
give the reading 'we found (εὕρομεν) her in the very act', most manuscripts use a passive formulation, 'she was taken' or 'caught in the very
act'. Who caught her? Where are they? Why are they not there to witness against the woman who has supposedly committed a capital

betrothed, see Blinzler (1957–58), followed by Beasley-Murray (1987: 145) and
Schnackenburg (1980: 164).

53. In her discussion of Ezek. 23, van Dijk-Hemmes remarks that although the
text is traditionally regarded as depicting two sisters who were insatiably promiscuous from their early youth, what Ezek. 23.3 and 23.8 actually show is that they were
acted upon in a sexual sense, and so they should be more adequately described as
having been sexually abused (1993: 166). She refers to this as an example of 'misnaming female experience', which causes women to be viewed as responsible for
their own violation (166). The same comment could well be applied to the woman
taken in adultery, since there is no distinction between rape and adultery in the law,
and even the form of the verb used to describe her so-called sin is in the passive
voice (Jn 8.4).

54. Thompson 1974: 201.

crime?[55] Under these circumstances, Jesus' reply to the accusers can be taken to mean, 'Let the one among you who is without sin in bringing this accusation be the first to throw a stone at her'. Their response to his words implies that their testimony is indeed deeply flawed; not one of them is prepared to stay and press the case once Jesus has spoken, and without the testimony of reliable witnesses against the woman the only proper course of action left to Jesus is to acquit her of the charge.

When Jesus' actions are seen in this light, it seems clear that he is not simply letting a guilty woman off the hook in what might be thought of as an unsatisfactory way. Rather, he is using the tools of the law that are available to him in order to prevent a miscarriage of justice. He is beating the accusers at their own game, and exposing the fact that although they claim to be upholding the law they are actually grievously misusing it—as is evidenced by their shamefaced dispersal when he challenges them. Not only are they laying a legally unjustifiable amount of responsibility on the lone woman, they are doing so without the support of reliable witnesses. But there is still the question of how the woman came to be accused in the first place. Surely she must be guilty, and therefore deserving of punishment, if she was caught in the very act of adultery? Assuming that the testimony of the accusers was in some way corrupt, as evidenced by their refusal to pursue the matter, a number of scenarios present themselves as possible explanations for how the situation might have arisen, although of course they must remain hypothetical. Derrett draws attention to the need to have at least two witnesses to the act of adultery itself, not just to the pair being seen together or in a compromising situation, and in view of the difficulty of achieving that, suggests that the woman's capture was a set-up: her jealous or suspicious husband had hired the witnesses to spy on her, and when she met with her lover they had allowed her to continue in her sin without making any attempt to stop her.[56] However, this assumes that the woman's guilt was beyond question, that she really had been involved in an act of voluntary intercourse with a man other than her husband. As indicated earlier, this need not have been the case, given the failure to distinguish in the law between voluntary and involuntary

55. Derrett (1963–64: 8) states, 'The witnesses will have been there', but this assumes that the charge was to some degree at least substantiated—and indeed, that the Pharisees were interested in substantiating the charge against the woman rather than simply trapping Jesus into an inflammatory response.

56. Derrett 1963–64: 4-8.

adultery in the case of a married woman. Indeed, it is possible that what the witnesses saw was in fact rape, and the reason for the woman's discovery was that she had cried out. In that case, the real sin would have been committed by those who chose to disregard the true nature of the woman's plight because they wanted to use her as ammunition in the battles with Jesus.

Alternatively, if the case was a set-up in order to make sure that there were witnesses, a man could have been paid to seduce the woman and then to appear as a witness against her. This would explain why her partner failed to be brought to justice, or even to appear in the scenario in any way. But there is also the possibility, perhaps the most attractive given the ambiguous nature of the narrative, that there were no witnesses to an act of adultery, and that the woman was being accused and virtually condemned on hearsay or suspicion. In this case, no assumptions can be made about whether she was guilty or innocent of the crime of which she was accused; indeed, it leaves open the very real possibility that she was guilty as charged. But Jesus' reply indicates that it is unacceptable to condemn a person to death merely on the basis of hearsay, even if that person is an adulterous woman who presents a threat to the whole ordering of society.

The whole episode is so compressed and therefore ambiguous that it lends itself to many different readings. However, it seems clear that the woman is a scapegoat, caught in the middle between other men's power games. Not only is she being made to bear a responsibility which legally is not hers to bear, she is being made to bear it in order to trap Jesus into giving an unfavourable response, regardless of what she herself may or may not have done or suffered. The incident can therefore be seen as an example of the attitudes discussed earlier, whereby men's honour and status were dependent upon their control of women, and the way to attack another man was to attack his women. Of course, this woman was not Jesus' wife or relative, but given his known tendency to associate with 'sinners', she was the kind of woman to whom he might well be expected to relate and with whom he could establish a rapport. Hence, his failure to save both her (and himself) from the situation would have demonstrated his inability to protect the very people he was supposed to be concerned with, and would have seriously undermined his credibility. But Jesus proves himself more than equal to the task of saving her from the conniving clutches of her accusers, thus establishing the rapport with her that enables him to treat her as a person in her own right and respond to her in an affirmatory rather than a condemnatory fashion. In vindicating her, even though she could be branded a 'sinner', he vindicates himself and what he stands for. Thus the story provides a sharp contrast with the Old Testament examples discussed above, where men vindicated themselves against other men by punishing not only the other men but also the women who were caught between them.

Conclusion

The Old Testament laws about marriage, adultery and divorce, the use of the metaphor of a (broken) marriage between Yahweh and his people, and the story of the woman taken in adultery all need to be understood on the basis of the androcentric nature of biblical society. When viewed from such a perspective, it is possible to appreciate nuances of meaning that are otherwise hidden, and in particular to recognize how the full meaning of these texts depends on a thoroughly subordinationist view of women and their sexuality.

BIBLIOGRAPHY

Barrett, C.K.
    1978   *The Gospel According to St John* (London: SPCK, 2nd edn).
Beasley-Murray, George R.
    1987   *John* (WBC, 36; Waco, TX: Word Books).
Bellefontaine, Elizabeth
    1979   'Deuteronomy 21.18-21: Reviewing the Case of the Rebellious Son',
        JSOT 13: 13-31.
Bird, Phyllis
    1989   ' "To Play the Harlot": An Inquiry into an Old Testament Metaphor', in
        Peggy L. Day (ed.), *Gender and Difference in Ancient Israel* (Philadelphia, PA: Fortress Press): 75-94.
Blinzler, J.
    1957–58   'Die Strafe für Ehebruch in Bibel und Halacha zur Auslegung von Joh.
        viii 5', *NTS* 4: 32-47.
Brodie, Thomas L.
    1993   *The Gospel According to John: A Literary and Theological Commentary*
        (Oxford: Oxford University Press).
Brown, Raymond E.
    1966   *The Gospel According to John I–XII* (AB, 29; Garden City, NY: Doubleday).

Carson, D.A.
    1991   *The Gospel According to John* (Leicester: IVP; Grand Rapids, MI:
                Eerdmans).
Cathcart, Kevin J., and Robert P. Gordon
    1989   *The Targum of the Minor Prophets, Translated with a Critical Introduc-
                tion, Apparatus, and Notes* (The Aramaic Bible, 14; Edinburgh: T. & T.
                Clark).
Cunliffe-Jones, H.
    1951   *Deuteronomy* (TBC; London: SCM Press).
Darr, Katheryn Pfisterer
    1992   'Ezekiel', in Carol A. Newsom and Sharon H. Ringe (eds.), *The Women's
                Bible Commentary* (London: SPCK; Louisville, KY: Westminster/John
                Knox Press): 183-90.
Davies, Eryl W.
    1981   'Inheritance Rights and the Hebrew Levirate Marriage: Parts 1 and 2', *VT*
                31: 138-44, 257-68.
Derrett, J. Duncan M.
    1963–64   'Law in the New Testament: The Story of the Woman Taken in
                Adultery', *NTS* 10: 1-26.
Dion, Paul-Eugène
    1980   ' "Tu feras disparaître le mal du milieu de toi" ', *RB* 87: 321-49.
Dijk-Hemmes, F. van
    1993   'The Metaphorization of Woman in Prophetic Speech: An Analysis of
                Ezekiel xxiii', *VT* 43: 162-70.
Driver, S.R.
    1895   *Deuteronomy* (ICC; Edinburgh: T. & T. Clark).
Eilberg-Schwartz, Howard
    1994   *God's Phallus and Other Problems for Men and Monotheism* (Boston,
                MA: Beacon Press).
Frick, Frank S.
    1994   'Widows in the Hebrew Bible: A Transactional Approach', in Athalya
                Brenner (ed.), *A Feminist Companion to Exodus–Deuteronomy* (The
                Feminist Companion to the Bible, 6; Sheffield: Sheffield Academic
                Press): 139-51.
Galambush, Julie
    1992   *Jerusalem in the Book of Ezekiel: The City as Yahweh's Wife* (SBLDS,
                130; Atlanta, GA: Scholars Press).
Goetze, Albrecht (trans.)
    1969   'The Hittite Laws', *ANET*: 188-97.
Hugenberger, Gordon P.
    1998   *Marriage as a Covenant: Biblical Law and Ethics as Developed from
                Malachi* (Grand Rapids: Baker Book House).
Keefe, Alice A.
    1995   'The Female Body, the Body Politic and the Land: A Sociopolitical
                Reading of Hosea 1–2', in Athalya Brenner (ed.), *A Feminist Companion
                to the Latter Prophets* (The Feminist Companion to the Bible, 8; Shef-
                field: Sheffield Academic Press): 70-100.

Lindars, Barnabas
    1972   *The Gospel of John* (NCBC; London: Marshall, Morgan & Scott).
Mace, D.R.
    1953   *Hebrew Marriage: A Sociological Study* (London: Epworth Press).
Mayes, A.D.H.
    1979   *Deuteronomy* (NCBC; London: Marshall, Morgan & Scott).
McKeating, Henry
    1979   'Sanctions against Adultery in Ancient Israelite Society, with Some Reflections on Methodology in the Study of Old Testament Ethics', *JSOT* 11: 57-72.
Moloney, Francis J.
    1998   *The Gospel of John* (Sacra Pagina, 4; Collegeville, MN: Liturgical Press).
Oden, Robert A., Jr
    1987   *The Bible without Theology: The Theological Tradition and Alternatives to it* (San Francisco, CA: Harper & Row).
Phillips, Anthony
    1973   *Deuteronomy* (CBC; Cambridge: Cambridge University Press).
    1981   'Another Look at Adultery', *JSOT* 20: 3-25.
Pressler, Carolyn
    1993   *The View of Women Found in the Deuteronomic Family Laws* (BZAW, 216; Berlin: W. de Gruyter).
    1994   'Sexual Violence and Deuteronomic Law', in Athalya Brenner (ed.), *A Feminist Companion to Exodus–Deuteronomy* (A Feminist Companion to the Bible, 6; Sheffield: Sheffield Academic Press): 102-12.
Sanders, J.N., and B.A. Mastin
    1968   *A Commentary on the Gospel According to St John* (London: A. & C. Black).
Schnackenburg, Rudolph
    1980   *The Gospel According to St John*, II (London: Burns & Oates).
Sherwood, Yvonne
    1995   'Boxing Gomer: Controlling the Deviant Woman in Hosea 1–3', in Athalya Brenner (ed.), *A Feminist Companion to the Latter Prophets* (A Feminist Companion to the Bible, 8; Sheffield: Sheffield Academic Press): 101-125.
Sloyan, Gerard S.
    1988   *John* (Interpretation; Atlanta, GA: John Knox Press).
Stienstra, Nelly
    1993   *YHWH is the Husband of his People: Analysis of a Biblical Metaphor with Special Reference to Translation* (Kampen: Kok).
Stone, Ken
    1996   *Sex, Honor, and Power in the Deuteronomistic History* (JSOTSup, 234; Sheffield: Sheffield Academic Press).
Stulman, Louis
    1992   'Sex and Familial Crimes in the D Code: A Witness to Mores in Transition', *JSOT* 53: 47-63.
Thompson, J.A.
    1974   *Deuteronomy* (TOTC; London: Inter-Varsity Press).

Weems, Renita J.

1995   *Battered Love: Marriage, Sex and Violence in the Hebrew Prophets* (Overtures to Biblical Theology; Minneapolis, MN: Fortress Press).

Wenham, Gordon J.

1972   '*Bᵉtūlāh* "A Girl of Marriageable Age" ', *VT* 22: 326-48.

White, Leland J.

1995   'Does the Bible Speak about Gays or Same-Sex Orientation? A Test Case in Biblical Ethics: Part I', *BTB* 25: 14-23.

Yee, Gale A.

1992   'Hosea', in Carol A. Newsom and Sharon H. Ringe (eds.), *The Women's Bible Commentary* (London: SPCK; Louisville, KY: Westminster/John Knox Press): 195-202.

ON THE TRAIL OF A GOOD STORY: JOHN 7.53–8.11 IN THE GOSPEL TRADITION

J. Martin C. Scott

There are few texts that provide a better insight into the process of Gospel formation than that of the story of the woman accused of adultery. As we shall see, the textual evidence overwhelmingly shows that it did not belong in the earliest manuscripts of the New Testament, yet later scribes chose to include it, most usually at the end of John 7, but occasionally elsewhere.[1] Despite its late inclusion, however, there is also evidence among early Christian writers that it was known as a separate story from fairly ancient times. Eusebius of Caesarea, writing his *Ecclesiastical History* in the early fourth century, quotes the second-century Papias as recording 'another story of a woman, who was accused of many sins before the Lord, which is contained in the Gospel according to the Hebrews' (3.39.16). Although we have no evidence that it did belong in this non-canonical writing,[2] the point of its early existence is nevertheless made.

More direct evidence comes from the third-century *Constitutions of the Holy Apostles* 2.24, which records the following:

> And when the elders had set another woman which had sinned before Him, and had left the sentence to Him, and were gone out, our Lord, the Searcher of the hearts, inquiring of her whether the elders had condemned her, and being answered No, He said unto her: 'Go thy way, therefore, for neither do I condemn thee'.

There can be little doubt that this is the account now placed at Jn 7.53. What is striking is that the writer places it alongside other quotations from New Testament writings (another quotation from a story of a

---

1.   Notably also in Luke's Gospel after Lk. 21.38, but also in several other places in the Johannine text.

2.   See the reconstruction of fragments in Vielhauer (1991).

woman 'sinner' [Lk. 7.47] immediately precedes it) without any distinction being made. Perhaps this is already an indication as to why it
was possible for some scribes to begin including it in later manuscripts.

Both its late *in*clusion and its earlier *ex*clusion from the Gospels are
matters which have puzzled scholars over the years. On the one hand,
its inclusion concerns those who see it as having the potential to provide a canvas upon which a picture of Jesus as less than stringent in his
condemnation of sexual sin may be painted.[3] On the other hand, its
exclusion from the canonical Gospels until a fairly late date exercises
the minds of those who suspect an attempt to play down Jesus' merciful
attitude, clearly acknowledged elsewhere in the tradition, precisely
because that disposition relates here to sexual impropriety.[4]

My purpose in this essay is to offer a narrative perspective on the text
as it most commonly occurs in Jn 7.53–8.11, to highlight the key issues
which arise in the story, and to see what new insight may be gained
from such consideration. This will allow me then to suggest possible
reasons for the story's initial exclusion from the canonical Gospels and
its eventual inclusion, and specifically its insertion in the Fourth
Gospel.

1. *The Textual Tradition*

The textual evidence relating to Jn 7.53–8.11 is comprehensively sur-
veyed by Ulrich Becker in his monumental work on the textual and
tradition history of the pericope (1963: 8-25).[5] A brief summary of
Becker's work may allow us a glimpse of the history of the emergence
of the story in the Gospel tradition.

---

3. It is against bishops who may be 'pitiless, not receiving the repentant sinner'
that the writer of the *Constitutions of the Holy Apostles* deliberately directs the story
(2.24). Calvin (1959: 209) was at his most vitriolic on this text, commenting that
'the Popish theology is that in this passage Christ has brought in the law of grace,
by which adulterers may be freed from punishment'. He then goes on to conclude
that 'although Christ remits men's sins, He does not subvert the social order or
abolish legal sentences and punishments'.

4. There is evidence from early Christian writings that adultery was considered
a sin so serious that even repentance might not bring forgiveness—see the discussion below for references.

5. Becker (1963: 145-50) also examines reports of the appearance of this text
in the *Gospel of Thomas*. See Aland (1967: 39-46) who updates, revises and offers
further insight on Becker's work.

The text is completely absent from the earliest Greek manuscripts of the New Testament, including the important papyri ($\mathfrak{P}$ 66 and $\mathfrak{P}$ 75) and both the major Codices which date from the fourth century (Sinaiticus and Vaticanus). Its appearance in later fifth- and sixth-century manuscripts such as D, E and H is always qualified by an asterisk or obelisk, indicating the scribe's opinion of its dubious nature. It is interesting to note that there are even some manuscripts which leave a space where the text could be inserted (Moir 1988: 172), suggesting that it was known in a written form and deliberately left out because of doubts about its authenticity.

A similar situation exists with regard to the absence of the text in manuscripts in all the other ancient languages of the New Testament. As Becker summarizes: 'The oldest and most important Greek, Syriac, Armenian, Georgian, Coptic and Latin witness to the New Testament text unanimously concur in not knowing the pericope of the adulteress' (1963: 25; my translation).

Even when the text begins to enter the manuscript tradition, it is by no means fixed in its position. Certainly the most common position is at Jn 7.53–8.11, but other notable settings for the pericope are after Jn 7.36 (minuscule 225) and after Jn 21.24—a kind of appendix to the Gospel, again betraying the scribes' doubt as to its validity. Some modern translations continue this tradition (notably NEB; REB), while the majority place it in brackets. The appearance of the pericope after Lk. 21.38 in a group of manuscripts merely goes to show both how widely known the story was, and how unsettled the text remained for a long period of time.

Although the text becomes most commonly fixed at the end of John 7, there is great variation in the wording, especially in the main section of the text, Jn 8.3-11. Ian Moir quotes C.R. Gregory's remarks on the extent of the variety in the transmission of the text:

> If I am not mistaken, there are in the whole New Testament no other dozen verses that exhibit such a manifold variation of reading. It is a section that in reference to its textual history and textual character stands totally alone. This multifariousness of form I am inclined to connect with its having been so very often read, and especially at a very early time (1988: 172).

Gregory also believed that the text was widely used in the early Church, even although it was not part of the Johannine text. He noted many manuscripts that contain new leaves and a new handwriting at this point, showing that the story had been deliberately added into older manuscripts at a later stage. His observation on the late oral trans-mission of the text is important, since it reflects the notion that the text had a life *within* the Church, rather than merely as an apocryphal tradi-tion drawn in from the edges by some later, interested party.

There seems to be some difference between Eastern and Western tex-tual traditions in terms of dating the first surfacing in the manuscripts. The pericope's provenance is stronger in the Western manuscripts, par-ticularly in Latin, and this trend is borne out by the fact that it is only among the Western 'Fathers' that the text receives any interpretative attention prior to the tenth century. Augustine is an interesting example at this point, since he offers full commentary on the pericope in his *Tractates on the Gospel According to St John*.[6] It may be that, although he knew it was not an original part of the Gospel, he considered it wor-thy of comment because of his opinion that it had once belonged to the text of John's Gospel—by all other standards a mistaken notion, but one to which I shall return.

Whatever the attitude of later Christian writers to this story, and however certain we may be that it was an ancient story, there can scarcely be any doubt that it was not an original part of the text of the Fourth Gospel, or indeed of any canonical writing. I shall turn now to read the text in its most common setting, at the end of ch. 7, before returning to the issue of its exclusion and inclusion.

2. Reading the Text

In the light of the textual tradition, how do we go about reading the story of the woman accused of adultery? This of all texts has proved difficult to approach using traditional historical methodology, not least because its lack of a secure context leaves it vulnerable to a high degree of speculation. The most widely acknowledged setting for the story is surely its position in the text of the Fourth Gospel at Jn 7.53–8.11. I shall therefore attempt a narrative reading of the pericope from within this commonly recognized position. The temporal setting is the end of the feast of Tabernacles and the physical setting of the main part of the text the environs of the Temple in Jerusalem. The action thus takes place at the heart of Israel's religious and cultural life.

6.   *Tractate* 33 is on Jn 7.40-53 and 8.1-11.

Although its original reference is unknown, the opening 'each of them' (ἕκαστος, 7.53) now refers to the departure of Nicodemus and the rest of the Pharisees. Despite the best efforts of Nicodemus, the Pharisees' purpose has been to find a pretext to arrest Jesus, and the failure of the Temple police to do so is a source of frustration to them. Jesus has escaped the grasp of his opponents once more and, for the only time in the Johannine story, spends the evening on the Mount of Olives. This geographical detail (8.1) is without exception seen by commentators as a point of disjuncture, and one of the reasons for the story finding a home after Lk. 21.38, which bears a number of similarities to Jn 8.1-2. From a narrative perspective, this misses a crucial intertextual link, which binds the story closely to Jesus prior words concerning 'living water' in Jn 7.37-39.

It is important to note that the Johannine account does not, in fact, use the same expression for 'Mount of Olives' which is found in Lk. 21.37 (τὸ ὄρος τὸ καλούμενον Ἐλαιῶν), but instead uses the form found in the LXX text of Zech. 14.4 (τὸ ὄρος τῶν ἐλαιῶν). This text in Zechariah is one of those that offer an echo of the theme of 'living waters' (Zech. 14.8; Jn 7.38).[7] As a prophecy of eschatological judgment, if an echo of the Zechariah text is heard in Jn 8.1, it provides both a link back to Jesus' preceding speech ('living water') and a perfect backdrop for what is to follow (judgment theme) in the Johannine context.

It is from this place *of* judgment that Jesus returns to be tested *in* judgment at dawn the next day (8.2). It is to the environs of the Temple that he once more comes, alerting the reader to the potential for entrapment, given the immediately preceding plotting of his opponents and the role of the Temple police in it. As so often in the Johannine narrative, many people are present to hear Jesus' wisdom, but crucially also to witness the events which follow in the unfolding drama.

The life-giving Word is interrupted in mid-flow by the merchants of death (8.3), who arrive abruptly on the scene, taking centre stage while the crowd appears for the moment at least to melt into the background. The Pharisees are joined here uniquely in the Johannine narrative by the scribes. Although difficult to see from our commonly used Greek texts,

7.   This text in Zechariah also connects with this section of John by reference to the feast of Tabernacles (Zech. 14.16). Jn 2.16 also alludes to Zech. 14.21, indicating the measure to which this text was known and reflected upon by early Christians.

it is notable that some manuscripts read 'chief priests' instead of 'scribes' here, which indicates that at least some copyists were alert to the nuances of Johannine language and sought to align it to the more familiar pattern found at Jn 7.32.[8]

The drama really begins to unfold with the announcement of the purpose of Jesus' opponents appearance: they bring a woman with them who they claim has been caught in adultery. The description is startling as she is thrust into the centre of the picture. As Gail O'Day describes it: 'She is an object on display, given no name, no voice, no identity apart from that for which she stands accused' (1992: 632). The reader here may recall an earlier story in the Fourth Gospel in which an unnamed woman is, at least implicitly, accused of sexual licence (Jn 4.16-18, the Samaritan woman). There the encounter with Jesus started a process of discovery by which the Samaritan woman entered into new faith and performed the task of true discipleship by calling others of her own people to an encounter with Jesus.[9] Here, however, the scene is much more threatening, since a woman's life clearly hangs in the balance. There remains every possibility that for her the outcome will not be life but death, as she becomes the scapegoat in a male power-game.

The positioning of the woman 'in the middle' (ἐν μέσῳ) is reminiscent of a courtroom scene. Schottroff quotes the tragic account of the modern-day stoning of a woman in an Iranian village, describing the way in which she was buried up to her neck, a circle drawn around her head, and the stoning commenced (1995: 183-84). While it is difficult to read this horrific practice directly back as a precise description of such a stoning in the Palestine of Jesus' day, it graphically illustrates for the modern reader the significance of being placed 'in the middle'.

This image also reminds us of the reality for the woman brought before Jesus: she is on trial for her life. Yet the reader becomes increasingly aware that the trial is not about any form of justice, but is a put-up job. First, if the woman was truly guilty of adultery, as the next verse tries to confirm, what need would there be to consult Jesus, for whose judgment his opponents to this point have shown only contempt (7.12,

8.   Brown 1966: 333. This reading is not evident from the critical apparatus of the Nestle–Aland twenty seventh edition. The edition by Constantine Tischendorf, *Novum Testamentum Graece* (1869), however, lists four miniscules which contain the reading 'chief priests'. It is significant insofar as it indicates the care taken by some copyists in inserting material in a manner sensitive to context.
9.   See Scott 1992: 184-98.

15, 20, 47-49)? Second, even the most obtuse of readers recognizes that it takes more than one person to commit adultery—yet only a woman is brought to Jesus. Third, the following verses show that Jesus is being placed in an impossible situation with regard to making a judgment, having to contradict the letter of either the Jewish or the Roman law.

The Pharisees appear to approach Jesus with a measure of respect when they address him as 'Teacher' (διδάσκαλος, 8.4). This may be evoked by the earlier description of his position, seated on the ground in the traditional manner of a rabbi with his disciples around him (8.2). Brown sees this as another link with Synoptic style (1966: 333), but it is in fact the most common way of addressing Jesus in the Fourth Gospel, and a title which the Johannine Jesus himself later acknowledges as an accurate description (Jn 13.13, 14) (Scott 1992: 152).

A significant narrative 'gap' occurs at this point. We hear that the woman was caught in the very act of adultery, but we are not told whether she has already been tried and sentenced or whether Jesus is being sought out as the 'judge' in a highly irregular court scene. Although Schnackenburg, after a whole page of discussion, concludes with some justification that 'the story itself shows no interest in the question' (1980: 164), it nonetheless remains an important interpretative crux for the narrative reader. Is Jesus being placed in the formal position of 'judge' by the Pharisees, or is he being, as it were, consulted in passing as the woman is taken already to her place of execution? The narrative setting into which the story has been placed by the copyists makes the former choice compelling, given the direct relationship which emerges on either side with Jn 7.24 and 8.15. The idea that, in addressing Jesus as 'Teacher', the Pharisees are 'in effect submitting the case to him for decision' (Schnackenburg 1980: 164), is attractive: the tone is set for what follows by alluding to Jesus as judge.

The designation of the crime as 'adultery' (μοιχεία) raises a number of issues for a narrative reading. Much of the discussion among historical critics has centred on the nature of the crime, the legality of the accusation in terms of proper witnesses and the marital status of the woman.[10] Again the text reveals nothing of any certainty here, even though the weight of argument seems to favour seeing her as a married woman. A significant aspect of the way in which the story is told is the uncovering of the hypocrisy of the woman's accusers, so the suggestion

10. See Blinzler (1957–58: 32-47); Derrett (1963–64); Becker (1963: 165-69).

that she is being used as a pawn in a deadly game in which the rules are being flouted sits well with the overall aim of the account. This would suggest that, whatever the legal niceties of the case, which Derrett (1963–64) is at pains to uncover, justice under the law is neither sought nor required by the accusers.

In the light of this, the theme of adultery takes on a different aspect within the Johannine narrative as a whole. It has long been noted that irony is a common technique employed by the Fourth Evangelist (Duke 1985), and this text fits the literary pattern of the Gospel well in this respect. As George Brooke has pointed out (1988: 107), there is a strong linguistic connection in the LXX between the two terms μοιχεία and πορνεία, the latter of which is used to describe Jesus' opponents in Jn 8.41. Whether or not the copyist saw this connection in placing the story where it now appears in the Fourth Gospel,[11] the close conjunction of the words now offers such a literary link to be made by the reader. The irony now lies in the fact that Jesus' opponents, who seek to condemn another of adultery, themselves come under such suspicion and innuendo within a matter of a few verses!

Adultery is used frequently in the Hebrew scriptures, especially in the prophetic materials,[12] as a metaphor for apostasy—turning away from the true God. This is precisely what the Fourth Gospel portrays the opponents of Jesus as doing in rejecting his message of truth for their own 'lies' (Jn 8.55). What irony, then, that those who seek to trap Jesus through complicity in 'subverting' the letter of the law on adultery, should themselves end up under accusation of the same charge. That the narrative does infer their guilt here is strengthened by another observation which Brooke makes regarding the use of language in Jn 8.44. Here the word ἐπιθυμία appears for the only time in the Gospel. Brooke connects it to the use of the word to translate the subject of the tenth commandment ('You shall not covet') in both of the LXX versions of the decalogue (Exod. 20.17; Deut. 5.21). He concludes:

> Since the first object of covetousness in the prohibition in the LXX is 'your neighbour's wife', it is perhaps not surprising to find an allusion to this commandment, the tenth, as the dialogue develops from the subject of adultery (1988: 107).

11. Brooke (1988: 107) suggests that this was the case, and I see no good reason to doubt the ability of an intelligent copyist in making this connection.

12. For details of the main texts, see Brooke (1988: 107).

In reading the unfolding narrative of John's Gospel, then, the insertion of the story of the woman taken in adultery at the end of ch. 7 serves to underline the hypocrisy of Jesus' opponents in the following dialogue. But it has a still wider connection to the theme of apostasy by means of yet another vital intertextual allusion: namely, to the figure of Sophia in Israel's wisdom literature.

The comparison between the adulteress, or prostitute and Sophia is a well-worked theme in Proverbs 1–9. The whole image of God's invitation to humanity, in the form of Sophia as the woman who invites 'men' to receive her gifts, functions successfully because it has a perfect foil in the image of the immoral woman who seeks to turn them away from God. This latter figure surely represents apostasy in the Wisdom tradition. Brooke also refers to the Wisdom literature, pointing to the identification of Sophia with Torah in Sir. 24.23 (1988: 107). To reject Sophia is to abandon the law, whose very purpose is to keep 'men' from the seductive powers of the adulteress (Prov. 6.23-29). Since the Fourth Gospel contains a sophisticated leitmotif of Jesus as the embodiment of Wisdom over against the idea that she is contained in the Torah,[13] the rejection of Jesus Sophia by his opponents in John 8 is an indication precisely of their apostasy. The huge irony which the insertion of a story concerning adultery throws up is that their supposed defence of the Torah is calculated at the expense of the true embodiment of Wisdom, Jesus Sophia. In Johannine terms, the attempt to entrap Jesus through Torah is the ultimate apostasy, since it puts false wisdom in place of true Wisdom.

The reference to Moses (8.5) recalls the words of the Johannine Prologue (1.17), where a direct comparison is made between Jesus and the lawgiver. Since at that point the contrast is made between law on the one hand and grace and truth on the other, the reader is already prepared for the potentiality of a merciful judgment from Jesus. In the story of the quite deliberate healing of a man on the *sabbath* (5.1-18), the Johannine Jesus has also demonstrated before that he is more than willing to flout the letter of the law to engage in the merciful work of God. When the story is placed into the context of John 7–8, the eventual outcome is less surprising in the light of what has gone before. Barrett notes that grammatically speaking the word 'you' (σύ) is placed

---

13. See Scott (1992: 105-106). The comparison begins in Jn 1.17 and continues throughout the Gospel.

'in a position of emphasis, inviting Jesus to set himself against Moses' (1978: 591). He duly takes up the challenge!

Although the story seems primarily concerned with the issue of Jesus' attitude to the Jewish law, on the level of the wider narrative a double dilemma is set up for Jesus in this challenge. On the one hand, if he refuses to condemn the woman to death, he will be accused of rejecting the authority of Moses and the Torah. Of course, the Johannine Jesus has already indicated his claim to superiority over Moses in a prior speech (5.46) and will do so again in the following dialogue (8.58), but the insertion of this story heightens the drama by appearing to make him explicitly override a legal prescription. On the other hand, if he accepts the verdict and allows the woman to be stoned, he not only subverts the portrayal of his role as the very embodiment of grace and truth (1.14), but also stands in potential conflict with the authority of the Roman law. Even if we cannot be certain whether the saying in Jn 18.31 was an accurate description of the functioning of Roman rule in Palestine at the time of Jesus, it is quite clear that on the level of a *narrative* reading, this conflict potentially exists for the Johannine Jesus.

The narrator interrupts the flow of the story at this point (8.6) to make explicit to the reader what has all along appeared to be the case: the woman is merely the bait in a plot to catch a bigger fish—Jesus. Although this aside does not appear in all manuscripts and is considered secondary by such a careful commentator as Becker, it fits well with Johannine style, as Johnson (1966) has pointed out.[14] The late addition of this statement[15] may again reflect the activity of knowledgeable scribes, who adjusted its style to echo Johannine usage. However much the aside now places the focus on the plot against Jesus, the reader remains conscious that it is the woman who lies in most immediate danger of death.

Jesus responds by bending down and writing with his finger on the

14. See also Trites (1974: 137-46).

15. We should note here the astonishing interpretation of Young (1995). He sees the addition of this verse to the tradition as an indicator of a quite different purpose in the *original* form of the story. Far from being a tale which sought to denigrate the Pharisees, he argues that the text is really about an attempt by the Pharisees to find a way to *save* the woman from the awful sentence of the law. In the young Rabbi Jesus they find an interpreter who enables them to achieve this end: 'They wanted to save her, and Jesus helped them' (1995: 70). Suffice it to say that only a *male* commentator was ever likely to think that one up!

ground. Perhaps predictably, this mention of ciphers in the sand, with its twin in v. 8, has been the subject of intense speculation by historical critics, who advance the claims of a variety of possible subjects. Some commentators assume that Jesus must have written out a text, which eventually pricks the consciences of the accusers. Others think he makes a more general accusation, for example by writing down the sins of his opponents. Yet others see it more in the form of a symbolic action, perhaps evocative of a particular text like Jer. 17.13: 'Those who have turned away from you will be written in the dust, because they have forsaken the Lord, the spring of living water'.

Among the texts advanced as possible subjects for Jesus' scribbling, Derrett is confident in identifying consecutively Exod. 23.1b and 23.7. This reflects his opinion that Jesus is challenging the legality of their witness and the honesty of their motives in bringing the charge (1963–64: 16-25). Derrett goes so far as to suggest that, from his position of crouching down, Jesus could only have written some 12 Hebrew characters—which miraculously coincides with the texts he quotes! Ingenious though this is, it is completely speculative and, as Brown comments, 'if the matter were of major importance, the content of the writing would have been reported' (Brown 1966: 334).

Brown's own conclusion about the action is untypically lacking in imagination. He thinks that Jesus is simply taking time out 'doodling on the ground' in order to contain his anger and revulsion (1966: 334). Even if this were the reason for the first such action, it does not explain the second occurrence. Strangely, too, the exhaustive treatment of Becker is somewhat banal at this point, since he sees the action of Jesus as merely an insertion by the narrator to offer a pause in the controversy dialogue (1963: 87). In his commentary on the text he calls it a 'novelistic-decorative detail' (1979: 283), rather ignoring the point, taken up by Schöndorf, that the double appearance of the motif in such a short text indicates a significant emphasis on it by the writer (Schöndorf 1996: 92).[16]

Schöndorf himself is almost triumphant in his identification of the significance of Exod. 31.18, the closing verse of the giving of the law on Sinai, with its telling phrase, 'the tablets of stone inscribed by the finger of God'. He concludes: 'Jesus' finger would be, in fact *is* the finger of God, which writes down the divine Law and thereby expresses

16. Also note Schnackenburg (1980: 165-66).

his opinion regarding sin' (1996: 92; my translation and emphasis). As an example of intertextual echo around the word 'finger' this would make some sense, but as a historical judgment it could scarcely justify Schöndorf's optimism.

In his analysis of the background to the text, Manson cites yet another possible approach to defining the content of the writing. He thinks it may well reflect the practice of the Roman courts, where the judge would first of all write out the sentence before delivering it to the accused (1952–53: 255-56). This might work with the first instance, the sentence being that announced in v. 7, but in terms of the unfolding of the narrative, the second occurrence, which would by Manson's analysis be the words of Jesus to the woman in v. 11, already anticipates the departure of the accusers in v. 9. Beasley-Murray also rightly cautions against reading wider Roman practice into the Palestinian context (1986: 146).[17] Luise Schottroff's comment probably contains more insight on the realities of the situation, however, when she says: 'I do not believe that Rome's representatives, especially the prefect in Caesarea, would have regarded a woman's execution by stoning as a trespass against Rome's sole jurisdiction over capital punishment' (1995: 184).

Schottroff rightly points to the assumption in both the narrative world of the text and the harsh world of the *Pax Romana,* that the woman is at best a disposable commodity.

Given this variety of suggestions from those approaching the text from a historical perspective, it is clear that there can be no simple single solution to the riddle of either its content or symbolism. From a narrative perspective, the action of Jesus presents a whole range of imagery for the reader open to its intertextuality. There is no question that Jer. 17.13 makes a compelling *narrative* link both with the internal discussion of the pericope (the apostasy theme noted above) and with the surrounding material in the text's present location in the Fourth Gospel. Jeremiah's reference to the 'spring of living water' has often been seen as a background to Jn 7.38. Then on the wider internal level of the Johannine narrative, the story would make a double connection to that of the Samaritan woman through the presence of a woman considered of dubious character and the identification of Jesus either verbally or symbolically as 'living water' (see Jn 4.14).

---

17. See also Schnackenburg (1980: 165).

I have already noted the potential narrative connection of the 'finger' to Exod. 31.18, and its further association with the Moses and the law. But the reader may also hear a link with another famous 'finger-writing' story—that of Belshazzar's feast, where the hand of God writes words of judgment on the wall condemning the King for his arrogance and apostasy (Dan. 5.5, 24-28). This is certainly the effect which Jesus' action has on the woman's accusers. It is also striking that the reward promised in Daniel to the one who would read the writing on the wall was to be dressed in a purple robe (Dan. 5.7, 29). This is precisely what happens to the Johannine Jesus during his mock coronation by the soldiers in Pilate's court (Jn 19.2).

The reader may also be encouraged to hear an echo of Daniel's account when we note the similarity between the whole of this story of a woman accused of adultery and the tale of Daniel and Susanna. In the story of Susanna, she is accused (falsely as it turns out) by two elders of Israel of committing adultery. She is initially sentenced to death on their evidence, that they caught her in the very act of adultery with a young man. In common with the Johannine story, this young man is not present at her trial, the excuse being that he escaped because he over-powered the elders. Susanna is only saved by the intervention of the hero, Daniel, who demands a retrial and brings about the conviction of the true culprits—the elders who first brought the charge.

Although the story of Susanna is often noted by commentators as having some similar content to the story of Jesus and the woman, it is usually deemed as unsuitable to provide a significant backdrop. Recently, for example, Iain McDonald has felt confident enough to state: 'The fact that the stories diverge in many important aspects removes any suggestion that this pericope is a gloss on the Susanna story' (1995: 421). In such an approach, Susanna is pictured as clearly innocent and falsely charged, whereas the Johannine woman is taken to be clearly guilty and subsequently 'let off' by Jesus.

Commenting on this issue, Sanders dogmatically states: 'The story... does not permit of the possibility that the accusation is false' (1990: 341). Yet, as we shall see, this approach to the Johannine text is based on quite slim evidence. The woman herself is never asked her side of the story and therefore has no chance of defending the charge. It is clear that even the narrator understands that she is being used in the story as a pawn in the Pharisees' game, so why should the reader believe their witness in the first place? The absence of the man strongly echoes the

Susanna story and raises at least the option for the narrative reader, that
the heroic intervention of Daniel on Susanna's behalf is being evoked.
The placing of the story between John 7 and 8, whose theme includes
the untrustworthiness of the witness of the Pharisees, offers the possibility to the reader that the woman may indeed, like Susanna before her,
be *innocent*.

The parallels between the two stories are, in fact, quite striking. In an
article commenting particularly on the legal issue of witnesses in the
Susanna story, Bernard Jackson summarizes the focus of that account:

> The story has a pronounced anti-judicial flavour. All the details point to
> the arrogance of the elders, and the humiliation heaped by them upon
> Susanna even before her condemnation... The point is given particular
> force, in terms of Jewish culture, by the theological dimension: the insuf-
> ficiency of the court's evidentiary safeguards is dramatically demon-
> strated by the fact that God himself is forced to intervene (1977: 38).

This description could easily be transplanted into the Johannine context. The whole of chs. 7–8 have a particular focus on the judicial process, with a clear emphasis on the unreliability of the witnesses who
come from the traditional Jewish religio-judicial hierarchy. There can
be little doubt that they have heaped humiliation on the woman by
dragging her publicly before Jesus, of all places in the heart of the religious institution, the Temple. Surely also, the insufficiency of the 'old'
legal system is precisely what the disputes of ch. 8 point to, and this
story of the woman's humiliation functions as a prime illustration of it
when placed at this point in the Gospel. Above all it is evident that the
theme of the pericope, taken in its Johannine context, is one of God's
intervention in the person of Jesus, whose very presence brings the
moment of *krisis*: the choice between life and death. The story of
Susanna, viewed from this perspective, acts as a perfect background
against which to hear the Johannine account and to recognize the
woman's innocence in the face of injustice.

Whatever intertextual echoes are evoked here, the story contains no
hint that the woman's accusers sought to argue with Jesus about what
was scribbled in the sand. A primary conclusion for the narrative critic
must be, then, that it is the *symbolism* of the action which combines
with Jesus' verbal challenge to force his opponents to back down in
disgrace. Given the range of potential intertextual echo we have noted,
there are two main themes which emerge: true interpretation of the law
(Exod. 23; 31), and judgment (Jer. 17; Dan. 5). Both of these themes

are prominent throughout the Fourth Gospel, and especially in the material of chs. 7–10 which surround the story. Those scribes who finally inserted the story at this point in John's narrative seem to have been aware of the appropriateness of their choice of venue.

Whatever Jesus may have written, his opponents are not content to let the matter lie: the text tells us that they put him under pressure ('They kept on asking', 8.7).[18] Although Schnackenburg suggests that they press Jesus because they are 'sure of their case' (1980: 166), the elements of injustice I have already noted make this unlikely. Rather, their behaviour is that of bullies who seek through pressure tactics to push someone they consider to be in a vulnerable position into a decision against the grain.

When Jesus' answer finally comes it is both dramatic and devastating. It is dramatic in that it adopts a high-risk strategy with regard to the woman's welfare; it is devastating in its insight and critique of the motivation of Jesus' opponents. While the commentators universally congratulate Jesus for the wisdom of his response, on the level of the narrative he nevertheless appears to condone the practice of stoning and invites death upon the woman. Just as the Magi, often called 'Wise Men', showed a certain lack of wisdom in going first to Herod, thus opening the way to the slaughter of the innocents, so too Jesus here runs the risk of encouraging his opponents to carry out their barbaric intentions towards the woman. As the narrator presents the story, whether we like it or not, she is a pawn not only in the hands of the opponents, but also in Jesus' reciprocation of their challenge to him.

Jesus' critique of his opponents is addressed in the first instance to the witnesses, since under Jewish law it was their duty to initiate the death penalty in the case of such a crime (Deut. 13.9; 17.7). What Jesus' words do is to introduce a different hierarchy of values to the criminal process here. Speaking of the role of the witnesses, Witherington sums it up in this way:

> They must not have any guilt in or legal responsibility for this particular crime themselves. Jesus then is questioning the motives of these men, for as leaders of Jewish society they had a moral responsibility to uphold the moral integrity of their community (1995: 364).

No longer, then, is the letter of the law in focus, but the motivation of the accusers. By this reading the word ἀναμάρτητος ('without sin')

18. See Schottroff (1995: 184).

surely does not mean 'sinless' but rather 'without moral responsibility' in the case. If we consider that no formal evidence has been brought in this case except the accusation that she was 'caught in the very act', and the bare fact alongside this is that no man is present, equally 'caught in the act', then the reader is left to fill a 'gap' which indicates that the witnesses do indeed share moral responsibility in the case. Either they are lying about the woman, in parallel to the Susanna story, or they have failed to bring to justice both parties involved in the case. This latter option would either mean that the male party was implicated in a scheme to entrap the woman (and so also Jesus), or that he was allowed to escape without being brought to justice.[19] The suggestion by Baltensweiler, that the man has already been executed 'does no justice to the text, because it does not explain the text's silence about this man'.[20]

Now for a second time Jesus stoops down and scribbles in the sand (8.8). As before, the action is symbolic, though on this occasion we hear that he 'wrote' (ἔγραφεν rather than the δακτύλῳ of v. 6). Sanders emphasizes the significance of kneeling down *twice*, seeing it as related to the giving of the two tablets of the Decalogue (1990: 341-42). Here he concurs with Schöndorf's view that the text in focus in the writing is Exod. 31.18 / Deut. 9.10, which talks of the two tablets written upon by the finger of God. Sanders suggests that Jesus initially bends and writes the first five commandments, in relation to which the accusers might declare themselves free from guilt, but when he stoops down and writes the second five, they are convicted by their consciences and leave. From the narrator's point of view the echo of the two tablets *might* be possible, but the second stooping down also provides a temporal space in which the embarrassed accusers may slink into a narrative void.

Gail O'Day provides another rationale for the double action of Jesus. She notes the pattern by which Jesus first bends down, then stands up to address his interlocutors, then speaks. Since Jesus does this twice, first directed towards the accusers and secondly towards the woman, O'Day thinks that this constitutes 'a narrative strategy of the text through which the scribes and Pharisees and the woman receive equal treatment from Jesus' (1992: 636). The story then becomes an invitation to both parties to 'give up the old ways and enter a new way of life'(O'Day

19. See Derrett (1963-64: 7), who notes that it was common practice for the male witnesses and the man involved in the act of adultery to come to an arrangement before trial whereby he was exonerated.

20. Schottroff 1995: 181. She is quoting here from Baltensweiler (1967: 125).

1992: 637). This is a clever and attractive reading of the text, even if it still assumes the guilt of the woman.

I have already noted how the insertion of this pericope into the Fourth Gospel provides further irony to a text which is well known for this literary technique. From a narrative perspective, Jesus' response to the woman's accusers sets up an ironic relationship to his own treatment later in the story. Questioned by Pilate about his lack of response to his interrogation, Jesus comments that the greater sin in his arrest and forthcoming death lies with his initial accusers—the Jewish leaders (19.11). The one who now releases a woman from injustice will himself become the victim of injustice perpetrated by the same accusers who, for the moment, cower off into the shadows. When this observation is read back into the story of this woman, the parallel with Jesus' innocence provides grist to the mill in the argument that the woman is *falsely* accused in John 8.

One by one, the accusers begin to drift silently away (8.9), starting with the eldest. This detail has been taken by commentators in different ways. It could be that those who are oldest are most conscious of their responsibility, or, as Lindars rather quaintly puts it, 'the more experienced senior men would be likely the first to acknowledge the falsity of their position' (1972: 310)! From the perspective of the narrative critic, however, there is a strong echo once again of the Susanna story, where it is old men, sufficiently frail that they can convince their audience initially that they were overcome by a single young man, responsible judges in Israel, who are the villains of the plot. From this angle it would be most appropriate for the oldest, and by implication the guiltiest to disappear quickly.

The final part of v. 9 is rather ambiguous, though this is rarely noted by commentators.[21] On the one hand we are told that Jesus is left 'alone' (μόνος) with the woman. Yet on the other hand, she is still curiously described as being 'in the middle' (ἐν μέσῳ). This echoes back to v. 3, where the reader is conscious that two distinct groupings are present: scribes and Pharisees who have dragged the woman in, and the crowd who were listening and learning before the others arrived. The narrator has thus left open the possibility that the accusers, those morally responsible, have departed the scene, while the seekers after truth, the crowd, remain as witnesses to the *entire* event.

21. Schnackenburg (1980: 167) is an exception here.

For the first time in the episode, Jesus now addresses the woman directly (8.10). In common with other stories involving women in the Fourth Gospel, Jesus calls her simply, 'woman' (γύναι), a formal term, but by no means cold or impolite.[22] Since he has stood up to address her, he must have observed that the accusing group have now departed, yet he asks her about them. It is highly significant that he does not interrogate her about the charge which had been brought, but instead seems to want to relieve her fear by calling attention to their departure. The reader is reminded here that the last words which Jesus spoke actually condemned the woman to be stoned—presumably she is still awaiting the impact of the first rock. The intertextual echo of the innocent Susanna's cry of despair to God as she awaits execution on a trumped-up charge sounds loudly to the informed reader of the story.

Now the woman begins to see clearly that, despite the risk of his strategy, Jesus has actually won her a stay of execution. Schottroff calls Jesus' action 'an act of civil courage', and goes on to comment on the effect that it has on the patriarchal system which perpetrated such injustice:

> The 'sin' of this woman is alike to the trespasses of those men, be it defamation, incest, theft, adultery, or any other offense. And Jesus disputes the particular status of adultery (shared with idolatry) as a capital crime. What this recognizes and critiques is the brutality that the patriarchal order brings into every woman's life through its power to regulate women's sexuality and the particular punishment meted out to women who have, or are alleged to have committed adultery. In terms of the text, Jesus, the messenger of God, takes sides with an afflicted and abased woman (1995: 185).

This is an important comment and has much in common with O'Day's analysis, since it moves the woman from her status as object to that of subject. In this respect the Johannine story goes beyond the comparable account of Susanna's experience, since she is never addressed, even by the 'heroic' Daniel. Even given this new-found status, however, in both stories the role of the woman is always held as secondary to the uncovering of the male 'hero'.

Jesus' question to the woman indicates that she has been released not merely from being 'judged' (κρίνειν—the normal Johannine usage),

---

22. Scott (1992: 179-80). He addresses his mother in this way at the foot of the cross (19.25-27).

but from being 'condemned' (κατακρίνειν).[23] Again this bears comparison with the story of Susanna, who is already on her way to execution before Daniel's intervention on her behalf brings release. Even at this late stage of the story, the question of the Johannine woman's guilt remains a matter of doubt under the influence of the Susanna account. It is especially important in narrative terms to recall the immediate connection of this theme of condemnation to Nicodemus's appeal on behalf of Jesus (7.51), who is being unjustly accused and condemned without trial by his opponents. The deliberate conjunction of these texts certainly makes way for a narrative reading which supports the innocence of the woman.

Finally the woman speaks for herself (8.11). There is now no longer an accuser in sight, so she must await only the judgment of the one who has saved her from her accusers' falsehood. Jesus' reply to her is swift and reassuring: he does not pronounce condemnation either. Here there are close echoes of the immediately surrounding material in the Fourth Gospel, especially Jn 8.15—'I pass judgment on no one'. But the echoes ring wider in the Gospel, for as Beasley-Murray points out, 'the story is a superb illustration of the dictum of 3.17' (1987: 147).

It might appear, then, that Jesus' pronouncement of freedom for the woman confirms her previous guilt. But is that really the case? Certainly the next statement seems to reinforce this—'Go and sin no more'—yet the narrative critic must point to a wider set of intertextual influences which offer another explanation for even this final statement. It has often been remarked that 8.11 bears close comparison with John 5.14, where Jesus exhorts the man healed on the sabbath to 'sin no more'—exactly the same words (μηκέτι ἁμάρτανε). Yet commentators working from a historical perspective want to distinguish between the two occurrences. Brown is typical of this: 'while the directive was a general one there (no particular sin had been mentioned), here the adulterous love affair is meant' (1966: 334).

That is an easy judgment which does not do justice to the wider Johannine picture, with which the woman's story now resonates. At least three other factors need to be borne in mind. First, as I noted above, the crowd is still part of the narrative in 8.11, making the address of Jesus audible and applicable to an audience wider than merely the woman herself. Second, the comparison with 5.14 also

23. See Brown (1980: 134, 334, 340-41).

needs to take account of a later resonance in 9.3, which breaks any *necessary* connection between sin and illness. This makes the comment in 5.14 very general indeed. Third, the text nowhere goes beyond making an *accusation* of adultery, so there is no reason why the expression in 8.11 has to be so specific. The woman is as much (and no more) a sinner as the man at the pool, or the blind man, or even the onlooking individuals in the crowd for that matter. The accused woman receives healing like the man in 5.14—though here it is healing from injustice and the oppression of a patriarchal system which would condemn her without a word and with no substantial evidence of guilt. When all is said and done, the man involved in this accusation of adultery is not there!

Similarly with the echo of the story of Susanna: she was innocent of the charge of adultery—but she was accused, falsely convicted, sentenced and led out to execution. That justice was done and she was later released did not, however, render her 'sinless'. It merely stopped a gross injustice being committed and allowed her to be restored to life and to regain her dignity. Her story, when allowed to echo into the story of the woman accused in John's Gospel, offers the reader a picture of false accusation righted by Jesus' action, a woman restored to life and, like the man at the pool before her, set free to live a life of possibility.

3. *Why Exclude the Story?*

We have already noted that there is firm evidence that the story of the woman accused of adultery was well known in the most ancient of circles. While the Fourth Gospel's rather obvious comment (Jn 21.25), that many scenes from Jesus' ministry are not included in the Gospel tradition, is undoubtedly true, it would nevertheless appear that this particular story is the *only* extra-canonical tale which gains any kind of regular attention from early Christian writers. This seems to point to the fact that it was a story seeking *inclusion* which met with resistance, rather than being a tale which was not picked up because it was not well enough known.

Commentators regularly remark that the linguistic evidence shows the text to be closer in form to the Synoptic Gospels than to John.[24] It is

24. For example: Schnackenburg (1980: 168) says that 'we are dealing with a synoptic type of narrative'; Beasley-Murray (1987: 145) remarks that 'the opening sentences are uncommonly reminiscent of Luke'; Barrett (1978: 590) concludes

certainly true that, on a statistical analysis, some words used in Jn 7.53–8.11 are distinctly unusual as part of the overall use of *Johannine* language. A good example of this is the introduction of the 'scribes' in Jn 8.3 alongside the Pharisees—a common enough Synoptic combination (Matthew has seven occurrences; Mark has four; and Luke has five), but one never used elsewhere in the Fourth Gospel. This might point to the story as something of a 'stray', which finally finds an uncomfortable home in a Gospel to which it could scarcely have belonged in the first place.

Johnson (1966) cautions, however, that there *are* stylistic elements in the story which mirror common Johannine usage, not least the use of explanatory interjections designed to alert the reader to the motives of the speaker (Jn 8.6 mirroring 6.6, 72; 11.13; etc.). Arguing that the textual difficulties are not so great as have been supposed, he concludes that the stylistic similarity to other instances shows the passage is 'an integral part of the whole Gospel' (1966: 96). Allison Trites (1974) builds on this argument by demonstrating that the pattern of the story is not inconsistent with the wider controversy pattern in the narrative of Jn 1–12. This leads to the conclusion that 'the case for the authenticity of the *Pericope Adulterae* does not appear as improbable as most New Testament scholars have supposed' (Trites 1974: 146). As we have seen, there is some merit in Trites's identification of the contextual suitability of the setting at the end of John 7. Both the stylistic similarities and the contextual suitability could also represent good redactorial skills on the part of the scribes who edited the story into the manuscripts, rather than an original Johannine provenance for the account.

There are other grounds than the textual tradition which point to this story as a later addition to the Johannine tradition. I have argued at length elsewhere that the Johannine tradition is unique in its use of stories involving women to illustrate for the reader the characteristics and qualities of discipleship (Scott 1992: 174-240; 1994). I have also argued that those stories consistently show traces of the influence of the same Sophia tradition which so thoroughly informs the Christology of the Gospel (Scott 1992: 83-173). Given that the first of these crucial elements of Johannine thinking is absent, and the second only present by way of intertextual allusion, it is not unreasonable to view the story as a non-Johannine interpolation. However well it may have been

that 'it closely resembles in form and style the synoptic narratives'.

known in the earliest Church tradition, it may not have appeared appropriate for inclusion in the earliest Johannine tradition because it did not serve the same ends as other stories about women encountering Jesus.

Given this situation, why was the story *excluded* from the canonical Gospel tradition? Several suggestions have been put forward by commentators over the centuries. Augustine thought it had originally been part of the Gospel tradition, but was removed at an early stage because church leaders felt it might offer license to wives (!) to commit adultery without regard to the consequences![25] The consistent absence of the text in the earliest manuscripts makes the idea of its deliberate *removal* unlikely, but the unremittingly patriarchal nature of the early Church hardly renders Augustine's thoughts on the reason for the absence of the pericope improbable. In his commentary on the text, he is at pains to point out that those who think of the story as a licence to sin should remember that God 'has made the day of death uncertain. Thou knowest not when thy last day shall come!'[26]

The most popular explanation of the exclusion of the tale relates it to the discrepancy between the portrayal of Jesus' reaction to the woman and the disciplinary codes of the early Church with regard to those deemed guilty of sexual sin. Typical of such an outlook is the comment of Riesenfeld:

> In all probability the contents of the account came to contrast in a disturbing and embarrassing way with the praxis of church discipline regarding offenses against the sixth commandment which naturally developed in the Christian communities…the climax of the pericope… must hardly have appeared to be in agreement with the way in which any regrettable cases of adultery were proceeded against in the communities. This disagreement must be thought to have led to more and more hesitation in quoting and using our pericope, which resulted in its slipping out of the mainstream of the tradition (Riesenfeld 1970: 98-99).

There are many texts among early Christian writings that indicate that discipline over sexual sin was extremely strict in the early Church. Commenting on the discipline of penance, Kelly notes: 'In the last decades of the second century adultery, homicide and idolatry (or apostasy) seem to have been treated in practice, if not in theory, as irremissible'(1977: 217).[27]

---

25. Augustine, *De con. adult.* 2.7.6 .
26. Augustine, *Tractate* 33.8.
27. See Riesenfeld (1970: 104-106); Burge (1984: 146-47).

He goes on to document writings from both Western and Eastern writers (Hippolytus; Tertullian; Origen) indicating both the general severity of the sanctions against adulterers and the hard line taken by some on forgiveness and restitution.

Burge tries to connect some aspects of the text to themes in Luke's writing, in particular Lk. 7.36-50, which does raise issues with regard to penance (1984: 141-48). It is clear from what we have seen that adultery was treated with the utmost seriousness in all quarters of the early Church. Where forgiveness was considered possible, it was always to be accompanied by *signs* of repentance. These would certainly include tears (*1 Clem.* 48.1), and some indication of submission, for example, kneeling or prostrating oneself. The *Did.* also suggests shunning as a policy for the community in respect of the miscreant (*Did.* 15.3). None of these elements is present in the text, thus giving a picture of a woman who is forgiven without condition of evident repentance, or even assurance as to future conduct. This could be seen as a point of considerable incongruity with the practice of the early Church.

This is not, however, the whole picture. It is clear from Hippolytus's 'highly prejudiced report' concerning Pope Callistus (Pope from 217–222), that this Bishop of Rome had adopted, 'as a matter of Church policy, a more generous attitude towards the sins of the flesh' (Kelly 1977: 218). Callistus clearly drew on some New Testament texts to support his position, but sadly the story of the woman taken in adultery is not listed among them. What his attitude does demonstrate, however, is that there were those in highly significant positions of leadership in the early centuries of the Church, for whom the story's content would *not* have caused particular problems in relation to the practice of Church discipline.

It is also significant in this regard that questions about the severity of action to be taken against those deemed guilty of adultery seem to come to a particular high point of discussion in the second century. There are a number of texts in the New Testament itself which rebuke immorality in general and number sexual sin among the grievous matters (1 Cor. 6.9-10; Gal. 5.19-21; Eph. 5.3-6; Col. 3.5-6), indicating the consequences of such action. Yet adultery is by no means singled out as the *most* grievous offence, being rather one among many things which led to defilement in the Christian community. Indeed there are many texts which need to be set against these condemnations of immorality, which indicate the merciful nature of God's attitude towards sin and the need for Christians to refrain from easy judgment of one another (Mt. 5.7).

The reasoning that the text was excluded primarily because of its clash with the practice of the Church is thus not altogether satisfactory. It is difficult to imagine what other outcome the story could have had. Did those who would have opposed its 'slackness' think Jesus should have upheld the decision and ratified the stoning—perhaps even cast the first one to show his sinlessness? We did note that his initial attitude is disturbing for the reader, since he does not condemn the men who have brought the woman, instead inviting them to carry out the sentence. It may be argued (with hindsight!) that this is a clever piece of bluff-calling, but it is at best a high-risk strategy from the woman's viewpoint.

Such ignoring of the plight of the woman as a pawn in male hands is not only a characteristic of the *ancient* writers. In the most recent major treatment of women as disciples in John, Robert Maccini, a male commentator who likes to think of himself as sympathetic to the women of the Gospel, comments on the account: 'This story is of the entrapment type commonly found in the Synoptics, and so it is not the woman but *Jesus* who is on trial' (1996: 235)! This completely misses the point that it is the *woman* who is under imminent threat of a horrific death. However true it may be that Jesus is also being tested in the story, it is the woman who faces the most immediate consequences of abuse and injustice.

Should it be argued that Jesus could have allowed the stoning to go ahead as a warning against adultery itself, but declaring forgiveness for the woman? This is also an absurd idea, not least because there is no evidence to support the idea that the early Christians saw stoning as an appropriate punishment for *any* crime. As long as the woman is considered guilty from the outset, the story contains the seeds of difficulty for the Church.

We are dealing, then, with a text which seems to have provoked deep anxiety in early Church circles. This may well have had to do with its relationship to structures of penitential discipline, but there are probably deeper underlying levels of discomfort. Approaching the pericope from a feminist perspective, Luise Schottroff concludes that it was excluded from the canonical text of the Gospels because it 'could not be harmonized with the interests of a church oriented toward dominance' (1995: 180). This comment goes to the heart of the matter, for nowhere is the issue of the abuse of the woman in the story addressed in the early writings. Nor is her potential innocence, which we have highlighted as a significant possibility, ever explored. The focus is always turned upon *Jesus* and what the text shows about his graciousness or his ability to outwit his opponents.

4. *Why Include the Story?*

Given that the pericope was excluded from the text for several centuries, there must eventually have been significant reasons for its inclusion in certain traditions. A number of such reasons have been alluded to in my narrative exegesis of the story, and I summarize them here. The most common explanation is that articulated in the early centuries by Augustine, who saw in the text an illustration of Christ's grace and mercy (*Tractate* 33). This attitude would be seen in contrast to that of Jesus' opponents, who are happy to use the unfortunate circumstances of the woman as a means to entrap Jesus.

O'Day's critique of Augustine's enormous influence on the history of interpretation is a telling one. She notes the way in which he polarizes the characters and in doing so dehumanizes the woman:

> To summarize the story as sin (woman) and grace (Jesus) is to objectify and dehumanize the woman the same way the scribes and Pharisees do in v.4. It is to define her away because of her sexuality rather than to treat her as a full person as Jesus does in vv. 10-11 (1992: 634).

The fact is that Augustine's bipolar approach to the text continues to influence modern commentators, including such major figures in recent Johannine scholarship as Schnackenburg and Brown.

A second option governing its late inclusion is that, although its content may have been considered too subversive and dangerous for original inclusion, it was kept alive in the lectionaries of the early Church.[28] It thus gains admission to the main text through copying into lectionaries and subsequently directly into the text. That it gains more established status after the fifth century reflects that fact that the Church by then was sufficiently secure in its disciplinary codes to be able to cope with the full inclusion of the text. Evidence for this is brought forward by van Lopik, who notes that some of the miniscules which contain the text in apparently odd places (such as minuscule 225, which has it after

---

28. See Moir (1988: 172), who quotes Gregory's study of this area.

Jn 7.36) are in fact lectionaries in the form of a 'continuous Gospel text' (1995: 289). He also challenges the view that the marking of the texts with obelisks always indicates the uncertain status of the text in the mind of the copyist. He thinks that many of these are simply lectionary markings (1995: 290).

A third area of speculation on the reasons for the admission of the text lies in its close relation to the surrounding material in the Gospels—and on this theme there are many variations! Such approaches assume that the text was sufficiently congruent with the Gospel tradition as to warrant its proper, if late, inclusion in a particular position in the canonical framework. This is easier to deal with in John than in Luke, though there are at least two connecting features to the Third Gospel: the close parallel in the introductory phrases (Lk. 21.37-38 = Jn 7.53–8.2), and the prior presence in the Lukan text of a story of a repentant woman 'sinner' accepted by Jesus (Lk. 7.36-50).

The most common connection noted in John is the theme of refraining from judgment. Sanders comments that 'nowhere else is the story's main point so enhanced as in the context of John 7 and 8' (1990: 340), and goes on to list links to 7.19—no one keeps the law, 7.24—not judging by appearances, 7.51—Nicodemus's defence of a fair trial, 8.13—challenge to Jesus' testimony, 8.15—I judge no one, 8.18—Jesus' defence of two witnesses, 8.21, 24, 26—Jesus' opponents accused of sin. These points have all been noted in my exegesis and form a formidable argument for the intelligence of the copyists in inserting the text at 7.53–8.11. Maccini (1996: 234-35) and Trites (1974) have similar kinds of approach to the text, seeing it as inserted because of its resonance with the theme of ongoing 'controversy' (Trites), or more specifically 'trial' (Maccini), between Jesus and the Pharisees.

A rather different analysis of the appropriateness of the Johannine setting is that which we noted from George Brooke (1988). He sees the unity of chs. 7–10 as resting in 'their treatment of the figure of Christ in relation to the law' (1988: 103), and more precisely in relation to the Ten Commandments. He demonstrates how each of the commandments is at least alluded to in this section of the Fourth Gospel, if not explicitly addressed. Brooke notes the issues at dispute in the long dialogue of ch. 8, and suggests that an informed reader of the text could easily have made the connection between descent through fornication and adulterous behaviour. He concludes:

> Perhaps the somewhat veiled allusion to the prohibition from adultery
> caused someone at a later time who recognised an interpretation of the
> decalogue in John 7-10 to insert a more obvious passage about adultery
> (7:53-8:11)! (1988: 107)

On this reading the pericope gains entry to the main text of John's
Gospel as an illustration. Although it assumes a fairly sophisticated
degree of insight from the scribes who inserted the story, there is sufficient evidence in the textual variants to render this at least plausible.
The ability to adjust language to fit what is recognized as common
Johannine usage certainly indicates that the copyists were not merely
mechanical scribes, but also intelligent observers of patterns and theological nuances in the texts.

Since history is always more complex than our attempts to put it into
neat little boxes of theory, the chances are that each of these theories
has some merit to it. There is, however, another dimension which the
reader operating within a hermeneutic of suspicion may wish to place
alongside the plausibility of the ideas and theories to which I have
pointed. Schottroff's comments, which I noted earlier, on the effect of
the story on the patriarchal system of justice, already point us in the
direction I want to take here.

It is widely recognized by commentators on this text that, by the end
of the fourth century, the disciplinary codes of the Church were well
established enough in respect of the treatment of sexual offenders. Systems of penance were in place, so that the shocking aspect of the text
was sufficiently diminished as to allow for it creeping into the canonical
text. Another way of putting this might be that the climate of male
dominance in the Church, and the systematic denigration of female
sexuality, were so overwhelmingly established, that the text's ability to
shock was well sanitized enough to allow it to find a home in the Gospel proper. That it found a good home in John 7–8 was thus more due to
its literary merits than its theologically explosive content. Given its
male power structures, the Church was ready to handle a subversive
text of this nature by the dawn of the fifth century.

But there's more! Not only was the traditional interpretation of the
text as one in which Jesus frees a condemned, sexually voracious
women from her just desserts sufficiently sterilized by the time of its
inclusion, but the other possible option for interpretation—that the
woman was in fact innocent and released from injustice—was completely submerged. My exegesis has pointed to this as a genuine alter-

native reading of this text, but nowhere has it been allowed to surface in the tradition. Only now, as the last male bastions of tradition begin to break down, may this unjustly treated woman, along with her parallel sister figure Susanna, finally begin to celebrate her true liberation from male oppression.

BIBLIOGRAPHY

Aland, Kurt
    1967   *Studien zur Überlieferung des Neuen Testaments und seines Textes* (Berlin: W. de Gruyter).
Baltensweiler, Hans
    1967   *Die Ehe im Neuen Testament: Exegetische Untersuchungen über Ehe, Ehelosigkeit und Ehescheidung* (Zürich: Zwingli-Verlag).
Barrett, C.K.
    1978   *The Gospel According to St John* (London: SPCK, 2nd edn).
Beasley-Murray, George R.
    1987   *John* (WBC, 36; Waco, TX: Word Books).
Becker, Ulrich
    1963   *Jesus und die Ehebrecherin: Untersuchungen zur Text- und Überlieferungsgeschichte von Joh. 7:53-8:11* (BZNW, 28; Berlin: Adolf Töpelmann).
    1979   *Das Evangelium nach Johannes, Kapitel 1-10* (ÖTBK; Gütersloh: Gütersloher Verlagshaus).
Blinzler, J.
    1957–58   'Die Strafe für Ehebruch in Bibel und Halacha zur Auslegung von Joh. viii 5', *NTS* 4: 32-47.
Brooke, George J.
    1988   'Christ and the Law in John 7-10', in Barnabas Lindars (ed.), *Law and Religion: Essays on the Place of the Law in Israel and Early Christianity* (Cambridge: James Clarke & Co.): 102-112.
Brown, Raymond E.
    1966   *The Gospel According to John I–XII* (AB, 29; Garden City, NY: Doubleday).
    1970   *The Gospel According to John XIII–XXI* (AB, 29A: Garden City, NY: Doubleday).
Burge, G.M.
    1984   'A Specific Problem in the New Testament Text and Canon: The Woman Caught in Adultery (John 7:53-8:11)', *JETS* 27: 141-48.
Calvin, John
    1959   *The Gospel According to St John* (Edinburgh: T. & T. Clark).
Campenhausen, Hans von
    1977   'Zur Perikope von der Ehebrecherin (Joh 7:53-8:11)', *ZNW* 68: 164-75.

Coleman, B.W.
1970 'The Woman Taken in Adultery, Studies in Texts: Jn 7:53-8:11', *Theology* 73: 409-410.

Derrett, J. Duncan M.
1963–64 'Law in the New Testament: The Story of the Woman Taken in Adultery', *NTS* 10: 1-26.

Dods, Marcus (ed.)
1873 *The Works of Aurelius Augustine, Bishop of Hippo.* X. *Tractates of the Gospel According to St. John* (2 vols.; trans. John Gibb; Edinburgh: T. and T. Clark) (for *Tractate* 33 see I, pp. 434-41).

Duke, P.D.
1985 *Irony in the Fourth Gospel* (Atlanta: John Knox Press).

Heil, J.P.
1991 'The Story of Jesus and the Adulteress (John 7,53-8,11) Reconsidered', *Bib* 72: 182-91.

Jackson, B.S.
1977 'Susanna and the Singular History of Singular Witnesses', in W. de Vos *et al.* (eds.), *Acta Juridica: Studies in Honour of Ben Beinart*, II (University of Cape Town: Faculty of Law): 37-54.

Johnson, A.F.
1966 'A Stylistic Trait of the Fourth Gospel in the *Pericope Adulterae*', *Bulletin of the Evangelical Theological Society* 9: 91-96.

Kelly, J.N.D.
1977 *Early Christian Doctrines* (London: A. & C. Black).

Lindars, Barnabas
1972 *The Gospel of John* (NCBC; London: Marshall, Morgan & Scott).

Lopik, T. van
1995 'Once Again: Floating Words, their Significance for Textual Criticism', *NTS* 41: 286-91.

Lührmann, D.
1990 'Die Geschichte von einer Sünderin und andere Apokryphe Jesus-überlieferungen bei Didymos von Alexandrien', *NovT* 32: 289-316.

Maccini, R.G.
1996 *Her Testimony is True: Women as Witnesses According to John* (JSNTSup, 125; Sheffield: Sheffield Academic Press).

Manson, T.W.
1952–53 'The Pericope *de Adultera* (Joh 7,53-8,11)', *ZNW* 44: 255-56.

McDonald, J.I.H.
1995 'The So-called *Pericope de adultera*', *NTS* 41: 415-27.

Migne, J.-P, (ed.)
1864 *Sancte Aurelii Augustus, Hippinensis episcopi, opera Omnia* (Bibliotheca Patrum Latina, 40; Paris: Apud Fratres Garnier).

Moir, Ian A.
1988 'Fam. 272: A New Family of Manuscripts in the "Pericope Adulterae"', in T. Baarda *et al.* (eds.), *Texts and Testimony: Essays on New Testament and Apocryphal Literature in Honour of A.F.J. Klijn* (Kampen: Kok): 170-76.

O'Day, Gail R.
  1992   'John 7:53-8:11: A Study in Misreading', *JBL* 111: 631-40.
Reisenfeld, H.
  1970   'The Pericope *de adultera* in the Early Christian Tradition', in *idem*, *The Gospel Tradition* (Philadelphia: Fortress Press; Oxford: Clarendon Press): 95-110. (orig. published as 'Die Pericope von der Ehebrecherin in der frühkirchlichen Tradition', *SEÅ* 17 [1952]: 106-111).
Sanders, J.A.
  1990   'Nor do I…': A Canonical Reading of the Challenge to Jesus in John 8', in R.J. Fortna and B.R. Gaventa (eds.), *The Conversation Continues: Studies in Paul and John in Honour of J. Louis Martyn* (Nashville: Abingdon Press): 337-47.
Schaff, P., and H. Wace (eds.)
  1976   A Select Library of Nicene and Post-nicene Fathers (Grand Rapids: Eerdmans [1890]).
Schnackenburg, Rudolf
  1969   *The Gospel According to St. John*, I (London: Burns & Oates).
  1980   *The Gospel According to St. John*, II (London: Burns & Oates).
  1982   *The Gospel According to St. John*, III (London: Burns & Oates).
Schottroff, Luise
  1995   *Lydia's Impatient Sisters: A Feminist Social History of Early Christianity* (London: SCM Press; Louisville, KY: Westminster/John Knox Press).
Schöndorf, H.
  1996   'Jesus schreibt mit dem Finger auf die Erde', *BZ* 40: 91-93.
Scott, Martin
  1992   *Sophia and the Johannine Jesus* (JSNTSup, 71; Sheffield: JSOT Press).
  1994   'The Women of the Fourth Gospel: Paradigms of Discipleship or Paragons of Virtue?', in *Festschrift für Günther Wagner* (Bern: Peter Lang): 169-89.
Trites, A.A.
  1974   'The Woman Taken in Adultery', *BSac* 131: 137-46.
Vielhauer, P.
  1991   'The Gospel of the Hebrews', in Wilhelm Schneemelcher and R. McL. Wilson (eds.), *New Testament Apocrypha. I. Gospels and Related Writings* (Cambridge: James Clarke & Co., rev. edn): 172-79.
Witherington, Ben
  1995   *John's Wisdom: A Commentary on the Fourth Gospel* (Cambridge: Lutterworth Press).
Young, Brad H.
  1995   ' "Save the Adulteress!": Ancient Jewish *responsa* in the Gospels?', *NTS* 41: 59-70.

A Woman's Plight and the Western Fathers[*]

Thomas O'Loughlin

One of the great, incidental benefits of the labour of the Vetus Latina Institut (situated in Beuron, Germany) to establish the pre-Vulgate Latin version of the scriptures is that it makes it possible to ascertain virtually every use in Latin of even a phrase from the Bible in the first Christian millennium.[1] This usually means that for a verse from the Gospels one finds a collection of slips which identify every textual witness to that verse whether the manuscript is Vulgate, non-Vulgate or some mixture, and then a collection of slips which contain every citation or allusion to that verse from Tertullian (c. 160–c. 225) to proto-scholastic writers (tenth–eleventh centuries). As can be imagined this is often a sizeable collection of slips; particularly in those cases where a New Testament text has some relationship to the Old, for in those cases it may be cited both for itself, and because it stands in some relationship (e.g. law prefiguring Gospel) to an earlier text which was the writer's immediate concern.[2] Such collections of slips then allow us to follow that text's theological career, within what was self-consciously a tradition,[3] so building up a mosaic picture of the relationships between Scripture, theology and preaching in the Latin church.[4] Given the

*. I wish to express my gratitude to the staff of the Vetus Latina Institut, Beuron, for facilitating research for this article; and in a special way to record my gratitude to its late director, Dr Hermann J. Frede, who welcomed me to carry out this research only weeks before his untimely death, *requiescat in pace*. I also wish to thank Dr Fergus O'Donoghue and Dr Kieron O'Mahony who provided me with editions of texts not held in Lampeter. The usual disclaimer applies.

1. For a convenient account of the Institut's work, see Petzer (1995: 113-30).
2. See O'Loughlin (1998: 475-85) where the variety of such relationships are noted.
3. See O'Loughlin (1997: 291-314).
4. For a study of how Gen. 2.2 was combined with Jn 5.17, see O'Loughlin (1999a: 217-39).

dramatic nature of the story of the woman caught in adultery, the links made in the text between Jesus and the demands of the law, the clash between Jesus and 'the scribes and Pharisees' (favourite hate-figures), and the light in which it presents Jesus as merciful, one would expect a large crop of slips in the Institut, as much from homilies as from exegetical works. However, and this is the key point of this article, the story hardly surfaces in the Latin Fathers. Indeed, in works by only four writers—Ambrose (c. 339–397), Jerome (c. 342–420), Augustine (354–430), and Cassiodorus (c. 485–c. 580)—does it receive more attention than an incidental reference or allusion. So my task here is twofold: to set out an account of how it was treated by those writers; and then to suggest reasons why it does not have greater prominence.[5]

1. *The Text of John*

Since the *pericope de adultera* is a disputed text, the first question to be addressed is the extent to which it was present in Latin copies of John's Gospel. This was summed up by Harald Riesenfeld: '[the pericope] appears sporadically before the Vulgate and then in the entire Vulgate tradition' (1970: 97). However, now through the work of Bonifatius Fischer we can quantify that judgment and add precision to the meaning of 'sporadically'. Fischer collated two passages from each Gospel from every surviving Latin Gospel text prior to the tenth century.[6] Of the 399 manuscripts (complete Gospels, lectionaries, missals, and fragments of all of these) examined by Fischer, 395 have the pericope, while 4 omit it. Of the manuscripts he collated he considered ten to be copies of the Vetus Latina, and in this group seven have the pericope, and three omit it. Only one Vulgate manuscript omits it: the rather strange Codex Brixianus.[7]

---

5. It might be objected that we do not know, at present, what would be a mean figure for comments on a verse or passage by these patristic and early mediaeval writers. However, the passages of great interest remain more or less the same, especially in texts that have an immediate appeal in preaching or which are easily imagined episodes in Jesus' ministry (e.g. the miracle at Cana [Jn 2] looms larger in the memory of people throughout Christian history than some of teaching passages in Jn 6). What is surprising in this case is the story's modern popularity with pastors and congregations, without a similar interest being manifested in the earlier period.

6. The information on the pericope can be found in 1991: 242.

7. Brescia, Biblioteca Queriniana s.n. (Lachmann, siglum 'f'; Fischer siglum 'Jg'). This is a de luxe purple codex written in silver and has a complex textual

That it is ubiquitous in Vulgate manuscripts is not surprising as Jerome had made a definite decision to include it in his version. He reveals that he was aware of the textual difficulty of its not being found in every manuscript of John when he referred to the text in his argument against the Pelagians thus: 'there is a story found in many [*multis*] Greek and Latin codices of the gospel of John' (*Dial. Pel.* 2.17). But equally he assumed that his decision to include it was neither a matter of controversy nor a case of following the minority of witnesses.[8] His reference allows for the possibility that it was not familiar to his readers, but he expected that it was known.[9] And, as with so many of his textual decisions, once he had included it in his revised text, the Vulgate, its survival as 'what the text should contain' became the basic working assumption for more than a millennium.

So given the presence of the pericope in the Vulgate, a textual omission will not explain the lack of attention in the later Latin tradition of exegesis. However, the Vulgate only gradually supplanted the earlier versions—and it is a matter of conjecture as to when the Vulgate became the most common text in various places in Europe, but for our purposes we could look on the fifth–sixth centuries as the period of transition[10]—so could the omission of the pericope from some of the

history: it is possibly a copy of a mixed text which is 90% Vulgate or a Vulgate corrected by reference to the tradition of the Gothic version (see Burkitt [1900: 129-34]). On this manuscript, see McGurk (1961: 85-86 n. 93; he describes it incorrectly as 'Pre-Jerome'). However, given that this is a display book—a witness to the religious reverence in which the Word of God conceived of as a *book* was held, rather than a text which anyone intended for reading—its value as a textual witness is reduced. It seems to be a feature of de luxe Bibles, then and now, that the more elaborate the layout, the less reliable they are as copies for actual reading!

8.   Bernard (1928: 716-17) stated that 'Jerome did not feel it practicable to expel it [from the text as Bernard himself had done]'. However, there is no evidence that Jerome had any doubts about the pericope's rightful place in the text.

9.   From the point of view of textual studies it is interesting that he does not appear to know of its presence in Luke in some Greek manuscripts.

10.   Much writing on the Latin Bible is vitiated by a mental image among modern writers that the replacement of the Vetus Latina by the Vulgate can be imagined in terms of the replacement of the AV by the RV, then the RV by the RSV, or the latter by some more recent version such as the NRSV. First, note that Pandects (whole Bibles) are extremely rare, and the normal book size is Gospels only, or the whole New Testament. Second, books were not replaced simply because they were now 'out of date', but only because a new or newer book was needed. Thus the spread of the Vulgate is one of it gradually becoming the acknowledged best exemplar, rather

copying traditions of Vetus Latina help explain the lack of attention in the earlier period?

Again, a textual omission is inadequate as an explanation. If we assume that copies of the Vetus Latina with the pericope have the same likelihood of survival—itself a matter of serendipity—as those without it, then on the basis of the ten surviving manuscripts we could say that it was twice as likely for a codex to contain it, than to omit it.[11] Therefore, on the evidence we possess, we can say that Riesenfeld's judgment that it only 'appears sporadically' underestimates the situation. That it was more likely than not to have been present prior to the dominance of the Vulgate also agrees with the remainder of the evidence. First, it accords with Jerome's numerical judgment that 'many' Latin codices contained it. Moreover, we know that it was in the text in common use in northern Italy in the later fourth century as it is assumed (without comment) as common knowledge by Ambrose of Milan. Likewise, it was in common use in Africa in the pre-Vulgate text which Augustine called the '*Itala*' (*De doct. Christ.* 2.15.22) for he took it for granted as a genuine event recorded in John's Gospel for in that context he commented upon it.[12] However, Augustine was aware that it was not present in every copy for he says in his work on adulterous marriages that 'men of little faith' had excised the incident lest the Lord's dismissal of the woman solely with the injunction 'sin no more' be inter-

than a dramatic decision that it represented a quasi-authorized text. The Vetus continued to be copied (hence our many manuscripts of it) where people either had not got access to the new version, or simply were unaware of its significance. Moreover, in a book which combined several biblical books, one might be copied from a Vulgate exemplar, another from a non-Vulgate exemplar: we shall never know what motivated such choices, but hum-drum explanations ('that Gospel book is hard to read' or 'this epistle book is easy to handle') are to be preferred to those which imagine definite theological choices. Such decisive clarity presupposes easily obtained books with ready uniformity—all functions of printing.

11. However, we have to note here the fallacy of 'small numbers', namely that when one's base is only ten units, a single extra survivor either way can alter the picture dramatically. At present we have 3.7 (i.e. 30% of Vetus manuscripts omit it); but let us imagine that the effects of fire in a library somewhere meant that one manuscript survived instead of another, then the picture could be 2.8—inviting the inference that only 20% of the Vetus omitted it; or 4.6 (40% omit) inviting the suggestion that it is a contentious point whether or not the pericope was widely accepted.

12. See below, pp. 94-99.

preted by their wives as an encouragement to adultery (*De. con. adult.* 2.7.6)![13] So Augustine not only has the pericope, but positively held that it was genuine even to the extent of having an explanation as to why those which did not have it were to be considered as deliberately mutilated. So I believe we are justified in accepting the proportions of the surviving manuscripts as indicative of the situation in Latin in the decades prior to fifth century: while not universally found, the pericope was both widespread and in the clear majority of texts.

2. Ambrose

Ambrose (c. 339–397; elected bishop, 374) is the first Latin writer to bring the text into his teaching in a significant way. He did this, however, neither in the course of either formal written exegesis nor in preaching upon the Gospel text within the liturgy, but in two letters, both of which are addressed to laymen.

a. *Epistola 50 (Ad Studium)*[14]
This letter was written sometime between 385 and 387 to Studius (who was probably a magistrate), and in it we see not only the concerns of the Christian bishop, but also of the one-time lawyer and governor. The topic of the letter is whether or not a Christian judge can order the death penalty without incurring excommunication from the Church. Ambrose's general teaching is that it is possible, for the necessary permission had been given by Paul in Rom. 13.4. Moreover, he held that there was a tradition of allowing Christian judges such powers, for unless 'their sword is feared, the madness of crime' would not be controlled but encouraged. Although Ambrose had been then a bishop for more than a decade, the civic official's fears that chaos loomed whenever the mailed fist was absent was still part of his basic perception of society (*Epist.* 50.1).

But, because a judge could execute without condemnation did not mean that he could not take another, more merciful, course which would then bring him praise. He could act towards his prisoners with

---

13. See below, where this statement by Augustine is examined in greater detail

14. There are several numerations in use for Ambrose's letters. I am following that of the most recent critical edition (*Corpus Scriptorum Ecclesiasticorum Latinorum* 82.2). This particular letter is found on pp. 56-59. In older editions, based on the seventeenth century Maurist edition, this is *Epist.* 25.

mercy, and free them of their bonds in the manner of a priest dealing with a sinner. Indeed, he ought to act in this way given that even some non-Christians could 'return from governing a province boasting that their axes were unstained by blood'. 'So', asks Ambrose, 'what should Christians do?' (*Epist.* 50.3) They can follow the example of Jesus who did not condemn the woman (*Epist.* 50.4). His lack of condemnation is equated with her redemption, for the lack of condemnation came from the one who is 'the redemption of sins'. The redemption is, for Ambrose, the act of forgiving her: 'he who is life restores her [and] like a fountain washes her clean' (*Epist.* 50.7).

Christ's action of non-condemnation, redemption and forgiveness is not, however, specific to that crime or exclusive to him. Ambrose sees Jesus' action of inclining 'his head' (an implication of his having had to look up at the woman in v. 10) as sacramental of his attitude to sinners: 'when Jesus inclines his head he does so that he might raise up those who have fallen' (*Epist.* 50.7). And in this action he has left a model for all judges to follow for there is always the possibility of correction for the guilty and they can hope for forgiveness through baptism (if not yet baptized) or penitence (it baptized already) (*Epist.* 50.8). So the primary significance of the pericope has nothing to do with adultery but with the relationship between justice and mercy: justice may justly condemn, but mercy can go beyond this and redeem. This additional act is praiseworthy, intimately linked to the person and work of Christ, and is deliberately offered as an example to Christians for their judgments in the secular order.

While the behaviour appropriate to Christian judges was the occasion for Ambrose's use of the pericope and the message he wished to draw from it is clear, he also deviated into a little exegetical excursion prompted by the context of the incident being a case of the scribes and Pharisees 'testing' Jesus (the Latin text has *temptantes* which has more sinister undertones than 'testing'), and his curiosity about what was written by Jesus with his finger in the ground. For Ambrose, 'the Jews' brought the woman to him out of malice and a deliberate attempt to catch him for the incident is part of the plot that would lead to his eventual arrest and crucifixion (picking up the phrase 'that they might have some charge to bring against him'); but more immediately it placed Jesus between the horns of a dilemma from which he must escape. One horn would be to deny the relationship that exists between him as the fulfilment of the law and the law itself—Ambrose quotes Mt. 5.17: 'I have come not to destroy the law, but to fulfil it'. The other horn would be to condemn the woman in accord with the law and so negate the very purpose 'for which he had come and the purpose of his plan [of salvation]'. Here lay their great crime: they were attempting to push Jesus into a position whereby he could not but deny himself and bring his own mission to nought. For Ambrose this is a fundamental crime and one for which those who committed it would have to be punished. The punishment is that they are, literally, 'written out' of the plan of salvation. Ambrose asserts that there is no doubt about what Jesus wrote on the ground (*in terra*): 'What did he write other than the prophetic saying: "O ground [*terra*], O ground, this man has been made sterile, none of his offspring shall succeed him" [Jer. 22.29-30] which is what the Prophet Jeremiah wrote about Jechonias?' (*Epist.* 50.4)[15] Now, sure of what Jesus had written, Ambrose expanded on the significance of this in terms of the contrast between Jews and Christians. The names of the Jews are written—possibly here we have an echo of other speculations of what Christ has written—on the ground and they are disowned by their Father for they have tempted him and insulted 'the Author of salvation'. By contrast, the names of the Christians are 'written in heaven' (an allusion to Lk. 10.20). Christ in speaking to them is passing judgment upon them (*Epist.* 50.5).

In passing it should be noticed that in Ambrose's perception of Scripture no detail is too small not to carry some universal meaning, a position that sometimes leads him to seeing detail in the text where it does not exist, and at other times leads to some absurd connections. We have examples of both in this short letter. Why did the elders leave first?[16] 'Either because they were greater sinners having lived longer or because they were held to be wiser...and they even began to weep more for their sins...' Weeping for sins is a common theme in patristic preaching, but it is not mentioned in John. Why has Jesus to bend down and then look up again to speak? 'When the Jews demand the payment [of the law] Jesus bows his head, but because he "has nowhere to lay

---

15. Following the LXX, both the Vetus Latina and the Vulgate harmonize the references to this king and give him the name *Iechonias* here (22.24, 28) and at 37.1 (where the Hebrew has Coniah), with the mentions of him at Jer. 24.1; 27.20; 28.4; and 29.2.

16. The text says 'beginning with the eldest'—Ambose imagines a formal ranking in the procession away from Jesus being led by men in order of age (*seniores priores*).

his head" [Mt. 8.20] he raises it again as if to give sentence...'(*Epist.* 50.6)

b. *Epistola 68 (Ad Irenaeum)*

In a second letter,[17] assuming knowledge of the earlier one, Ambrose returns to the question of whether Christians can exercise secular power in punishment. Now the question has a more focused form: if now bishops are accusing criminals in the imperial courts and seeking the death penalty, are these bishops not doing the same thing as 'the Jews' in demanding the death of the woman? Christ would not allow one woman to be punished according to the law, so what of these bishops (*Epist.* 68.3)?

Ambrose did not answer this main question—in all probability as it would have involved criticism of fellow bishops and he detested dissent among the Catholic bishops lest it play into the hands of the Arians— but instead twists the question to one of a detail: 'But where did Christ pass this judgment [that he would not let her be condemned]?' (*Epist.* 68.4). Ambrose then set off on a long digression examining various incidents where Christ was seen as merciful (the widow's contribution to the temple, the good Samaritan) and the symbolic representations of penance in the Old and New Testaments. Eventually he adds: 'But let us move on to discuss the forgiveness of the woman charged with adultery' (*Epist.* 68.5-10). However, what follows is a verse-by-verse commentary rather than a reply to the question posed to him—Ambrose will not return to that until the letter's closing paragraphs.

As to the explanation of the passage from John, Ambrose repeated almost every detail mentioned in the earlier letter, while adding a few extra, symbolic interpretations.[18] The first concerned the statement 'Let him who is without sin cast the first stone' (8.7). This he sees as 'godlike' in that one who is without sin is the one that should punish sin. In all other cases there is the prospect of hypocrisy: seeking to condemn others when oneself is the greater sinner. This leads him to quote Mt. 7.5, and then in turn to note that here we have an instance of a speck in another's eye being seen by those who have a beam in their own. Adultery (characterized simply as 'lust') as 'a crime is like a speck', while the crime of trying to trap and refusing to acknowledge 'the author of salvation' is like a beam. The accusers are greater sinners than

17. In older editions, this is *Epist.* 26.
18. This exegesis is found in §§ 11–19 of the letter.

the accused, and as hypocrites are blinded to their own massive evil while being able to see specks in others. These statements by Ambrose may appear very harsh towards the Jews, but in a context where adultery was preached as one of the three great sins, it is a remarkable statement about the seriousness of sexual sins.

The remainder of his treatment examined details of the pericope that he had not noticed earlier. The first of these was the significance of Jesus writing *with his finger*. Ambrose never considered the possibility that this was just what one does when one doodles when near dusty ground or sand. Just as earlier he imagined Jesus writing out an oracle from Jeremiah, now he images the act of writing as a formal theandric gesture. Jesus, the Logos, had written the law with his finger (he quotes Exod. 31.18); now with the same finger he writes again and this too has the status of law. Ambrose imagines the whole incident in a formal and forensic manner: a legal case has been brought to the author of the law. He now bends down and writes in a formal and deliberate way and begins to write as he did when he wrote the law—the result is that the legislator writes the sentence on those in front of him. While the names of the righteous are written in heaven (again he quotes Lk. 10.20), the names of the sinners are written on the ground.[19] But why, Ambrose asks, did the Logos write with his finder this *second* time (v. 8)? So that the Christian reader would know that the Jews are condemned in *both* testaments.

It is worth contrasting our image of the incident with that of Ambrose: for many of us Jesus' gesture is informal, and one which 'buys time' while he thinks of a way out of the trap; then he buys more time waiting for his statement 'to sink in'. For Ambrose such associations with our experience seem to have little place: Jesus' actions are keyed to the whole plan of salvation, and deliberately chosen to communicate, through a code of signs, with all who would read of or imagine this event. It is because every detail has sacramental significance that Ambrose can next turn to analyse why the Jews *went out* (*exibant*) one by one; and why Jesus was left *alone* with the woman. They went out because 'the letter' is outside (2 Cor. 3.6), the mysteries within; as

---

19. In the first letter, as we saw, there seems to be a certain confusion about what Jesus wrote on the ground: explicitly a verse from Jeremiah, but implicitly, a additional idea, the names of the accusers. In this second letter that ambivalence has disappeared: there is no mention of a verse from the Old Testament, but an explicit statement that he has written the names of the guilty Jews on the ground.

they wanted the leaves rather than the fruit (Mt. 21.19); and 'the shadow of the Law' (Heb. 10.1) rather than 'the Sun of Justice' (Mal. 4.2). So these words are a further condemnation of the Jews. That the woman is left alone with Jesus is presented as linked to Jn 16.32 and because 'no one can share with Christ the task of forgiving sins'. Finally, Ambrose adds further significance to Jesus lowering and raising his head: he lowers it when there is an accuser, but raises it when the accuser is no longer there, for 'he wishes none condemned, but all forgiven'.

Having concluded this lengthy sermon on Christ's mercy as seen in John 8, in the final sections of the letter he had to return to the initial question: are not the bishops accusing people in the courts failing to follow Christ's example? Should they not forgive as he forgave? Ambrose, himself a lawyer, dodged the heart of the charge (escaping either condemning fellow bishops or weakening the force of the law) in this way. He points out that Jesus did not want to be accused of forgiving the woman, hence his statement 'Neither will I condemn you' (*Epist.* 68.19). Despite what he had written just paragraphs earlier about standing alone, implying that only Jesus could forgive, he now said that Jesus did not forgive her, but simply sent her away uncondemned. This judgment he sees reflected in the final command ('Go, and from now on do not sin'): 'Jesus reformed the guilty woman, he did not forgive her crime'. Ambrose closed his letter at that point. He did not point out that if Jesus reformed the woman taken in adultery, then the demands on his fellow bishops to reform people, rather than accuse them, would be even more onerous (*Epist.* 68.20).

3. *Jerome*

No other patristic writer took as great an interest in the details of human sexuality as a source of sin than Jerome, so a priori one expects that this pericope will provide an excuse for some moralizing on the demands of Christ's law. However, he neither dwells on the nature of the woman's sin, nor mentions it in any of one of his writings where sexuality looms large as a topic. The context in which the pericope is brought up is a discussion of the possibility of human sinlessness as part of his campaign against 'the Pelagians'.[20] Jerome assumes that his opponents

20. The references to Jn 8 are found in *Dial. Pel.* 2.17; however, the precise question which gives rise to the citation is to be found in *Dial. Pel.* 2.16. With these

believe that sinlessness is possible as result of a decision of a free human will; he, by contrast, admits its possibility but only as a result of God's mercy—and this divine act is unrelated to the merits of the one receiving that mercy. A strong free will would amount to a denial of the need for mercy and divine help. So here we have the standard parody of 'Pelagianism' and the usual sledgehammer logic that is found in condemnations of 'Pelagius'.

If his opponents' heresy turns on the question of sinlessness, then John 8 becomes a text which can support Jerome's position: there Jesus asks if there is anyone who is sinless, and no one is found. Presumably, for Jerome, that none could be found in the group who brought the woman to Jesus is an indication that in any similar group the answer to the question would be the same. So John 8 is a proof of the universal need for forgiveness by mercy for no one can be sinless by his or her own choice and efforts.

While the Pelagian debate was Jerome's focus, his use of the pericope allows us to learn, indirectly, other details of how he interpreted it. First, he speculates about what Jesus wrote on the ground. For Jerome, this is surely lists of the sins of the woman's accusers. This action is a fulfilment of Jer. 17.13 read as a prophesy pointing to the Christ: 'they that depart from you shall be written in the earth'. In the context of the argument this point reinforces the idea that everyone is a sinner, and that every sinful detail is known to God. Second, when Jesus commanded the woman to 'sin no more' this was no more than the other things he commanded 'according to the law', and Jerome adds 'but whether she did or not, Scripture does not record'. Jerome's interest here is not in the command as a moral injunction about sexual licence, but that it did not imply that sinlessness was a matter of will for those who choose to follow the law. Here we meet the great conundrum of the Pelagian controversy: why did God give a law if it was impossible to keep it? However, that is not my topic here. Suffice to note that Jerome's fear is not that Jesus' non-condemnation would seem to minimize adultery, but could be seen to suggest that the woman could elect not to sin by simply following Jesus' command. Indeed, it is this precise point that led to Jerome's use of the pericope. Jerome's opponents say that they 'can be without sin' (*possum sine peccato esse*), but

polemical writings it would be wrong to treat the opinions attacked by Jerome as an expression of the opinions of any other individual or group—Jerome's enemies are always easy targets in his writings—so I place 'Pelagians' in inverted commas.

this is the exact phrase of Jn 8.10: 'whoever is without sin' (*qui sine peccato*), and no such person was found. Then Jerome makes this curious statement: 'When "without sin" is used, then the Greek [text of the Gospel] has ἀναμάρτητος which literally means "without sin"'. That he stresses the equivalence between the terminology of his opponents and that of the Gospel suggests that these words, and hence the pericope, was an established item of dispute. However, this passage of Jerome apart, if there was such a debate it has left no other trace in the record.[21]

4. *Augustine*

a. *The Tractates in the Gospel According to St John*
Among the Latin patristic writers only Augustine writes about the pericope in the context of formal exegesis in his work on John. The book, composed over a three-year period between 414 and 417, covers virtually the whole of the Gospel in 124 homily-length discourses. The pericope is dealt with in *Tractate* 33, which examines Jn 7.40 to 8.11. Here is the first point about Augustine's view: not only does he not express any doubt here about the authenticity of the text as a part of John's book, but sees it as just a part of a longer section of the Gospel. His commentary makes this explicit: this section relates two historically connected attempts by Jesus' enemies to discredit and capture him. The first part is the discussion among 'the chief priests and Pharisees' after the officers reported back to them after some had come to a decision to arrest Jesus (7.40-52). For Augustine, the result of their decision was their next attempt to test him by bringing the woman to him. So the pericope is integral to the text, and narrated in correct historical sequence with its occurrence in the life of Jesus.[22] What the incident brings out about the person and message of Jesus is that he was himself gentleness and truth, and the message Augustine wishes his hearers to take from the Gospel is that just as his opponents tried to drive a wedge

21. I have attempted to find other uses of Jn 8 in the context of the Pelagian controversy, but, to date, have been unsuccessful.

22. Augustine, as a basic principle of hermeneutics, allows for a narration of events in the Gospels in sequences which do not correspond to their temporal succession. This is the notion of 'recapitulation' which Augustine adopted from Tyconius (it was Rule 6 in Tyconius) (see Burkitt [1894: 66-70]), and for how Augustine explained it, see *De doct. christ.* 2.36.52-54.

between these aspects of the Christ, so must they respond to him as *both* gentleness *and* truth.

The starting point for Augustine in this trial of Jesus is that his enemies perceived his gentleness and wished to force him into a position whereby he abandoned that gentleness—and so his attraction to many—by adhering to justice; or he retained his gentleness as the expense of justice. Augustine analyses the action of 'the scribes and Pharisees' as placing Jesus within a dilemma (*Tractate* 33.4)—in much the same way as Ambrose had done. The way out of this trap is the reply of Jesus, 'let him...', which Augustine describes as 'The wondrous response of Wisdom!' (*Tractate* 33.5). The Jews had decided to trap Jesus by making him relinquish one of the divine attributes of gentleness or justice, now they had, in addition, heard the voice of truth and wisdom, and by Jesus' writing in the ground they would now see that he was also lawgiver.

'What', asks Augustine, 'was the sign he wished to convey by writing with his finger?' Because 'the Law was written "with the finger of God" but written "on stone" [Exod. 31.18] because of their "hardness of heart" [Mk 10.5]' (*Tractate* 33.5).[23] However, Augustine does not speculate as to what was written by Jesus but contrasts the actions of the lawgiver writing on stone in Exodus with writing on the ground. To write on the ground symbolizes the desire to obtain 'fruit'—picking up on the Johannine image that a relationship to Jesus manifests itself in the desire to bear fruit.[24]

Augustine, a trained rhetor, knew that if one was challenged with a dilemma, then one should rebut it with a counter-dilemma; so having analysed the action of the Pharisees as a dilemma, he now analyses Jesus' response as its counter. Justice versus gentleness is countered by 'letting the woman escape punishment' versus 'punishment with her'. During the time Jesus continued to write on the ground (v. 8), his opponents recognized that his reply was equivalent to the challenge that they must either let the woman go free or else receive with her the penalties of the law for their own transgressions of it. In this challenge they heard the voice of justice: 'let the sinner be punished but not by sinners, the law be fulfilled but not by its transgressors'.

Augustine's interest now shifts to the woman alone with Jesus. Now

23. While Augustine uses Exodus and Mark to supply him with phrases, the origin of the fundamental image is the contrast of heart and stone in Ezra 36.26.

24. See Jn 4.36; 12.24; 15.2-8, 16.

we, who are the ideal readers, 'having heard the voice of justice, hear the voice of clemency' (*Tractate* 33.6). But we also see at this point Augustine with his keen sense of human situations, for unlike earlier writers he speculates on the mental state of the woman at this moment: now alone in the presence of the sinless Lord—she recognized him for she replied 'No one, Lord' (v. 11)—she would be 'I suppose more frightened than ever'.

Augustine's exegesis alters its focus abruptly from interest in the text to interest centred on the moral lives of his audience.[25] Does Jesus' clemency imply that he is the 'patron of sin' or that she could live as she willed, sure of forgiveness and of being delivered from the torments of hell? Augustine's answer is a resounding 'No!' Having being delivered, the woman is told to sin no more: this shows that while he did not condemn her, he did condemn the sin. He then invokes a distinction he used elsewhere: the Lord condemns the sin and not the person. The Lord's forbearance is aimed at leading the individual to repentance (*Tractate* 33.7). The remainder of the *Tractate* is devoted to exploring how the Christian faced with both God's law and his mercy must hold several elements in tension: love the Lord's gentleness yet fear his truth, while avoiding the extremes of presumption of the Lord's mercy or despairing of his forgiveness (*Tractate* 33.7-8). He ends on this note: the Lord's pardon of the woman made her past secure, but she still had the demands of the law for the future; so with Christians for whom the past can be put behind them, but there is still the challenge of finding what the Lord has promised. This interpretation of sin and forgiveness in terms of an individual's life history in the hourglass of time is a theme he merely hints at, but one which—in the light of subsequent praxes or theologies of repentance—must be seen as a great missed opportunity in the history of doctrine.[26]

Before leaving the *Tractate* we should note that there is some evidence in Augustine's treatment that he knew of Ambrose's letter to Irenaeus. We have noted that both analyse the aim of the scribes and Pharisees as that of trapping Christ with a dilemma (although each

---

25. For Augustine's conception of the 'senses' of Scripture at this period of his life, see O'Loughlin (1999b: 168-72).

26. The notion that sin–repentance–forgiveness are linked to the temporal nature of human existence is a theme which Augustine hints at in several places in his writings, most notably the *Confessiones*, but it is a theme which has not, to my knowledge, been explored; it deserves a proper study.

frames it differently) and both invoke Exod. 31.18 (although it is clear that Augustine has looked at the text and not merely taken the image from Ambrose). With regard to the use of a dilemma, given that both were trained in dialectic (one as a lawyer, the other as a rhetor) it would be natural for both men to analyse any contest using these formal rhetorical figures—which, as the manuals of logic always pointed out, were the weapon of the accuser rather than the tool of the logician. So they could have developed this point independently. More significant is the use of Exodus, since patterns in the use of scriptural texts is one of the best methods of identifying dependencies among patristic and early mediaeval Christian writers. Thus it is very probable that Augustine had read Ambrose, but not certain.[27]

b. The *De conjugiis adulterinis*
In this text written in 419 we have the sole case where the pericope was used as a material part of teaching in the area of sexual morality. The purpose of Augustine's argument is to defend the teaching that among Christians an act of adultery does not end the marriage contract and leave the innocent party free of the marriage contract, but rather spouse should be reconciled with spouse, and the original obligations of marriage continue.[28] Therefore, Augustine's scriptural starting point is the divorce texts in the New Testament, especially Mt. 19.3-10. Augustine recognized that this teaching on a spouse being reconciled with an adulterous partner would be perceived as harsh by his own audience (*De con. adult.* 2.6.5), just as it was found difficult by Jesus' disciples (Mt. 19.10). It is to explain the harshness of this new law that the pericope is invoked. Augustine begins by noting that under the Old Law there was no sacrifice which could wipe away a crime, hence a man could not take back an adulterous woman.[29]

27. Such relationships should be laid out with parallel columns of the text in Latin. However, such a procedure would be out of place here as my purpose is to examine the reactions to the pericope rather than the book-use of the Latin church in the early fifth century.

28. For an account of the work, and its place in Augustine's teaching, see Mackin (1989: 219-20), who points out how Augustine argues the case for the continuance of the 'bond' of marriage; and Reynolds (1994: 207-212 [on the *De conjugiis adulterinis* itself] and 213 and 220-24 [on the situation regarding divorce and remarriage in his diocese in which he wrote the book]).

29. Augustine was also aware that his statement that under the Old Covenant men could not take back adulterous wives was not watertight: did not David wish to

However, crimes can now be washed away by the blood of the New Covenant, hence Christ's statement: 'Neither do I condemn you, go and sin no more'. Here Christ has provided the example which husbands must follow: they must take back their adulterous wives rather than condemn them. Moreover, they must no longer call those wives 'adulteresses' as their sin has been eradicated 'by the mercy of God as a result of their penances' (*De con. adult.* 2.6.5).

While we note that Augustine views the matter from a wholly male point of view (he writes to husbands, assuming that it is only a woman who is being labelled an 'adulteress' [*adultera*] for the crime and divorced), we should note that his action within that culture is to mitigate its severity towards woman. Husbands who have faith must forgive their wives, even if they do not like the prospect. They must even stop calling their wives 'adulteresses' for that would deny the possibility of repentance opened up by Christ. Augustine then adds that such forgiveness is alien to 'the pagan mind' (i.e. Christians who do not think as Christians should but as the pagans do) as they imagine it as tantamount to giving a permission to sin—hence his argument that husbands remove the text from the codices. Indeed, such a rejection of the obligation to take back a wife after adultery is equivalent to a rejection of Christ, for it denies that sins can be healed by him as 'the divine Physician' (*a medico Deo*). But Augustine also injects a note of social realism into his argument by rejecting claims by such men that their sternness is the result of their own high moral standards: they are among those standing around the woman before Jesus who are not without sin themselves, and therefore should not be casting stones at others. They censure the physician's medicine of forgiveness, but need it themselves (*De con. adult.* 2.7.6).

c. *A Subversive Reading?*

Augustine's second treatment of the pericope brings out an aspect of its history that is unique among the patristic references to it, and one which we may pass over today without notice. The internal dynamic of the pericope is that it is a trial to trap Jesus (vv. 3-6) and an expression of his message of mercy and forgiveness (vv. 7-11)—it is not primarily a

---

take back Michal (2 Sam. 3.14), his wife (see 1 Sam. 18.27), after she had married Paltiel the son of Laish (1 Sam. 25.44 and 2 Sam. 3.15)? However, this exception does not act as a counter-indicator to the general demand of the law because in this case, argues Augustine, David is a prefiguration of the new law.

piece of teaching on adultery in society, or on the consequences for those caught. Equally, the treatments of Ambrose, Jerome, and Augustine in the *Tractates* focus on this original purpose of the pericope or upon some other issue connected with crime/sin/forgiveness in order to draw general theological lessons. However, in the case of its use in *De conjugiis adulterinis* we see the pericope functioning in a different way: it is held up as a challenge to the society, and the society's values, in which it is read. Augustine uses it as a direct *exemplum* for Christian attitudes, and as a precedent for action. In this situation the text poses a threat to that society's behaviour and it becomes subversive in removing threats to women. Viewed from this perspective, his statement that the pericope is absent from some copies of John's Gospel is not a case of naive textual criticism, but recognition that for many men—although Christian in name in that they own copies of the Gospels—the demands of that faith are secondary to their own desires that religion be a buttress of social control by the dominant group in society. Thus, *De conjugiis adulterinis* can be seen as one of the first recorded instances of the use of a subversive reading of a biblical text: the pericope is being used as a mirror to the society as to how it should behave towards women, in contrast to how it actually behaves.

5. *Cassiodorus*

The *Expositio Psalmorum* is Cassiodorus's greatest exegetical work in which he comments on every verse of the Psalms from the position that they foreshadow,[30] and so help the Christian reader to understand, the Christ-event.[31] He invokes the pericope once, in commenting upon Ps. 57.6: 'They set a net for my steps; my soul was bowed down. They dug a pit in my way, but they have fallen into it themselves.'[32]

The 'Christ-ian' reading of that verse is that it refers to the traps the Jews will set for Jesus, and the particular trap is the incident recorded in John 8. The basis for this identification is the charge of the evangelist that they brought the woman 'to test him, that they might have some

---

30. On this hermeneutic in Cassiodorus, see O'Loughlin (1998).

31. On the general background of Cassiodorus, see O'Donnell (1979; this is now available *in toto* with an updated bibliography on the Internet). For background to his commentary on the Psalms, see Walsh (1998: 226-34); for an account of Cassiodorus's relationship to Augustine's exegesis, see O'Loughlin (1999c).

32. Cassiodorus used the LXX numeration of the Psalms, where this is Ps. 56.7; his comments can be found after that lemma in the *Expositio*.

charge to bring against him' (Jn 8.6). Cassiodorus describes it as a 'malicious questioning'. Then Jesus physically bent down (Jn 8.6), which expresses how his soul bowed down (Ps. 57.6) at the failure of the 'wicked Jews' to believe. Then he interprets the pit (Ps. 57.6) as signifying a sentence of death 'which sends men to the pit', which is the sentence set before Jesus for the woman, 'but they fell in it themselves' for 'an unjust sentence harms its giver, before it harms the one sentenced'.

For Cassiodorus, the three correspondences between the two texts make it clear that it was the incident with the woman that David was prophesying in the Psalm.[33] That it could be foretold by David implies that for Cassiodorus there can be no doubt about the canonicity of the text nor of the historical truth of the incident in the life of Jesus. From our perspective it is regrettable that he only mentioned the text incidentally (his focus was on the Psalm text), rather than making a direct comment upon it.

6. *The Silence*

When we survey the evidence for the use of the *pericope de adultera,* the overwhelming impression is that of the scarcity of use and comment. The small number of commentators apart, it is only used accidentally by Ambrose, Jerome and Cassiodorus. Only two writers, Ambrose and Augustine, were interested in its details—except for Jerome's suggestion as to what Jesus wrote—and can be said to have provided an exegesis of it. Only one writer, Augustine, used it in the context of sexual or moral teaching. The most common element in all the comments is the condemnation of the Jews for seeking to trap Jesus and expose him as a religious fraud; however, the most common lesson drawn from it was that Jesus is mercy and forgiveness (even if Ambrose would try to argue otherwise verbally) for sinners.

But why the paucity of use? Any attempt to answer this question must be prefaced by two notes. First, it is by nature a fraught question for it is an argument from silence: the historian works with factual evidence speculating once something has happened—but speculation about a silence in history, which is not just a silence in evidence for we have no shortage of Gospel commentary, is little more than guesswork.

---

33. Cassiodorus read the Psalms in the light of New Testament texts such as Acts 1.16—David predicting the life of Christ.

Second, if the pericope did not appeal to many writers—and it is perhaps significant to note that we are dealing with almost exclusively male writers—then there probably was no single reason for their silence.

This lack of interest has been addressed by several writers who account for it primarily in terms of the availability of the text, and secondly, in relation to the fact that since the early Church considered adultery one of the three capital sins which demanded stern public penance that it was rejected for its 'leniency'.[34] On closer examination neither of these appears to me to take us very far. That the text was not available to early writers may be a partial explanation, for it was not ubiquitous in Latin—though on the extant manuscript evidence it was more widely found before the fifth century than Riesenfeld believed. However, it is no explanation at all once the Vulgate had become dominant. Moreover, while both Jerome and Augustine knew it was not ubiquitous, both firmly believed the pericope was genuine—indeed there is not one extant statement which argues that it is not genuine Scripture, and so some lingering doubts or hesitations about its canonicity can discounted as a factor in its being ignored.

That the simple dismissal of the woman by Jesus with the command to change her life in the future might undermine the preaching of public penance is a far more plausible explanation. Early Church discipline in the West focused on a trio of capital sins (which were seen to derive from Acts 15.29): murder, apostasy and adultery.[35] These sins, perceived as crimes by analogy with civil law, could not be remitted by the ordinary course of prayer and penitence that was seen to be intrinsic to Christian living, but required formal penitence by exclusion from the eucharistic community, together with special acts of reparation of prayer, fasting and almsgiving (a trio they based on Mt. 6.2-6 [alms, prayer]; and 16-18 [fasting]), followed by a liturgical action of being brought back into communion. While this was preached with constant intensity, in practice it was an almost complete failure.[36] Moreover, those who attempted to break away from this discipline in favour of a

34. These arguments can be traced back from Riesenfeld (1970: 100) to Bishop (1934: 40-45); to Bernard (1928: 715-21). It has surfaced most recently in Burge (1984: 146-48).

35. See O'Loughlin (2000: 100).

36. See O'Loughlin (2000: 93-102); and O'Loughlin and Conrad-O'Briain (1993: 65-83).

practical pastoral approach to the forgiveness of sins-after-baptism, had
to contend with the reproach that they were 'going soft on sin'.[37] In
such a context, to dwell on the fact that Jesus simply told the woman
that she was not to sin in future—in effect that she could put the past
behind her—could be seen as the kind of example that one would not
want to dwell upon. However, while this seems plausible, and no doubt
caused some to pass over the pericope, its value as an explanation is
limited: it is a hypothesis, and so is vulnerable to hypothetical assaults
on its reasoning. First, it could be argued that the dismissal of the
woman with the injunction to begin a new life was a type of baptism—
when previous sins were remitted without penalty—rather than of penance which only concerned sins committed after baptism. This was a
fundamental premise within the whole debate and so it could have
come naturally to preachers, indeed we have seen an example of how
Ambrose used it. Moreover, there were many ways around any text
which proved awkward with regard to practice, so a perceived challenge to practice would not stop the use of a text which otherwise found
favour. We must note that in the period in which we are concerned
there was a general contentment that both church structures regarding
penance and the scriptures came from the same divine source: suggesting that the pericope was glossed over as showing up a practice 'without warrant' in Scripture is the retrojection of a later logic of controversy. Second, in the one homily we possess on the pericope, Augustine's *Tractates*, we have a case where the incident is integrated seam-
lessly—without any controversial note—into the standard preaching of
penance, and the need for penitence in the Christian life. Ambrose,
likewise, saw the woman's dismissal in terms of the ecclesial discipline
of penance without any apparent difficulty.

---

37. There sees to be some curious internal dynamic linking religious authorities,
concerns about sin, and intellectual blindness, which recoils from the idea that
unless they insist on awful suffering by the sinner, they are condoning sin. And this
fear becomes so important that they ignore the whole purpose of religious commandments, as well as the most elementary psychology of human encouragement.
Be they 'the scribes and Pharisees' in the text, the bishops of the fourth to sixth centuries (some, e.g. Theodulf of Orleans, were still shouting about 'getting back to the
purity of public penance' in the ninth century), or more recent preachers, this fear
by preachers of 'going soft' often destroys not only the spiritual lives of people, but
also their happiness. Perhaps here is the value of the pericope: preachers should not
worry that they are not standing up for 'God's law', but rather realize that everyone,
themselves included, have to move one step forward in discipleship tomorrow.

We have only one hint from antiquity as to why the pericope was ignored—Augustine's explanation of its absence from many texts through its inconvenience to husbands—and perhaps here we have a key to its lack of prominence. The pericope challenges some very deep-seated fears by men about the behaviour of their wives, the fear of sexuality without control among women whose sexuality was considered accounted for, and the notion that religion must support the structures of the society. One recalls Voltaire's desire that his tradesmen and his wife should be believers—his fear of being cheated in business and bed providing a rationale for the irrational! Augustine identified this as a text which many would find sensitive, one which went against the grain of his society, and which many Christians would prefer to do without lest it gave their wives ideas or lessened their threats and controls. Here I suspect lies the omission of the text from comment. Even if not excised from the canonical text, it was excised from the mental canon of the readers—'bad women' were 'bad women' no matter what Jesus said or did. Augustine's argument may not be good text criticism, but he may have been more profoundly correct than he imagined.

BIBLIOGRAPHY

Bernard, J.H.
    1928   *A Critical and Exegetical Commentary on the Gospel According to St John* (2 vols.; Edinburgh: T. & T. Clark).

Bishop, E.F.F.
    1934   'The *Pericope adulterae*: A Suggestion', *JTS* 35: 40-45.

Burge, G.M.
    1984   'A Specific Problem in the New Testament Text and Canon: The Woman Caught in Adultery (John 7:53-8:11)', *JETS* 27: 141-48.

Burkitt, F.C.
    1894   *The Book of Rules of Tyconius* (Texts and Studies, 3.1; Cambridge: Cambridge University Press): 66-70.
    1900   'The Vulgate Gospels and the Codex Brixianus', *JTS*: 129-34).

Fischer, Bonifatius
    1991   *Die lateinischen Evangelien bis zum 10. Jahrhundert* (Freiburg: Herder).

Mackin, Theodore
    1989   *The Marital Sacrament: Marriage in the Catholic Church* (New York: Paulist Press).

McGurk, P.
    1961   *Latin Gospel Books from A.D. 400 to A.D. 800* (Paris: Standaard Boekhandeln).

O'Donnell, James Joseph
    1979   *Cassiodorus* (Berkeley: University of California Press).

O'Loughlin, T.
    1997   'Individual Anonymity and Collective Identity: The Enigma of Early
                Medieval Latin Theologians', *Recherches de théologie et philosophie
                médiévale* 64: 291-314.
    1998   'Christ and the Scriptures: The Chasm between Modern and Pre-modern
                Exegesis', *The Month* 259: 475-85.
    1999a   'Tradition and Exegesis in the Eighth Century: The Use of Patristic
                Sources in Early Medieval Scriptural Commentaries', in *idem*, (ed.), *The
                Scriptures and Early Medieval Ireland* (Turnhout: Brepols): 217-39.
    1999b   *Teachers and Code-Breakers: The Latin Genesis Tradition, 430–800*
                (Turnhout: Brepols).
    1999c   'Cassiodorus', in Allan D. Fitzgerald (ed.), *Augustine through the Ages:
                An Encyclopedia* (Grand Rapids: Eerdmans): 143-44.
    2000   'Penitentials and Pastoral Care', in G.R. Evans (ed.), *A History of
                Pastoral Care* (London: Cassells): 93-111.
O'Loughlin, T. , and H. Conrad-O'Briain
    1993   'The "baptism of tears" in Early Anglo-Saxon Sources', *Anglo-Saxon
                England* 22: 65-83.
Petzer, J.H.
    1995   'The Latin Version of the New Testament', in B.D. Ehrman and M.W.
                Holmes (eds.), *The Text of the New Testament in Contemporary
                Research: Essays on the Status Quaestionis* (Grand Rapids: Eerdmans,
                1995): 113-30.
Reisenfeld, H.
    1970   'The Pericope *de adultera* in the Early Christian Tradition', in *idem*, *The
                Gospel Tradition* (Philadelphia: Fortress Press; Oxford: Clarendon Press):
                95-110 (orig published as 'Die Pericope von der Ehebrecherin in der
                frühkirchlichen Tradition', *SEÅ* : 17 [1952]: 106-111).
Reynolds, Philip Lyndon
    1994   *Marriage in the Western Church: The Christianization of Marriage dur-
                ing the Patristic and Early Medieval Periods* (Leiden: E.J. Brill).
Walsh, P.G.
    1998   'Cassiodorus Teaches Logic through the Psalms', in J. Petruccione (ed.),
                Nova et Vetera: Patristic Studies in Honor of Thomas Patrick Halton
                (Washington: Catholic University of America Press): 226-34.

A Place for Mercy: Some Allegorical Readings of 'The Woman Taken in Adultery' from the Early Middle Ages (with Particular Reference to Bede, the *Heliand* and the Exeter Book[*]

Mark Atherton

During the first millennium, the peoples of England and Germany were Christianized, and the religion of the Book gradually took a hold on their minds and cultures. Interestingly, the story of the woman taken in adultery occurs only occasionally in their biblical exegesis and in their (originally oral) poetry. Why this should be so is a matter of speculation. On the whole, of course, the literature that has actually survived was dependent on the literate class of mainly monastic writers and scribes who copied the manuscripts, and possibly it was they who found the theme uncongenial. But the problem can also be seen as part of a wider question of inculturation and accommodation that the educators faced: which aspects of the Bible and the Christian message should be emphasized?

In the two case studies presented here I will consider the processes by which a challenging episode from the Gospels was explicated and adapted for people who had been converted to Christianity only two or three generations before. The first text is by the historian Bede, writing in the 720s in Northumbria; the second by an unknown poet writing a life of Christ in Saxony in the 840s. To place the story of Jn 8.1-11 in context, both authors emphasize the setting: in the former instance by explicating the topography, in the latter by transforming the same topography of the episode into a cultural world of much greater familiarity to his intended audience. Thus Bede focuses on the Mount of Olives, while the Old Saxon poet sets the scene carefully in the Temple

* I would like to thank Dr Hugh Magennis, of The Queen's University Belfast, and Mr Peter Jackson, of the *Fontes Anglo-Saxonici* research project, for their useful comments on an earlier draft of this chapter.

as a royal hall and a centre of law-making and power. As we shall see, in both cases the emphasis on significant setting allows the episode to resonate with other literary texts, poems and stories from the period. In particular, 'The Wife's Lament', a poem from the celebrated Exeter Book (the major surviving collection of Old English lyric poetry), provides a foil to the two case studies in its mysterious and perhaps pagan setting of 'the oak-tree in the grove'.

1. *Literary Background*

Bede (c. 673–735), the humane Northumbrian monk, historian, biblical scholar and poet, was the most learned and prolific writer of Anglo-Saxon England and, indeed, the greatest scholar in the Europe of his time. His famous work, the *Ecclesiastical History of the English People*, which survives in over 130 English and continental manuscripts, was widely read and copied throughout the Middle Ages and beyond.[1] Written in the tradition of Eusebius's *Ecclesiastical History*, its topic, the general history of the church in southern Britain from the Roman empire until his own time—treating in detail the story of the English Church following Pope Gregory's mission in 597—is a masterly work of art, with a clear rhetorical purpose and an impressive array of documentary and oral sources. It remains to this day a major source for the early history of England.

Thematically, Bede's *Ecclesiastical History* derives from his biblical commentaries on the Acts of the Apostles, in which he was a pioneer, and from his work on the literal meaning and typological significance of Old Testament history.[2] In his commentaries and sermons, Bede adapted the patristic writings of Augustine, Ambrose and Jerome, as well as those of the 'Apostle of the English', Pope Gregory the Great.[3] On the strength of his exegetical works, later writers such as Alcuin, Ælfric, Abelard and Dante regarded Bede as one of the Fathers of the Church.

1. The most easily available translation is that of Sherley-Price (1990). The edition by Colgrave and Mynors (1969) of the original Latin provides a reliable translation on the facing page; the other major edition is Plummer (1896).

2. Cf. Martin (1989) and Connolly and O'Reilly (1995).

3. Gregory the Great (c. 540–604), Pope 590–604, instigator of the mission to England in 597 under Augustine of Canterbury; his policy of accommodation of the harmless rituals and traditional customs of the pagan English is reported in Bede's *Ecclesiastical History* (1.30); on this see Markus (1970).

Among his many exegetical activities, Bede found time to compose two sets of homilies on the Gospels,[4] to be read aloud at appointed times throughout the ecclesiastical year, either in the monastery church or in the refectory where the monks listened to edifying texts while taking their meals. Again his model was Gregory—in this case, his Forty Gospel Homilies[5]—but Bede showed his originality by choosing to treat pericopes which had not been covered by the missionizing Pope. These include the sermon for Lent on Jn 8.1-12, which will be considered in more detail below.

Despite the Classical standard of his Latinity, Bede also championed the use of the vernacular language, for, as he remarked in one famous passage, 'verses, however masterly, cannot be translated literally from one language into another without losing their beauty and dignity'.[6] According to a pupil, the monk Cuthbert, Bede was translating the Gospel of John into English shortly before he died in 735.[7] Unfortunately, this translation has not survived, though another English work attributable to him is reproduced in Cuthbert's account; this is 'Bede's Death Song',[8] a four-line poem written in the ancient Germanic alliterative style most famously preserved in the Anglo-Saxon epic poem *Beowulf*.[9] Further evidence of Bede's encouragement of literature in English (rather than exclusively in Latin) is his famous story in the *Ecclesiastical History* (4.24) of the illiterate cowherd Cædmon at Abbess Hild's monastery at Whitby, who miraculously acquired the inspired ability to compose artful religious verse after a dream in which a man told him to 'sing the creation of all things'.

Bede's example of encouraging literature in English was followed in later centuries. It should be noted (though the policy probably did not begin with Bede) that copies of the Vulgate Gospels were regularly equipped with interlinear running glosses in English, and the four

4.   CChr, 122; trans. by Martin and Hurst (1991).
5.   *PL*, 76: 1075-1314; translated by Hurst (1990).
6.   Cf. *Eccl. Hist.* book 4 ch. 24 (henceforth such references will be given on the pattern: '4.24').
7.   Cuthbert's 'Letter on the Illness and Death of the Venerable Bede the Priest' is translated in Sherley-Price (1990: 357-60).
8.   Sherley-Price (1990: 358); Hamer (1970: 125-27); Bradley (1982: 6).
9.   The poem survives from what is normally referred to as 'Anglo-Saxon' (i.e. pre-Norman) England; the language in which it is written is commonly known as 'Old English'.

Gospels were properly translated in the tenth century.[10] Though we are far from certain, the written tradition of vernacular religious verse appears to have spread from Northumbria to Mercia and finally to the collections of late Anglo-Saxon England, such as the Exeter Book and the *Beowulf* manuscript.[11] The Cædmonian model of the inspired vernacular poet from among the people perhaps also inspired the ninth-century Old Saxon poem on the life of Christ known as the *Heliand* ('The Saviour').[12] This poem, composed in the ancient alliterative metre with a newly converted Old Saxon (i.e. North German) audience in mind, may reflect a tradition of vernacular religious poetry begun by the Anglo-Saxon mission to the region in the eighth century.[13] But there is evidence of reciprocal relations between the Anglo-Saxons and their Continental cousins.[14] The Old Saxon poetry in turn influenced the late Anglo-Saxon verse collections; the Old Saxon 'Genesis' was adapted into Old English, in a poem preserved in the so-called 'Junius manuscript'[15] and the *Heliand* itself was copied (and presumably read) in mid-tenth-century England.[16]

2. *Attitudes to Women and Marriage in Bede's Writings*

Before turning to Bede's exegesis of the story of the woman taken in adultery, it is worth considering briefly the status of women in Bede's thought and the frequency with which women occur in his historical writings. At first sight, his story of synods, battles and dynasties might

---

10. Liuzza (1994); the text of John's Gospel includes the story of the woman taken in adultery.

11. These two books contain poetry written in vernacular Anglo-Saxon, or Old English, as it is usually called. For introductions to Old English literature, see Godden and Lapidge (1991); Greenfield (1972); Bradley (1982). The Exeter Book survived as a gift of Bishop Leofric to the library of Exeter Cathedral in 1072 (Barlow 1972; Conner 1993; Gameson 1996); the origin of the *Beowulf* manuscript, now in the British Library, is unknown.

12. Edited by Behaghel (1922); the Preface containing the allusion to Cædmon is discussed by Haubrichs (1973).

13. A racy and controversial introduction is Murphy (1989); a good collection of scholarly research is that edited by Eichhoff and Rauch (1973). See below for further discussion of the *Heliand*.

14. Schwab 1988; Magennis 1999.

15. Doane 1991.

16. Priebsch 1925.

appear to preclude the occurrence of women. This is not so, for a number of powerful women appear in the *Ecclesiastical History*. Christian queens, for instance, play their part in the conversion of their husbands. Thus, at the point where Bede's narrative effectively gathers momentum—with the arrival in 597 of the Roman bishop, Augustine, sent by Gregory as leader of the mission to the pagan King Æthelberht of Kent—we learn that the King's Frankish wife, Bertha, is a Christian, and has (so it appears) favourably disposed him to allow the mission to establish its see at Canterbury (*Eccl. Hist.* 1.25). In the next generation, as the mission moves northwards, the then Pope writes to Æthelberht's daughter, Æthelburh, now married to King Edwin of Northumbria and anxious to effect his conversion; Gregory's letter is recorded verbatim in the *Ecclesiastical History* (2.11). In it the Pope cites Paul's discussion of marriage in 1 Cor. 7.14 and urges Æthelburh to persevere 'so that the warmth of divine faith may set his mind on fire through your constant encouragement and remove the deadening errors of paganism'. No doubt there are political factors at play as well as theological in this letter of a Roman pope to an influential Northumbrian queen.

Other evidence in Bede's writings for the power and prestige of women (at least those of aristocratic rank) is the establishment in the seventh and eighth centuries of double monasteries ruled by an abbess. This institution, which consisted of separate houses for monks and nuns, is celebrated in book 4 of Bede's *Ecclesiastical History* in the accounts of the two powerful abbesses Hild of Whitby (4.23) and Æthelthryth of Ely (4.20). The former is the abbess who 'discovers' Cædmon and encourages him to develop his poetic gift. The latter is praised by Bede in a Latin hymn on her sanctity, which consisted, in the earlier part of her life, in refusing for reasons of piety to consummate her marriage with her husband Ecgfrith, King of Northumbria (670–684). This was despite the heavy pressures he subjected her to before he finally permitted her to leave him for the monastery.[17]

The respect for women in Bede's world is documented even in the prominence of place-names derived from women's names, such as Bebbanburh, now Bamburgh, which Bede describes as 'the royal city which is called after a former queen named Bebba' (*Eccl. Hist.* 3.6). Such evidence points, as most scholars have argued, to a very high status for Anglo-Saxon women as compared to other European women of the

---

17. Note the discussions of the hagiographies of these important figures by Fell (1981) and Leyser (1995: 34-35).

same period.[18] Later documents support this, at least in part. In the Domesday Book of 1086 (which is essentially a census ordered by the Normans but based on the earlier Anglo-Saxon records), some of the major landowners are women, and the surviving Anglo-Saxon wills show that male and female heirs were treated equally, with no undue preference shown to sons.[19]

Such evidence is generally supported by the great Anglo-Saxon law-codes, which are also highly informative on the procedures for marriage and divorce. The first English law-code was compiled, probably by Augustine of Canterbury, for Æthelberht of Kent in about 602–603.[20] The compilation is noted by Bede (*Eccl. Hist.* 2.5), and he presumably knew the text (which survives now only in a much later manuscript). Clauses 77–81 of this code, along with other evidence,[21] show that Anglo-Saxon marriage involved a contract between a prospective bride-groom and the bride and her relatives. The groom undertook to pay her a 'bride-price', and the relatives were involved in order to protect her interests both before and after the marriage, since husband and wife retained independent property rights. After the wedding itself, the bride received a 'morning-gift', which she kept as her personal property and bequeathed to her relatives if she died childless. An example mentioned already is Bebbanburh, which was apparently given to Bebbe as her 'morning-gift' in the seventh century.

The stipulations of the law-code find support in the poem 'Maxims I' from the Exeter Book. Whether Bede knew the poem is uncertain, but it is likely that poetry of a similar kind existed in his day. 'Maxims I' is a series of gnomic sayings and proverbial wisdom, which evoke tradi-tional customs and practices, the ancient and probably pre-mediaeval world of the 'mead-hall':

18. The question has generated much interest and discussion. Recent studies of many aspects of women in the Anglo-Saxon period include Damico and Olsen (1990); Dietrich (1980); Fischer (1986); Hollis (1992); Klinck (1982); Leyser (1995).

19. This generally held view is qualified somewhat by Stafford (1994).

20. Attenborough (1922); Liebermann (1903); Whitelock (1979: 391-94).

21. Especially the tenth-century tract entitled 'Be wifmannes beweddunge' ('Concerning the Betrothal of a Woman'); see Liebermann (1903) and Whitelock (1979). On engagement, wedding and marriage in Old English, see also Fischer (1986).

A king has to procure a queen with payment, with goblets and with rings. Both must be pre-eminently liberal with gifts. In the man, martial war-like arts must burgeon; and the woman must excel as one cherished among her people, and be buoyant of mood, keep confidences, be open-heartedly generous with horses and with treasures; in deliberation over the mead, in the presence of the troop of companions, she must always and everywhere greet first the the chief of those princes and instantly offer the chalice to her lord's hand, and she must know what is prudent for them both as rulers of the hall.[22]

In the hierarchy thus presented, women 'are given an honoured place in the community and can act as major influences upon it'.[23]

As an earlier passage in the same poem shows, the duties of men and women in this shame-culture are based on codes of expected behaviour and allotted roles, in which reputations must be guarded and all actions kept in the open:[24]

Woman belongs at her embroidery; a roving woman gives rise to talk—she is often accused of sordid things; men speak of her insultingly... A person nursing guilt must needs move about in darkness; the candid person belongs in the light.[25]

The hierarchy in which women must find their place is also the world of the 'comitatus', the retinue of companions in the service of a chosen leader, a relationship symbolized by the banqueting hall and its 'gift-stool'. In such a world, ties of loyalty and service must be honoured and paid for. The above passage continues as follows:

---

22. Bradley 1982: 348; cf. Muir 1994. A similar scene occurs in the epic poem *Beowulf* when, at the celebration feast in the mead-hall, the Queen Wealhtheow offers the cup to the hero (l. 1168-74; Wrenn 1973; Bradley 1982: 442).

23. Magennis 1996: 107.

24. Ll. 63-66; Bradley 1982: 348.

25. Ll. 63-66; Bradley 1982: 348. Line 64b, 'she is often accused of sordid things' ('oft hy mon wommum belihoð) is repeated again word for word at l. 100b in a context which speaks first of the joyous loving welcome the Frisian wife gives to her husband home from the sea (ll. 23-29), but then goes on to sound a note of warning. 'A woman must keep faith with her man', the poet says, since 'often they are accused of sordid things; many are constant, but many are promiscuous and love strange men when the other is travelling far away' (ll. 100-102). The motif of separated husbands and wives waiting by the sea occurs in two other Exeter Book poems, 'The Wife's Lament' and 'The Husband's Message', discussed further below.

The head must influence the hand; treasure must wait in its hoards—and
the gift-throne stand prepared—for when men may share it out. Eager for
it is he who receives the gold; the man on the high seat has plenty of it.
There must needs be a return, if we do not mean to deceive, to the one
who afforded us these favours.[26]

The social relationships which this passage expresses are typical of
many poetic and legal texts of the period, and must be assumed also to
lie behind many of the historical and theological writings, such as those
of Bede.

Like the Old English poetry just discussed, the law-codes themselves,
particularly the early ones, are similarly archaic in nature, for they are
based on an ancient 'Germanic' principle of compensation.[27] In the
early period, all crimes and transgressions were considered to be against
the injured party rather than against society. When brought to light,
crimes had to be redeemed by a payment of compensation or fine calculated by the monetary status of the person concerned, known as a
'wergild' (literally, 'man-payment'). Thus, if a person was killed, the
appropriate wergild was paid to his or her relatives to prevent the outbreak of a feud. The system applied also to other transgressions and
breaches of contract such as adultery. In Germanic law on the continent,
the aggrieved husband who apprehended his adulterous wife and her
lover *in flagrante delicto* was at liberty to kill them outright if he so
wished.[28]

Evidence for the harsh punishments against adulterous women in the
pagan areas of eighth-century Germany is contained in a letter of 746–
747 (admittedly highly rhetorical) from Bede's contemporary Boniface
(c. 675–754) to Æthelbald, King of Mercia. Like Tacitus's *Germania*
criticizing the Romans by contrasting their morals with those of the
noble barbarians, and drawing on similar rhetoric in the letters of Paul,[29]
Boniface contrasts the free sexual behaviour of the Mercian court and
monasteries with the strict monogamy of the Old Saxons, arguing that
'even by pagans is this sin reckoned a shame and a disgrace'. He goes

---

26. Ll. 67-70; Bradley 1982: 348.
27. On law-codes, see Leyser (1995: 40-52). See also Fischer Drew (1991: 32-
39) on the 'Frankish judicial system'; as she aptly remarks, 'all criminal law was
civil law'.
28. Schulze 1986: 479.
29. Namely Rom. 2.14-15.

on to list the punishments of execution or torture of adulterous women that 'sometimes' occur in the Saxon villages.[30]

By contrast, in the gentler law code of Æthelberht, clause 31 required payment of wergild in compensation: 'If a freeman lies with the wife of a freeman, he is to atone with his wergild, and to obtain another wife with his own money and bring her to the other's home'.[31]

Whether this was the offender's or the injured party's wergild remains uncertain, as the pronoun *his* in the original Old English is ambiguous:[32] 'Gif friman wið fries mannes wif geligeþ, *his* wergelde abicge, and oðer wif his agenum scætte begete and ðæm oðrum æt ham gebrenge'.[33]

As Rivers suggests, what is probably meant in this seventh-century law is that either the lover paid the husband's wergild as compensation, or he was to make amends by securing a new wife for the husband.[34] All in all, when compared with the brutal punishments for adultery on the continent, this penalty, though heavy, is relatively humane.

Moving from the early seventh century to the year 673, the time of Bede's birth, we find a further stipulation on marriage at the Synod of Hertford (*Eccl. Hist.* 4.5), here based not on civil law but on canon law (i.e. the law of the Church, as passed by Church councils and supplemented by local ecclesiastical councils). From the tone of approval with which Bede quotes Archbishop Theodore, it is clear that he fully accepts the decree of the Synod on marriage. Bede's text reads:

> On marriages: 'That lawful wedlock alone is permissible; incest is forbidden, and no man may leave his lawful wife except, as the gospel provides, for fornication. And if a man puts away his own wife who is joined to him in lawful marriage, he may not take another if he wishes to be a good Christian. He must either remain as he is, or else be reconciled to his wife'.

30. Talbot 1954: 123.

31. Whitelock 1979: 393.

32. Text from Attenborough (1922: 8); cf. Liebermann (1903: 5). Although Whitelock (1979: 393) notes that 'grammatically, it is possible that her wergild is meant', I think it more likely that the pronoun *his* refers to one or other of the two males involved.

33. For readers who are unfamiliar with Old English, the two letters ð and þ represent the sound of the modern English digraph 'th', as in 'bath' or 'bathing'.

34. Rivers 1991: 24. For more discussion of the Kentish laws, see Hough (1994).

From the cumulative evidence of references in the *Ecclesiastical History* and from parallels in Old English poems and law-codes, a reasonably coherent picture can be pieced together. With regard to his attitude to women and marriage, Bede's views can be seen as the product of an eclectic society: on the one hand a shame-based, highly traditional culture with an elaborate legal system based on compensation; on the other hand a Christianized (and in many ways monastically organized) society where chastity was admired and encouraged for its own sake— even within marriage—but where (at least in Bede's day) punishments for adultery, though severe, were not harsh or brutal. Such an attitude must be borne in mind when considering Bede's Lenten homily on Jn 8.1-12; although the relative leniency of the time is not a sufficient explanation for Bede's exegesis, it remains constantly present as a backdrop to the interpretation he adopts.

3. *The Mount of Olives and Augustine's Oak*

In the opening of his homily, Bede makes the following statement:

> It is customary for the scriptures to signify the sort of things that are going to be told about later, sometimes by a circumstance of time, sometimes by a circumstance of place, and sometimes by both. So when the evangelist was about to refer to the tempering of the severity of the law by our Redeemer's mercy, he first mentioned that Jesus made his way to the Mount of Olives, and that at daybreak he came again to the temple.[35]

As becomes clear later, the predominant message that Bede draws from his pericope—and repeats and develops throughout his verse-by-verse exposition—is one of mercy. As he says when referring to the Mount of Olives but at the same time implying the whole of his exposition, his theme is 'the height of the Lord's benevolence and mercy'.

The crux of the homily is its comment on Jn 8.4-5 (p. 246): the woman's wicked accusers confront Jesus with a choice of two wrongs, by which, so it seems, he can only condemn himself. Bede presents the dilemma in a highly memorable and influential formulation, a double conditional sentence (i.e. with two *if*-clauses):

> If he also determined that she was to be stoned they would scoff at him inasmuch as he had forgotten the mercy which he was always teaching;

---

35. Martin and Hurst 1991: 245. All citations of the homily are based on the page numbers of this translation.

if he forbade stoning, they would gnash their teeth at him, and, as they
saw it, rightly condemn him as a doer of wicked deeds contrary to the
law.[36]

Bede follows this with the image of a double-bind or 'catch' from
which it seems that Jesus cannot escape. 'From this side and that', Bede
says, 'the scribes and Pharisees spread traps and snares for the Lord,
supposing that in judging he would be either unmerciful or unjust' (p.
247). But, as Bede develops the exegesis at v. 7, Jesus 'foresaw their
treachery, and as it were passed through the threads of their net', for his
solution is both merciful and just: 'Do you want to hear about his
restraint as he shows mercy?—"*Let one who is without sin among you*".
Again, do you want to hear about his justice in judging?—"*be the first
to throw a stone at her*".'

Since his pericope ends at v. 12, Bede regards Jesus' subsequent
speech 'I am the light of the world' as the coherent resolution to the
episode. 'Far be it from blind wickedness,' he points out, 'to stand in
the way of the Sun of justice to keep him from giving light to the
world.'

As well as mercy, therefore, Bede's homily is also about Christ's
power; as he writes on vv. 6-10:

> It is good that he was bent over when he wrote on the ground [but]
> upright when he uttered the words of mercy, since through his unity with
> human infirmity he promised the gift of his benevolence, [but] through
> the power of his divine might he delivered it to human beings.[37]

Allegory and typology are at work in this passage, above all in the
semiotics of gesture. In particular, there is a a dialectic of distinctions

36. Note the use of this passage in the *Heliand*, ll. 3856-62: 'The adversaries
wished to catch him with words: if he said that they should allow her to live, and
save her life, the people of the Jews would say that he contradicted the law of their
ancestors, the legal code of the people; if he ordered the crowd to take the girl's life,
then they would say that he did not bear in his heart the merciful attitude that the
Son of God should have.' Bede's text was transmitted in the eighth century directly
in copies of his homilies, and indirectly in the work of Alcuin. It is interesting that
the same text is used by the poet Otfrid of Weissenburg in his mid-ninth-century
Old High German Life of Christ (ch. 17, ll. 21-34; cf. Erdmann 1973: 132-33) and
by the late tenth- and early eleventh-century Old English homilist Ælfric (cf. Sup-
plementary Homily 13, in Pope 1967–68: 506, ll. 206-211). The two if-clauses,
used in a very similar way by all these writers, essentially prove the strength of
Bede's influence.

37. Pp. 249-50.

made between stooping down and standing upright, between the longer
action of writing and the single act of speaking, between human
infirmity and power, between law and grace, judgment and mercy. Bede
is concerned to bring out the full significance of the 'ciphers in the
sand'. Writing with the finger represents 'subtlety of discernment' (p.
247); the writing on the ground allows time for a person to contemplate
the 'ground' of his or her own heart first (p. 247); it is also the means of
recording the law, like the Ten Commandments written on stone (p.
249). In addition writing records a promise, here the 'promise of the gift
of his benevolence', which is only delivered through the power of
speech (p. 250). By contrast to the activity and record of writing, therefore, there is the act of speech, which theorists of orality have shown is
more immediate, more concerned with human action and presence.[38] In
Bede, speech represents acts and gestures: acts of accusation, of judgment, of power, and in the end of forgiveness and mercy.

As Bede also makes clear, gestures of bodily movement accompany-
ing the dialogue are a notable feature of the pericope itself, and he
highlights Christ's sitting down to teach in v. 2 and his twice-repeated
actions of stooping down to write and standing up to speak (vv. 6-7, 8,
10). (Perhaps surprisingly, he makes no mention of the fact that the
woman—in her status as the accused—remains standing throughout the
encounter.) As Bede remarks earlier in the homily, Christ's sitting to
teach represents typologically 'the humility of his incarnation' (p. 246).
Similarly, Christ's stooping is associated with humility, but here has
both a literal and a figurative meaning: literally he stooped down and
looked away to give the tempters the opportunity to leave (p. 248); morally, the action teaches people that they should first 'subject themselves
to a suitably humble examination' before making any public judgments
on others (p. 249). In the passage just quoted, the gesture of bending
down closer to the earth is again associated with Christ's unity with
human infirmity, whereas his standing to utter the 'words of mercy'
reflects his divine power and authority.

The repeated emphasis on human gesture and its motivational significance is revealing, for there is a near parallel in the *Ecclesiastical History* (written probably 11 years after the Lenten homily). The famous
story of 'Augustine's Oak' in book 2 is apparently unique in the

---

38. Ong (1982); the distinction between speech and writing will be seen to be of
relevance in the discussion below of the poems from the Exeter Book: 'The Wife's
Lament' and (especially) its companion piece 'The Husband's Message'.

Ecclesiastical History in placing the (Roman) Archbishop Augustine in a bad and the native British Christians in a good light, since Bede usually severely criticized the British (i.e. the Welsh) for playing no part in the Christianization of the English newcomers and for refusing to work in unity with the Roman Church.[39]

As in the Lenten homily, the opening section of the story of Augustine's Oak is concerned with the setting and its significance:

> Meanwhile with the aid of King Ethelbert, Augustine summoned the bishops and teachers of the nearest British province to a conference at a place still known to the English as St Augustine's Oak, which lies on the border between the Hwiccas and the West Saxons. He began by urging them to establish brotherly relations with him in Catholic unity, and to join with him in God's work of preaching the gospel to the heathen.

This meeting, along with the miraculous healing of a blind man which accompanies it, takes place at 'Augustine's Oak' and thereafter retains—for the English—some special religious significance. The location is a place of enlightenment, for Augustine prays that the man's lost sight will be restored 'and prove the means of bringing the light of spiritual grace to the minds of countless believers' (*Eccl. Hist.* 2.2). The healing is successful and, as Bede says, 'all acknowledged Augustine as the true herald of the light of Christ', a phrase which recalls one of the main points of Bede's homily on the woman taken in adultery: 'Far be it from blind wickedness to stand in the way of the Sun of justice to keep him from giving light to the world'.

On a second occasion in the same chapter, however, a meeting occurs at 'the most famous monastery which the English call Bancornaburg' (Bangor-is-y-Coed, Clwyd). Here the British bishops and scholars consult a 'wise and prudent hermit' on whether they should abandon their own traditions and submit to Augustine. The hermit tells them they should ascertain first of all whether Augustine is a man of God, by testing his humility:

> 'Our Lord says, *Take my yoke upon you and learn of me, for I am meek and lowly in heart*', he replied. 'Therefore if Augustine is meek and lowly in heart, it shows that he bears the yoke of Christ himself, and

---

39. The confrontation between Augustine on the one hand and the indigenous Welsh (or 'Celtic') bishops on the other is now the subject of Peter Oswald's interesting play *Augustine's Oak*, which uses the story and its setting to explore the relationship of other faiths to Christianity. See Shortt (1999: 18).

offers it to you. But if he is haughty and unbending, then he is not of
God, and we should not listen to him.' Then they asked, 'But how can
we know even this?' 'Arrange that he and his followers arrive first at the
place appointed for the conference', answered the hermit. 'If he rises
courteously as you approach, rest assured that he is the servant of Christ
and do as he asks. But if he ignores you and does not rise, then, since
you are the majority, do not comply with his demands.'

Needless to say, when the meeting took place, Augustine did not rise,
and no agreement was reached, though otherwise his behaviour seems
to have been exemplary, at least as far as we can tell from Bede's narrative perspective. In the rest of the chapter, Augustine remains the 'man
of God', while many of the British priests and monks are 'faithless
Britons' who incur 'the punishment of temporal destruction' when
attacked by King Ethelfrid's men at Chester. Evidently the point of
Augustine's remaining seated was to demonstrate his power and authority, which the Britons failed to acknowledge. To emphasize this point
Bede highlights the significant setting of Augustine's Oak, where the
first meeting took place and where Augustine was also able to show his
divinely sanctioned power by healing the blind man and bringing
enlightenment to those present.

At this point, we should return to the Lenten homily and reconsider
Bede's discussions of the circumstances of time and place that give a
significant structure to the whole sermon. Bede places the story of the
woman within two frames: the Mount of Olives and the statement 'I am
the light of the world'. This is reminiscent yet again of Bede the historian seeking—as he regularly does in his *Ecclesiastical History*—to
place his characters and their actions in a wider moral and theological
framework.

Thus at the start of the homily Bede explains the circumstances of
place and time and emphasizes the sacred significance of the setting on
the Mount of Olives and the return to the Temple. To explain the name
of the place, Bede employs biblical reminiscence and pushes the allegorical method to its limits in arguing that oil floats on the top of other
liquids and so 'suggests the grace of heavenly mercy, concerning which
it was written, *The Lord is gracious to everyone, and his compassion is
over all his works*'. The circumstance of time—daybreak—is similarly
fraught with meaning for Bede, since it signifies 'the dawn of grace by
which the light of the gospel truth was to be revealed when the shadow
of the law was taken away', and furthermore the arrival at the Temple
symbolizes that the radiance of the New Testament is beginning—at a

time when 'the same mercy was to be disclosed and presented to the temple, namely to his faithful ones'.

At the end of the homily, just before the closing exhortation, as he discusses Jesus' statement 'I am the light of the world', Bede closes the frame, drawing all his ideas together on the significance of setting, time and events in the interpretation of the story of the woman taken in adultery:

> Here he clearly taught, not only by what authority he had forgiven the woman's sins, but also what he himself had expressed figuratively by making his way to the Mount of Olives, by coming again at daybreak to the temple, and by writing with his finger on the ground: that he himself is the summit *of mercies and the God of all consolation*,[40] the herald as well as the bestower of unfaltering light,[41] the source of the law as well as grace.

In this Lenten homily, then, we have a monastic sermon on the theme of enlightenment, the written promise of consolation and the spoken word of mercy. Despite its devotional tone, it nevertheless reveals something of Bede the historical writer, attaching psychological significance to the actions of characters and drawing out the wider importance of time and place. For the period in question Bede's homily is the only full and wide-ranging interpretation of the episode of the woman taken in adultery. Given the popularity and wide dissemination of Bede in the mediaeval period, his exegesis is a touchstone for the evaluation of later interpretations. The fact of Christ's mercy towards the woman remains a theme in later exegetes, but none emphasizes it quite as strongly as Bede.

4. *Temple as Royal Hall: The Setting in the* Heliand

In the eighth century, the Anglo-Saxons, now part of Christendom, turned their attention to the continental *Ealdseaxoni* or Old Saxons, described by the principal missionary Boniface as being 'of one blood and one bone' with their English cousins, the Anglo-Saxons.[42] A vigorous mission followed with some successes based on preaching and heavy persuasion, but not yet achieving full Christianization.[43] Under

40. 2 Cor. 1.3.
41. Sir. 24.6.
42. Talbot 1954: 96.
43. Keep 1982.

Charlemagne (742–814), however, the problem of the aggressive pagan neighbours to the north and east was dealt with by a more focused policy of suppression and coercion. By the early ninth century, as a result of the military campaigns of Charlemagne between 772 and 804, the Saxons had been subdued, a symbolic sacred tree (the Irminsul) destroyed, and the whole area (from the Rhine north of the Ruhr eastwards to the Elbe) subjected to forcible Christianization;[44] as the *Capitulatio de partibus Saxoniae* or 'Law-code of the Saxon Territories' of 797 testifies: 'From now on, should anyone hidden among the Saxons as a non-baptized person wish to remain in concealment, who disdains to come to baptism and wishes to remain a pagan, let him be put to death'.[45]

With the region now pacified, there was room for other approaches. An influence for change was Alcuin (c. 735–804), the Anglo-Saxon scholar from York who became chief adviser at the Frankish court of Charlemagne and ended his career as Abbot of Tours. Alcuin advised a relaxation of the oppressive Carolingian policy.[46] Evidently he preferred the policies of Gregory, Bede and Boniface to direct aggression. Another important figure is Hrabanus Maurus (780–856), who appears to have championed the use of the vernacular German language while serving as Abbot of Fulda (the monastic foundation of Boniface). The composition of the *Heliand* in the period 830 to 850 mirrors this new and different attitude, much closer to Gregory's policy of accommodation in the conversion of England, or to Abbess Hild's promotion of Christian poetry in the vernacular at Whitby.

The *Heliand*, or Old Saxon 'The Saviour', is a life of Christ written in verse and based on Tatian's *Diatessaron*, which was in use at Fulda.[47] In its use of the old Germanic alliterative metre and verse-

44. For a short, lively account of the 'Frankish drive to the East', see Fletcher (1997: 193-227). A general survey of England and the Continent in the eighth century is provided by Levison (1946). An interesting account of the possible 'Germanization' of Christianity in this period is proposed by Russell (1994).

45. Von Schwerin (1918: 40); translation by Murphy (1989: 11).

46. Allott (1974: 71-76).

47. The standard edition of the *Heliand* is Behaghel (1922), and there are translations by Scott (1966) and Murphy (1992). It was at Fulda that an Old High German version of Tatian's *Diatessaron* was completed, probably at the behest of Hrabanus Maurus (Sievers 1964). The *Heliand* poet may have used this text as a source (Baesecke 1948; disputed by fon Weringha 1965). Other sources are discussed by Huber (1969).

form, its style is reminiscent of 'Cædmon's Hymn' and other Old English poems, and scholars have speculated that the poetic tradition to which it belongs was established during the earlier Anglo-Saxon mission.[48] The question of its place of composition is unresolved, but whether written in Frankish territory at the Anglo-Saxon foundation of Fulda, or in Saxon territory at Werden,[49] it is remarkable for its use of what must have once been pagan vocabulary in a poem on the life of Christ. For instance, words in the semantic field of 'mind, thought, heart' such as *hugi* and *mod* indicate different notions of the soul and spirit to those of Christianity.[50]

Such connotations may be subconscious, merely a lower stratum in the history of the language. However, a look at the poem itself reveals changes in the concrete details of the Gospel story that are more obvious evidence of a consciously different attitude on the part of the poet to his material and audience. Where appropriate, the world of the Gospel is transformed into that of the Saxons, who apparently had a high regard for their traditional customs.[51] As in the Old English verses of 'Maxims I', there is an emphasis on the close 'comitatus' relationship between lord and retainer. Linked to this is the prominence of the theme of kingship. The poet emphasizes the idea of noble birth, both of John the Baptist and of Jesus Christ. John's physical appearance and perfection of body are described in glowing terms, and in the Nativity episode the infant Christ is guarded by *ehuscalcos*, that is, grooms or squires, rather than being visited by lowly shepherds. For the calling of the disciples, Christ as 'mead-giver' selects and calls 12 companions in a description highly reminiscent of the reciprocal comitatus relationship. The twelve accompany him to the mountain, where Christ takes his seat as a great and wise king 'gracious in thought and generous in spirit'. The subsequent Sermon on the Mount takes up 8 of the 72 'fitts' (the

48. There is a full summary and discussion in Schwab (1988); Edwards (1994) gives an English summary of German vernacular literature in this period.

49. See the discussions on place of origin in Baesecke (1948) and Drögereit (1951).

50. Eggers (1973). The poem's vocabulary of kingship is similarly well developed, and draws on what must be traditional Germanic diction and secular experience; see Weisweiler and Betz (1974: 70). For a discussion of the 'pagan words and Christian meanings' in Old English poetry, see North (1991).

51. As in a preface by the Saxon cleric Walbert of Wildeshausen cited in Brown (1996: 310). Further evidence of syncretism and pagan survival is discussed by Karras (1986).

songs or sections into which the poem is divided). In short, Christ is the *landes hirdi* ('guardian of the land'), the bringer of *heil*, a concept not simply translated as 'salvation of the soul', but rather having connotations of the health of the kingdom and the nation.[52] These vernacular concepts appear to be still present in the depiction of the Saviour of the *Heliand*.

The poet's policy of redressing the Christian gospel in his native idiom is likely to have originated in the writings of Bede and his successors, and in the effects of the Anglo-Saxon mission, particularly at Fulda, to which much of the vernacular literary activity of the early ninth century points. Bede's original homilies were certainly available in Saxony, and were perhaps used during the Anglo-Saxon mission to the area. The Anglo-Saxon missionary Boniface wrote letters back to England requesting copies of Bede, particularly the homilies, 'because it would be a very handy and useful manual for us in our preaching'.[53] There is evidence that they were also translated, at least in part, into the Saxon vernacular. An Old Saxon translation of a passage from Bede's homily for All Saints' Day was added to a tenth-century Latin manuscript of Gregory's Gospel Homilies. The passage is illuminating, for it deals with an instance of accommodation of pagan customs with the newer Christian practices—the re-use of the Parthenon at Rome for Christian purposes and the establishment of the festival of All Saints' Day.[54]

For his handling of the story of the woman taken in adultery, the *Heliand* author appears to have used Bede's Lenten homily on Jn 8.1-12 as his source. As we have seen, his wording demonstrates clearly that he had read the main passage in that homily on the significance of the question put to Jesus by the scribes and Pharisees in their attempt to 'catch' him and force him to condemn himself. The poet may also have had access to the passage in a mediated version, for instance that by Alcuin. Further evidence of the availability of this Bedan interpretation

52. The role of the king in the early Germanic peoples was 'leader of the war-hosts but also the charismatic mediator with the divine, the sacral holder of the tribal "luck"' (Chaney 1970: 14) and 'the living embodiment of the tribe in a single nation' (Myers and Wolfram 1982: 348-49).

53. Talbot 1954: 128, 138.

54. The homily is edited by Gallée (1894: 118-19) and Wadstein (1899: 18-19), and discussed by Ahlsson (1973), who emphasizes that it is a complete text rather than a fragment.

of the story is the fact that Otfrid of Weissenburg, a vernacular writer of the next generation, also paraphrases the same Latin passage at the appropriate point in his poem, the *Evangelienbuch*.[55]

In order to understand the probable effect that the *Heliand* episode of the woman taken in adultery had on its implied audience, it will be necessary to recall Boniface's letter of 746–47 on the subject of the punishments for adultery in Saxony. Since there is no reason to doubt the validity of his testimony, scholars accept Boniface's account of the Saxon justice system as accurate.[56] If such attitudes and practices were still prevalent at the time of the *Heliand*'s composition,[57] then it is likely that the theme of mercy was one which the poet wished very strongly to put across to his audience. At the same time, however, given his audience, and given the Saxon colouring with which the poet has everywhere embellished his poem, he adapts the story to the character of Christ that he has so far developed.

In the events preceding fitt 47 (which deals with the woman taken in adultery), the power of Christ is constantly affirmed: all power is in Christ's hand not only over the life of the people, but also—as earlier in the poem—over the land itself (end of fitt 46). Christ is variously given the epithets 'Ruling Christ', 'Healing Christ', 'Guardian of the land', as well as 'Saviour'. In fitt 47 itself, an immediately striking effect is the emphasis on the nobility of Christ, apparent in the depiction of Christ's regal bearing in the episode. There is a total absence of the theme of Christ bending down and writing on the ground. Given the significance of this in Bede as an outward sign of Christ's humility, it is not difficult to see why this 'noble warrior' version of the Gospel should omit it and present instead a strong-willed, unbending figure.

In keeping with the Christ of such a cultural world, the setting for this episode strongly recalls the royal 'mead-hall' of the Old English poem 'Maxims I', where 'the candid person belongs in the light'. Even more vividly, it bears comparison with the hall of the Danish king Hrothgar in *Beowulf*:

55. On the poet's use of Bede's Lenten homily, see n. 36 above.

56. The entry by Schulze (1986: 480) in a standard reference work accepts the account as reliable, though (perhaps for subjective reasons) it tones down its violence.

57. As Rathofer shows (1962: 63), the poet is careful to include earlier in his poem the condemnations of adultery from the Sermon on the Mount at Mt. 5.27-28 (Tatian 28; *Heliand*, fitt 17, ll. 1475-83).

It came into his mind that he would command a hall-building to be made, a banqueting-chamber, greater than the children of men had ever heard tell of, and that there inside it he would share out to young and to old all of such as God gave to him... I have heard that this labour of embellishing a place of the people was proclaimed far and wide to many nations throughout this earth. In due course, quickly in the sight of men, it came to pass that it was brought to final completion, the greatest of hall-buildings. He devised the name Heorot for it, he who far and wide exercised the authority of his word. He did not leave unfulfilled his vow: he shared out rings and jewels at the feasting. The hall towered aloft, high and wide gabled...[58]

In Old English, the last few words of this passage are 'Sele hlifade, heah and horngeap', a phrase which as we shall see has a strong echo in the *Heliand*. Another fine passage of poetry on the same theme is Beowulf's visit and approach to the hall of the Danes: he and his men hurry along 'until they were able to make out a timber-built hall, magnificent and agleam with gold: of buildings here below the heavens this one in which the great ruler lived was the most eminently cele-brated among earth's inhabitants'.[59] Line 311 then tells us that the lustre of the hall cast light over many lands, or in Old English: 'lixte se leoma ofer landa feola'. The symbolism of the hall is emphasized by the 'clear song of the bard' within Heorot, who tells of God's creation of the bright earth and 'each of those species which go their vital ways'. Outside, however, is the darkness of the marches and wasteland, inhabited by the monsters of the race of Cain, a threat to the joy and happiness of the hall. Hrothgar's royal hall is thus both a literal place and also a symbolic location of light, life, power, authority, patronage, generosity and community.[60]

Comparable imagery occurs in the *Heliand*. During the Sermon on the Mount (in a passage adapting Mt. 5.15-16), the Saviour tells his audience not to hide their light under a bushel in terms reminiscent of the hall-light symbolism in *Beowulf* (*Heliand*, ll. 1400-1409):

lâtad iuuua lioht mikil liudiun skînan, manno barnum...

Let your great light shine on the people, the children of men, that they may know your thoughts, your action and your will, and so also praise in this light the ruling God, the heavenly Father, with clearness of mind,

58. Ll. 67b-82a; trans. Bradley 1982: 413.
59. Ll. 307-10; trans. Bradley 1982: 419.
60. On the hall as an image of community, see Magennis (1996: 35-40).

that he gave you such teachings. No one who has a light should hide it from people or keep it secret, but they should hang it up high in the chamber that all alike who are within, the heroes in the hall, may see it.

Later, in the entry to Jerusalem, as 'the ruling Christ, the best of men' rides to the city, he looks across and sees 'blîcan thene burges uual endi bû Iudeono, hôha hornseli endi ôk that hûs godes, allaro uuîho uunsamost', words which translate roughly as 'the city wall shining, the dwelling of the Jews, the high horn-gabled halls and also the house of God, the fairest of sanctuaries' (ll. 3683-87). It is in this building that Christ, presented as a wise and regal law-giver, pronounces his solution to the predicament of the woman taken in adultery.

Unlike in Bede's exegesis, there is a different timescale, with no mention of the Mount of Olives being made at this point,[61] and most of the action being set in the Temple itself. In fitt 45, Jesus enters Jerusalem and clears the Temple. Appropriately, given that he has just ejected the money-lenders, he remains in the Temple for fitt 46, the main theme of which is twofold: 'the widow's penny' and the question about 'Caesar's coin'. Here, events separated in the Gospel accounts, and separated also in the major source, the gospel harmony of Tatian's *Diatessaron*, are brought together because of their thematic connections. The whole scene is couched in terms of a legal disputation. Christ is described as teaching in the Temple every day, surrounded by crowds of listeners. Among these, however, is a group of people who are evilly disposed to Christ's teachings and who are plotting with 'Herod's thane' to arrest him and put him in chains. Described as the 'evil adversaries', they are clearly the opponents in this litigation, and they try to test his reactions first of all to 'Caesar's tax'. Fitt 47 continues immediately, almost as if it is the same day and the same occasion, with a renewed attack on Jesus by his envious and malicious opponents, who having failed with the test of Caesar's coin, now bring into the Temple the woman charged with adultery.

The point to be stressed here is the poet's critical attitude to the law. The emphasis at l. 3845 'so uuas an iro eu gescriben' ('thus it was written in their law') sounds like an oblique criticism—by the narrator—of practices in the contemporary Old Saxon society. The rest of the fitt only confirms this. Whereas in the biblical text, Jesus asks the

---

61. The Mount of Olives appears in fitt 51, with the Temple again associated with light imagery.

woman if anyone has condemned her and assures her 'Neither do I condemn thee', the *Heliand* text changes the idea of 'condemn' (Latin *con-
demnare*) to 'harm' (Old Saxon *derian*). Note in passing also that the
woman is given more words to say (though in reported speech) in the
Heliand version of the dialogue:

> Then the woman answered him,
> and said that no one there—through the Holy
> Saviour's help—had done her any injury
> in recompense for her crime. Then the Ruling Christ spoke,
> the Lord of men: 'I do not harm you either', he said,
> 'but depart from here in safety, and take care in your spirit
> that you never after this become sinful again'.[62]

The change of verb seems deliberate, for the poet sums up this half of
the fitt by saying 'thus he had helped the woman, and saved her life'—
unlike, one is tempted to add, the contemporaneous Saxon villagers with
their brutal punishments of adulterous women. The model of behaviour
presented here is clear and unequivocal. In a version of the story interesting for its cultural setting and rearrangement of events, it is clear that
the *Heliand* poet is using the message of mercy as a deliberate challenge to his Old Saxon audience's harsh tradition of rough justice
against adulteresses, and allowing the story to speak for itself as an
exemplum of the need to show mercy to others.

At the same time, like the story of Augustine's Oak, the setting and
characterization are so adapted as to portray the central protagonist in a
literally powerful light. Thus in the rest of the fitt, having withstood his
opponents, Christ moves to centre-stage and becomes a figure of great
authority; once again the poet takes up the theme of light:

> He stood in the midst
> and taught the people with bright words
> in a loud voice.[63]

Departing from the *Diatessaron* gospel harmony of his source, and
unlike Bede, though using his ideas, the poet changes the order of the
Johannine narrative at this point. In a rhythmical passage of intensi-
fying poetic strength, the Christ of the *Heliand* goes on to speak of the
believer, from whom will flow 'a living flood':[64]

62. Ll. 3888-94; Cf. Behaghel (1922).
63. Ll. 3908-10.
64. Ll. 3917-19; As pointed out by Ohly-Steimer (1955–56: 103), the poet
passes over eight Tatian chapters from 120 (Jn 8.3-11) to 129 (Lk. 19.47-48, Jn

> I can tell you this:
> whoever believes in me of the children of men,
> firm in the nation, from him will flow,
> out of his body, a living flood,
> rushing water. A great wellspring
> will come from him, a life-giving source!

Developing this in a final comment, the poet gives a fitting conclusion to the episode of the woman taken in adultery, a story of how Christ first overcomes his opponents and then proclaims the promise of his salvation. As the poet goes on to say, the waters refer to the Spirit, and to the promise that the children of men will receive:

> Light and learning, life eternal
> The height of heaven and the grace of God.[65]

Like a homily, this section of the poem ends on a 'ringing theme' of illumination and wisdom.[66] At the same time, in contrast to Bede, the episode of the woman taken in adultery is situated in a subtly transformed sacred setting in which the Temple assumes aspects of a Saxon royal hall, with all the attendant imagery which such a comparison entails. In such a setting, there is no place for 'what was written in their law' or for 'ciphers in the sand'. The *Heliand* is about the power of the Word, and there is a corresponding emphasis on the spoken word of authority and mercy.

5. *The Oak in the Grove*

As I stated at the beginning of this essay, there are very few treatments of the story of the woman taken in adultery in Anglo-Saxon literature. But given the two versions by Bede and the *Heliand* author, both of which were available in England, the question of influence elsewhere arises. Is there any trace of the biblical passage and its cxcgcsis in any of the canonical texts of Old English literature? The question dodges the problem of the relative dating of the various texts, but can be use-

7.32-52, of which the poet uses only Jn 7.37-39 and perhaps Lk. 19.48b).

65. Ll. 3924-3925.

66. Ohly-Steimer (1955–56: 104) points out that this theme of heavenly light, a development here of Alcuin's Commentary on John (*PL*, 100: 851), is used also to conclude many of the other sections, e.g. fitts 22, 24, 30, 33, 44. There are parallels in the sermons of Hrabanus Maurus and in the closing exhortations of many Insular homilies (Hill 1969). This occurrence of light imagery pertains to Weber's observation (1927) that the central episode of the poem is fitt 38—the Transfiguration.

fully approached by focusing on 'the late Anglo-Saxon period, the period in which we know the poems to have been read'.[67] In the late tenth and the eleventh centuries, at Canterbury, Worcester, Exeter and other great centres of ecclesiastical renewal—with their strong emphasis also on vernacular literature—we can imagine communities of like-minded readers.[68] To judge by the surviving manuscripts, their staple reading matter in English consisted of the hortatory and exegetical homilies of their contemporary, the homilist Ælfric,[69] who (as I have already noted) gives a translation of Jn 8.1-11 in one of his later sermons. Arguably, such an audience would share a knowledge of Bede and Ælfric—and perhaps the Old Saxon *Heliand*—with an interest in compiling and reading collections of the older poetry, such as the Exeter Book.

As the present study has sought to demonstrate, in Bede the circumstances of the story of the woman taken in adultery signify light and mercy. A similar image is taken up in the *Heliand*, though altered by the vernacular setting in which the poet places his work. Contrast this picture with the setting of the Old English 'The Wife's Lament'. In the poem, a wife has been forced to take refuge after her husband's kinsmen have plotted against her; whether she is an adulterous woman is uncertain, but she is certainly an accused woman. Moreover she is a woman able to give voice to her feelings in a rare example of 'women's language' in Old English.[70] 'Now', the first person narrator says to her absent husband, 'it is as though our marriage and our love had never been'. They have made her live, she continues, *on wuda bearwe* (l. 27), that is, 'in a forest grove',[71] under an oak tree, in an ancient 'earth-cave'

---

67. Magennis 1996: 5.

68. The kinds of books available are suggested by the booklist in the Leofric bequest to Exeter Cathedral; cf. Swanton (1975: 20-21).

69. A good introduction to Ælfric is Wilcox (1994).

70. Belanoff 1990.

71. A forest grove occurs as the site of a monastery in Bede's *Ecclesiastical History* at the site where Chad founded a new monastery (4.3): 'King Wulfhere gave him fifty hides of land to build a monastery at a place called At-Barwe—that is, At the Wood—in the province of Lindsey, and evidences of the regular observance that he established remain to this day'. Here the setting and the name may well be significant, for the original Latin has 'in loco qui dicitur Ad Baruae, id est Ad Nemus'. Here *Ad Baruae* is a Latinization of the Old English *Æt bearwe* (at the wood). Evidently, Chad—following the instructions of Gregory to Mellitus (*Eccl.*

surrounded by dark valleys and hills. Such a setting is mysterious—at least for the modern reader—and has provoked much discussion. Is this a hermit's cell, or perhaps an old chambered barrow used as a refuge?[72] And what of the 'oak in the grove'? Is this a significant site, as in the case of 'Augustine's Oak' in Bede's *Ecclesiastical History*? As many critics have pointed out, such details suggest an ancient pre-Christian religious site where the wife has been forced to take refuge or sanctuary.[73] In many ways, then, the setting is the antithesis of Bede's depiction of olive plantation, bright dawn and sacred temple; it is a place of darkness and exile rather than of mercy.

In contrast also to Bede, 'The Wife's Lament' is a poem characterized by 'the saturation of the text with emotion-packed words'.[74] The anonymous poet focuses on the woman's feelings:

Joyless is the place. Full often here
The absence of my lord comes sharply to me.
Dear lovers in this world lie in their beds,
While I alone at crack of dawn must walk
Under the oak tree round this earthy cave,
Where I must stay this summer-long day.[75]

The essential emotion of the wife is summed up in the phrase 'mec longade', literally 'I longed', or 'my heart yearned', and the last statement (ll. 53-54) is one of desolation:

Wa bið þam þe sceal
of langoþe leofes abidan.

Grief must always be
For him who yearning longs for his beloved.

Such a message is a world away from that of Bede. But it differs also

---

Hist. 1.30) on the preservation of the older pagan sites—first sanctifies the place before building his church there.

72. Leslie 1988: 56.

73. Bragg 1991: 93; Doane 1966: 87; Pearsall 1977: 56. Kershaw (1922: 173) and Malone (1962: 114) argue that the textual crux in l. 15b *herheard*, should be interpreted as *hearg-eard* ('sanctuary'). The Old English place name *ac-leah*, which survives in the modern names *Oakleigh*, *Ockley* and *Oakley*, implies 'an oak in a grove', perhaps for religious use. See also Wentersdorf (1981: 504).

74. Renoir 1977: 19.

75. Ll. 32-37. Text and translation (here slightly altered) in Hamer (1970: 74-75). See also the edition by Leslie (1988).

from parallel statements that occur in other poems of the Exeter Book. These treat similar themes of exile and longing, but with a clear Christian perspective. So in another tale of coping with exile, 'The Wanderer', the poet concludes with a statement having a parallel syntactic structure to the end of 'The Wife's Lament'—but a very different message:

> Wel bið þam þe him are seceð,
> frofre to Fæder on heofonum, þær us eal seo fæstnung stondeð.

> Well shall it be for him who looks for grace
> And comfort from our father in the heavens,
> Where is ordained all our security.[76]

Given the Christian context of the collection as a whole, the reader is entitled to wonder whether, like 'The Wanderer', the wife of 'The Wife's Lament' will also come to grace, comfort and security.

One other poem in the Exeter Book suggests that she does in fact achieve this goal. Seven pages further on in the manuscript is a text which seems, to many critics, to provide an answer to the wife's dire situation. This is 'The Husband's Message', a poem which begins with a riddle on the theme of writing, as—by the rhetorical device of *prosopopoeia*—the writing tablet or rune-stave speaks, at first to the general reader or hearer, and subsequently to an implied recipient of the message. The same speaker then continues at the beginning of the poem proper, and it becomes clear that the actual physical message itself (presumably inscribed on wood) is addressing a woman:[77]

> Now I have come here in a ship and now you shall know how you may think in your mind of my lord's heartfelt love.[78]

As the plot continues we see that the husband of the poem is sending to his long-suffering wife a message of optimism and reconciliation:

> Go to the sea, the country of the gull,
> And board a ship, that you may southwards thence
> Rejoin your man across the water's ways,
> There where your lord is waiting for your coming.[79]

Many critics have seen 'The Wife's Lament' and 'The Husband's

---

76. Ll. 114-15; Hamer 1970: 183.
77. The speaker of the poem is discussed by Orton (1981).
78. Trans. Bradley 1982: 399.
79. Trans. Hamer 1970.

Message' as complementary poems of elegy and consolation,[80] and some have argued that the wife is an allegory of the Church yearning for Christ, who eventually calls her.[81] Pearsall, thinking of the manuscript context of the Exeter Book, which contains a large collection of short enigmatic riddles on secular and religious themes, has even suggested that the text of the poem is deliberately obscured, as 'an exercise in moralistic interpretation' for its monastic readers.[82] Such a situation would fit our constructed audience of the late tenth century, approaching the poem with all the cultural experience of the developed Latin and vernacular literature of the late Anglo-Saxon church.

Given the biblical themes of Jn 8.1-12 which may have been known to these readers, could this allegory perhaps have been extended even further? If so, then the wife of the biblical story and of the two poems represents, typologically, benighted humanity: the woman, perhaps a priestess of the old religion, is confined in the darkness of sin in her 'earth-cave' and awaiting the summons to the hall or temple where she will receive the spoken word of remission and the written message of invitation from the Lord, as promised in 'The Husband's Message'. As in the Gospel episode of the woman taken in adultery, there is a distinction in this poem between the voice of the Lord himself, and the 'voice' of the written message, a distinction which would be of more significance in a semi-oral or transitionally literate society.

What of the writing itself? Is there a riddle or mystery in this 'message', apart from its summons to the woman to return to her lord? The enigmatic quality of 'The Husband's Message' seems to suggest this, for it finishes with a kind of solemn vow based on selected letters and their corresponding names from the runic alphabet, the old form of writing used throughout northern Europe in the pagan and early Christian period:

> I conjoin S (sun) together with R (road)... and EA (earth) and W (joy) and M (man) to declare on oath that he would fulfil, by his living self, the pledge and the covenant of friendship which in former days you two often voiced.[83]

The critic S.A.J. Bradley hazards a symbolic solution to the enigma:

---

80. Howlett 1978.
81. Swanton 1964.
82. Pearsall 1977: 56.
83. Ll. 49-54; trans. Bradley 1982: 400.

> The runic clue at the end suggests an interpretation: 'sun' is conjoined
> with 'road' to make 'sun-road', that is 'heaven', and with 'earth' and
> 'joy' and 'man' to witness the fulfillment by 'his living self' of the cove-
> nant. If these are tokens of what is conjoined in the incarnate, resurrected
> and ascended Redeemer then the message affirming them is perhaps 'the
> good news', that is the Gospel or the whole Bible....[84]

There is clearly some link with the riddle prefacing 'The Husband's
Message', which declares:

> I used to be by the sand, close by the sea-cliff at the ocean's edge; firm in
> my first state I stood. It was few only of humankind that observed my
> dwelling-place there in solitude but with each dawn the tawny wave
> would lap me with watery embrace. Little I imagined that early or late I
> should ever speak, mouthless, across the mead-bench, and communicate
> words. It is something of a wonder, perplexing to the mind of him who
> knows nothing of such, how the point of a knife and the right hand, a
> man's ingenuity and the point together, deliberately pricked me so that I
> should confidently declare a message in the presence of us two alone, so
> that no more people might gossip our converse further afield.[85]

The solitude of exile, the message in the mead-hall, the wonder of the
written message; these are the images presented by this riddle. Again
one solution appears to be 'Gospel' or 'good news'. To the late-Anglo-
Saxon (tenth-century) users of this manuscript, well versed in both the
seventh-century sermons of Bede and the ninth-century poetry (such as
the *Heliand*), this text may have been replete with symbolic and allegorical significance. For them, 'The Husband's Message' is literally a
husband's message spoken by a messenger, but allegorically it is also
the 'good news' of the Gospel writings.

6. *Conclusion*

For the readers of the period, 'The Woman Taken in Adultery' is a
story about bringing light and illumination, about spoken words and
written promises, about mercy and benevolence. Four themes emerge.
First, from a legal and moral standpoint, the story almost certainly challenged its readers to reconsider the role of mercy in tempering the
severities of the law; this is particularly true of the situation of the Tem-

---

84. Bradley 1982: 398.
85. Bradley 1982: 398.

ple as royal hall or assembly place as pictured in the *Heliand*. Secondly, in sociological terms the various alterations made by this poet suggest ways in which biblical stories are transformed and accommodated by writers from a very different cultural background to that of the Greek, Roman and Hebrew world of the Bible. Thus the cultural world of the *Heliand* is also that of *Beowulf* and of poems from the Exeter Book. Thirdly, from a hermeneutical point of view, there is a marked highlighting of the background and the setting, which offers interesting and novel suggestions for modern approaches to the story. In Bede's homily, his story of Augustine's Oak, and the anonymous 'The Wife's Lament', a tree in a grove can be surprisingly significant, and the circumstances of place and time are at once both convincingly literal and also typological and allegorical. Fourthly, there is the relationship between language and gesture, and speech and writing: the notion that the spoken word brings forgiveness; the written word the promise of grace. The idea is explored by Bede in his homily, touched on in the *Heliand* and suggested in 'The Husband's Message', and when viewed in conjunction with Jn 8.1-11, the latter poem provides a rather different perspective on the much discussed meaning of the enigmatic 'ciphers in the sand'.

BIBLIOGRAPHY

Ahlsson, Lars-Erik
    1973   'Die altsächsische Bedahomilie', *Niederdeutsche Mitteilungen* 29: 30-41.
Allott, Stephen (trans.)
    1974   *Alcuin of York, c. A.D. 732 to 804: His Life and Letters* (York: William Sessions).
Attenborough, Frederick L.
    1922   *The Laws of the Earliest English Kings* (Cambridge: Cambridge University Press).
Baesecke, Georg
    1948   'Fulda und die altsächsischen Bibelepen', *Niederdeutsche Mitteilungen* 4: 5-44 (repr. in Jürgen Eichoff and Irmengard Rauch [eds.], *Der Heliand* [Darmstadt: Wissenschaftliche Buchgesellschaft, 1973]: 54-92).
Barlow, Frank
    1972   *Leofric of Exeter: Essays in Commemoration of the Foundation of Exeter Cathedral Library in A.D. 1072* (Exeter: University of Exeter Press).
Behaghel, Otto (ed.)
    1922   *Heliand und Genesis* (Halle: Niemeyer [rev. Burckhard Taeger, Tübingen: Max Niemeyer, 1984]).

Belanoff, P.A.
1990   'Women's Songs, Women's Language: *Wulf and Eadwacer* and *The Wife's Lament*', in Damico and Olsen (eds.) 1990: 193-203.

Bradley, S.A.J. (trans. and ed.)
1982   *Anglo-Saxon Poetry* (London: J.M. Dent).

Bragg, Lois
1991   *The Lyric Speakers of Old English Poetry* (London: Associated University Presses).

Brown, Peter
1996   *The Rise of Western Christendom: Triumph and Diversity AD 200–1000* (Oxford: Basil Blackwell).

Chaney, William A.
1970   *The Cult of Kingship in Anglo-Saxon England: The Transition from Paganism to Christianity* (Berkeley: University of California Press).

Colgrave, Bertram, and R.A.B. Mynors (eds. and trans.)
1969   *Bede's Ecclesiastical History of the English People* (Oxford: Clarendon Press).

Conner, Patrick W.
1993   *Anglo-Saxon Exeter: A Tenth-Century Cultural History* (Woodbridge: Boydell).

Connolly, Seán, and Jennifer O'Reilly
1995   *Bede: On the Temple* (Liverpool: Liverpool University Press).

Damico, Helen, and A.H. Olsen (eds.)
1990   *New Readings on Women in Old English Literature* (Bloomington: Indiana University Press).

Dietrich, S.C.
1980   'An Introduction to Women in Anglo-Saxon Society (c.600–1066)', in Barbara Kanner (ed.), *The Women of England from Anglo-Saxon Times to the Present* (London: Mansell, 1980): 32-56.

Doane, Alger N.
1966   'Heathen Form and Christian Function in *The Wife's Lament*', *Medieval Studies* 28: 77-91.

Doane, Alger N. (ed.)
1991   *The Saxon Genesis* (Madison: University of Wisconsin Press).

Drögereit, R.
1951   *Werden und der Heliand: Studien zur Kulturgeschichte der Abtei Werden und zur Herkunft des Heliand* (Essen: Fredebeul and Koenen).

Edwards, Cyril
1994   'German Vernacular Literature: A Survey', in Rosamond McKitterick (ed.), *Carolingian Culture: Emulation and Innovation* (Cambridge: Cambridge University Press): 141-70.

Eggers, Hans
1973   'Altgermanische Seelenvorstellungen im Lichte des Heliand', in Eichoff and Rauch 1973: 270-304.

Eichhoff, Jürgen, and Irmengard Rauch (eds.)
1973   *Der Heliand* (Darmstadt: Wissenschaftliche Buchgesellschaft).

Erdmann, Oskar (ed.)
1973   *Otfrids Evangelienbuch* (Tübingen: Max Niemeyer).

Fell, Christine
    1981   'Hild, Abbess of Streonshalch', in Hans Bekker-Nielsen *et al.* (eds.), *Hagiography and Medieval Literature* (Odense: Odense University Press): 76-99.

Fischer, A.
    1986   *Engagement, Wedding and Marriage in Old English* (Heidelberg: C. Winter Universitätsverlag).

Fischer Drew, Katherine (trans.)
    1991   *The Laws of the Salian Franks* (Philadelphia: University of Pennsylvania Press).

Fletcher, Richard
    1997   *The Conversion of Europe: From Paganism to Christianity 371–1386* (London: Fontana).

Gallée, J.H. (ed.)
    1894   *Old Saxon Texts* (Leiden: E.J. Brill).

Gameson, Richard
    1996   'The Origin of the Exeter Book of Old English Poetry', *ASE* 25: 135-85.

Godden, Malcolm, and Michael Lapidge
    1991   *The Cambridge Companion to Old English Literature* (Cambridge: Cambridge University Press).

Green, Martin (ed.)
    1983   *The Old English Elegies* (London: Associated University Presses).

Greenfield, Stanley B.
    1972   *The Interpretation of Old English Poems* (London: Routledge & Kegan Paul).

Hamer, Richard (trans.)
    1970   *A Choice of Anglo-Saxon Verse* (London: Faber & Faber).

Haubrichs, Wolfgang
    1973   'Die Praefatio des *Heliand*', in Eichhoff and Rauch 1973: 400-35.

Hill, Thomas D.
    1969   'The Seven Joys of Heaven in "Christ III" and the Old English Homiletic Texts', *Notes & Queries* 214: 165-66.

Hollis, Stephanie
    1992   *Anglo-Saxon Women and the Church* (Woodbridge: Boydell).

Hough, Carole
    1994   'The Early Kentish "Divorce Laws": A Reconsideration of Æthelberht, chs. 79 and 80', *ASE* 23: 19-34.

Howlett, David R.
    1978   '*The Wife's Lament* and *The Husband's Message*', *Neuphilologische Mitteilungen* 79: 7-10.

Huber, Wolfgang
    1969   *Heliand und Matthäusexegese: Quellenstudien besonders zu Sedulius Scottus* (Munich: Huber).

Hurst, David (trans.)
    1990   *Gregory the Great: Forty Gospel Homilies* (Kalamazoo: Cistercian Publications).

Karras, Ruth M.
1986 'Pagan Survivals and Syncretism in the Conversion of Saxony', *CHR* 72: 553-72.

Keep, David
1982 'Cultural Conflicts in the Missions of St. Boniface', in Stuart Mews (ed.), *Religion and National Identity* (Studies in Church History, 18; Oxford: Basil Blackwell): 47-57.

Kershaw, Nora
1922 *Anglo-Saxon and Norse Poems* (Cambridge: Cambridge University Press).

Klinck, A.L.
1982 'Anglo-Saxon Women and the Law', *Journal of Medieval History* 8: 107-121.

Leslie, R.F. (ed.)
1988 *Three Old English Elegies* (Exeter: University of Exeter Press, rev. edn).

Levison, Wilhelm
1946 *England and the Continent in the Eighth Century* (Oxford: Clarendon Press).

Leyser, Henrietta
1995 *Medieval Women: A Social History of Women in England 450–1500* (London: Weidenfeld & Nicolson).

Liebermann, Felix
1903 *Die Gesetze der Angelsachsen*, I (Halle: Max Niemeyer).

Liuzza, R.M.
1994 *The Old English Version of the Gospels* (EETS, OS 304; Oxford: Oxford University Press).

Magennis, Hugh
1996 *Images of Community in Old English Poetry* (Cambridge: Cambridge University Press).

Malone, Kemp
1962 'Two English *Frauenlieder*', *Comparative Literature* 14: 106-117.

Markus, Robert A.
1970 'Gregory the Great and a Papal Missionary Strategy', in G.J. Cuming (ed.), *The Mission of the Church and the Propagation of the Faith* (Studies in Church History, 6; Cambridge: Cambridge University Press): 29-38.

Martin, Lawrence T. (trans.)
1989 *The Venerable Bede: Commentary on the Acts of the Apostles* (Kalamazoo: Cistercian Publications).

Martin, Lawrence T., and David Hurst (trans.)
1991 *Bede the Venerable. Homilies on the Gospels* (Kalamazoo: Cistercian Publications).

Muir, B.J. (ed.)
1994 *The Exeter Anthology of Old English Poetry* (2 vols.; Exeter: University of Exeter Press).

Murphy, G. Ronald
1989 *The Saxon Savior: The Germanic Transformation of the Gospel in the Ninth-Century Heliand* (Oxford: Oxford University Press).

Murphy, G. Ronald (trans.)
    1992   *The Heliand: The Saxon Gospel* (Oxford: Oxford University Press).
Myers, William A., and Herwig Wolfram
    1982   *Medieval Kingship* (Chicago: Nelson-Hall).
North, Richard
    1991   *Pagan Words and Christian Meanings* (Amsterdam: Rodopi).
Ohly-Steimer, Marianne
    1955–56   '*huldi* im Heliand', *Zeitschrift für deutsches Altertum* 86: 81-119.
Ong, Walter
    1982   *Orality and Literacy: The Technologising of the Word* (London: Rout-
            ledge).
Orton, P.
    1981   'The Speaker in the *The Husband's Message*', *LSE* 12: 43-56.
Pearsall, Derek
    1977   *Old and Middle English Poetry* (London: Routledge & Kegan Paul).
Plummer, C. (ed.)
    1896   *Venerabilis Baedae Opera Historica* (2 vols.; Oxford: Clarendon Press).
Pope, John C. (ed.)
    1967–68   *Homilies of Ælfric: A Supplementary Collection* (EETS, OS 259 and 260;
            London: Oxford University Press).
Priebsch, Robert
    1925   *The Heliand Manuscript, Cotton Caligula A. VII in the British Museum:
            A Study* (Oxford: Clarendon Press).
Rathofer, Johannes
    1962   *Der Heliand: Theologischer Sinn als tektonische Form* (Cologne and
            Graz: Böhlau Verlag).
Renoir, Alan
    1977   'A Reading of *The Wife's Lament*', *English Studies* 58: 12-19.
Rivers, T.J.
    1991   'Adultery in Early Anglo-Saxon Society: Æthelberht 31 in Comparison
            with Continental Germanic Law', *ASE* 20: 19-25.
Russell, James C.
    1994   *The Germanization of Early Medieval Christianity: A Sociohistorical
            Approach to Religious Transformation* (Oxford: Oxford University Press).
Schulze, R.
    1986   'Ehebruch', in Johannes Hoops (ed.), *Reallexikon der germanischen
            Altertumskunde*, IV (Berlin: W. de Gruyter): 479-80.
Schwab, Ute
    1988   *Einige Beziehungen zwischen Altsächsischer und Angelsächsischer
            Dichtung* (Centro italiano di studi sull'alto medioevo, 8; Spoleto: Centro
            italiano di studi sull'alto medioevo).
Schwerin, Claudius von (ed.)
    1918   *Leges Saxonum und Lex Thuringorum* (Hannover and Leipzig: Hahnsche
            Buchhandlung).
Scott, Mariana (trans.)
    1966   *The Heliand Translated from the Old Saxon* (Chapel Hill: University of
            North Carolina Press).

Sherley-Price, Leo (trans.)
  1990   *Bede: Ecclesiastical History of the English People* (rev. R.E. Latham with introduction and notes by D.H. Farmer; Harmondsworth: Penguin Books).
Shortt, Rupert
  1999   'Bough Down', review of a performance of the play *Augustine's Oak*, by Peter Oswald, in *TLS* (August 20): 18.
Sievers, Eduard (ed.)
  1964   *Tatian: Lateinisch und Althochdeutsch mit ausführlichem Glossar* (Paderborn: Ferdinand Schöningh).
Stafford, Pauline
  1994   'Women and the Norman Conquest', *TRHS*, 6th series, 4: 221-49.
Swanton, Michael
  1964   '*The Wife's Lament* and *The Husband's Message*', *Anglia* 82: 269-90.
Swanton, Michael (trans. and ed.)
  1975   *Anglo-Saxon Prose* (London: J.M. Dent).
Talbot, Charles H. (trans.)
  1954   *The Anglo-Saxon Missionaries on the Continent* (London: Sheed & Ward).
Wadstein, Elis (ed.)
  1899   *Kleinere altsächsische Sprachdenkmäler* (Norden: D. Soltau).
Weber, Carl August
  1927   'Der Dichter des *Heliand* im Verhältnis zu seinen Quellen', *Zeitschrift für deutsches Altertum* 64: 1-76.
Weisweiler, Josef, and Werner Betz
  1974   'Deutsche Frühzeit', in Frierich Maurer and Heinz Rupp (eds.), *Deutsche Wortgeschichte*, I (Berlin: W. de Gruyter): 55-133.
Wentersdorf, K.
  1981   'The Situation of the Narrator in the Old English *Wife's Lament*', *Speculum* 56: 492-516.
Weringha, Juw fon (ed.)
  1965   *Heliand and Diatessaron* (Assen: Van Gorcum).
Whitelock, Dorothy
  1979   *English Historical Documents*. I. *c.500–1042* (London: Eyre & Spottiswoode, 2nd edn).
Wilcox, Jonathan (ed.)
  1994   *Ælfric's Prefaces* (Durham: Durham Medieval Texts).
Wrenn, C.L. (ed.)
  1973   *Beowulf with the Finnesburg Fragment* (London: Harrap).

'REVEALING THE AFFAIRS OF THE HEART': SIN, ACCUSATION AND CONFESSION IN NATHANIEL HAWTHORNE'S *THE SCARLET LETTER*

Larry J. Kreitzer

Within the great literature of the world there are many tales of fallen women, sad and heart-breaking women who have been caught in the snare of an illicit relationship and are made to bear the social consequences of it. The theme is an enduring one and seems to capture the imagination of every age and every culture. Yet nowhere is this topic dealt with in so moving and memorable a fashion as it is in Nathaniel Hawthorne's *The Scarlet Letter* (first published in 1850).[1] Although Hawthorne's character Hester Prynne does not lend her name to the title of the work which gains her literary immortality, she nevertheless takes her place alongside other fictional adulteresses whose names appear in such classic works as Gustave Flaubert's *Madame Bovary* (1857), Leo Tolstoy's *Anna Karenina* (1875–77), Theodor Fontane's *Effi Briest* (1895), and D.H. Lawrence's *Lady Chatterley's Lover* (1928).[2] Yet it would be inaccurate to say that *The Scarlet Letter* is primarily a tale about the trials and tribulations of the adulteress Hester Prynne, even though she is undoubtedly the character around whom the story is built. This is *not* simply a story about a fallen woman who is condemned to a lonely and isolated existence at the hands of her fellow Puritans in Boston within the seventeeth-century Massachusetts Bay Colony. Despite the obvious temptation to render it so, the story is not one which is preoccupied with the theme of adultery per se. In fact, it may come as something of a surprise to note that Hawthorne is careful to ensure that the words 'adultery' and 'adulteress' never appear in the book at all. He

---

1.   Throughout this article I shall designate references to *The Scarlet Letter* using both the chapter number and title, and shall use page numbers from the Penguin Classics edition of 1986 and abbreviated as *SL*.

2.   On the theme of adultery in fiction, see Armstrong (1976); Tanner (1979); Greiner (1985); White and Segal (1997).

is more concerned with the *effects* of the transgression upon the principal characters, the tragic consequences of hidden and secret sin in their lives and in the lives of those who dare to risk judging them, rather than with the sinful act itself. In this respect *The Scarlet Letter* shares an important feature with the so-called story of the woman taken in adultery of Jn 7.53–8.11. These two stories cannot be reduced simply to tales of adulterous women; both have larger concerns at their heart and it is this which attracts my attention within this study.

My task here is to explore some of those wider issues and come to a better understanding, not only of the biblical story contained in John's Gospel, but also of Hawthorne's classic tale itself. In this respect Hawthorne's novel can be used as a convenient lens through which to view the biblical story afresh.[3] I shall divide the study into five parts: (1) Hawthorne's writing of *The Scarlet Letter*; (2) the story and the characters, *The Scarlet Letter* summarized; (3) Hawthorne's use of biblical imagery; (4) sin, accusation and confession in *The Scarlet Letter*; and (5) some film interpretations of *The Scarlet Letter*.

1. *Hawthorne's Writing of* The Scarlet Letter

From an early age Hawthorne displayed an intense love of reading and writing.[4] He attended Bowdoin College in Maine from 1821 to 1825 and profited greatly from his education there, cultivating the disciplines and habits necessary for a writer to succeed at his profession. He was a meticulous researcher and within his writing often made use of his historical investigations, particularly those concerning the Puritan period of New England history. Yet it would be going too far to describe him as a historian of seventeenth-century Puritanism, for he really only uses the period as a backdrop against which to set his fiction. In this way he was able to use his knowledge of the past in creating literary works of great imagination and power. This is certainly the case with *The Scarlet Letter*.

From where does Hawthorne draw his inspiration for this story, now universally acknowledged as a classic which has helped to establish

---

3.   Abel (1988: 305) argues that Hawthorne has the story from Jn 7.53–8.11 in mind when creating the characterization of Hester. Waggoner (1963: 155) also describes the New Testament story as helping to set the scene for Hawthorne's tale of religious legalism.

4.   Warren 1935; Keil 1992.

American writing as an independent literary force in the modern era? Hawthorne created in Hester Prynne the first true heroine in American fiction, a woman who, in the words of one admirer 'is perhaps the only woman in nineteenth-century American literature who could stand before Melville's Ahab and never blink'.[5]

There are many sources upon which Hawthorne drew in the composition of *The Scarlet Letter*. No writer worth his salt works entirely in a vacuum, and Hawthorne was certainly no exception.[6] He was well conversant with the classical tradition of Greece and Rome and no doubt this influenced him to a large degree.[7] Many critics of his work have noted the importance of the biblical story of the Fall as a mythology which Hawthorne adopts (Hester Prynne thus becomes an Eve-like figure who leads the Dimmesdale/Adam character into error).[8] However, it is to his own family history that we must turn if we are to appreciate more fully what he has accomplished within *The Scarlet Letter*.

Nathaniel Hawthorne was born in the town of Salem, Massachusetts on 4 July 1804 and throughout his life considered the town, with which he had a love–hate relationship, as his native soil.[9] Salem is perhaps

---

5. Bigsby 1992: xvi.

6. Hawthorne had been toying with the image of 'the scarlet letter' for a number of years, as his short story, 'Endicott and the Red Cross' (1838) demonstrates. The sketch contains a brief paragraph describing a young Puritan woman who is forced to wear an embroidered 'A' on her dress as punishment for her adultery. Also worth noting is a suggestive comment made in his *The American Notebooks*. He records in an entry for 27 July 1844 the idea for a story as 'The life of a woman, who, by the old colony law, was condemned always to wear the letter A, sewed on her garment, in token of her having committed adultery' (Hawthorne 1972: 254; Martin 1994: 346). Almost certainly Hawthorne has in mind, at least in part, the life of Mary Latham, who was executed in 1644 for having committed adultery with a number of men (Martin 1994: 36). Mary Latham was married to an older man, who was unloving and apparently sexually dysfunctional (features which are applied to the fictional Hester Prynne).

7. Wall (1988) puts forward a powerful case for viewing *The Scarlet Letter* as Hawthorne's creative adaptation of the classical myth of the rape of Callisto by Zeus. Similarly, Green (1980) offers some interesting suggestions about the idea of a 'descent into hell' (as found in the works of Homer, Virgil and Dante) as a background to Hawthorne's effort here. Girgus (1990: 49-78) sees echoes of the Oedipus myth in operation within Hawthorne's life and work.

8. For more on this idea, see Erlich (1968).

9. Hawthorne has been the subject of considerable biographical interest over the years. The most recent biography of his life is Miller (1991).

most famous for its witch trials of 1692, the story of which forms the
historical setting of Arthur Miller's award-winning play *The Crucible*
(1953).[10] Hawthorne did, on occasion, live elsewhere than Salem,
including England (he was American consul in Liverpool from 1853 to
1857), but it was to the town, and to the Massachusetts area, that he was
rooted, not only in terms of family history, but also in his literary interest and artistic temperament. He drew upon his own family history and
heritage in constructing his imaginative tale of the town of Boston as it
was during the time of the Puritans. We detect something of this within
Hawthorne's essay entitled 'The Custom House', a 50-page introduction to *The Scarlet Letter* which sets up a quasi-historical framework
for the story which follows, perhaps even providing a clue to the germi-
nal idea for it.[11] Here, for example, Hawthorne recounts, almost in
passing, a tantalizing reference to his own great-great-great grandfather
William Hathorne (1607–1681),[12] who had emigrated to the Massachusetts Bay Colony in 1630. He says:

> He was a soldier, legislator, judge; he was a ruler in the Church; he had
> all the Puritanic traits, both good and evil. He was likewise a bitter per-
> secutor; as witness the Quakers, who have remembered him in their his-
> tories, and relate *an incident of his hard severity towards a woman of
> their sect*, which will last longer, it is to be feared, than any record of his
> better deeds, although these were many (*SL*: 12; emphasis mine).[13]

This forefather, whom Hawthorne describes as the first to arrive in
the New World from England, came 'with his Bible and his sword'. He
had a son named John Hathorne (1641–1717) whom Hawthorne also
briefly describes in 'The Custom House'. This second ancestor was
actually one of the magistrates in the witch trials of 1692, and as such
has gone down in history as one of the 'villains' of the era. Puritan
history may also yield another historical figure, which Hawthorne used

10. In 1996 Miller's play was made into a big-budget film directed by Nicholas
Hytner and starring Daniel Day-Lewis and Winona Ryder. The screenplay for the
film was written by Miller himself. See Decter (1997) for a discussion.

11. Occasionally Hawthorne's novel has been published without this introductory essay; this is unfortunate for it stands as an integral part of the work as a
whole. Lee (1982) discusses the importance of the essay for understanding the
story. See also McCall (1966–67); Stouck (1971); Bayer (1980–81); Weber (1992);
and Martin (1994: 331-38).

12. Hawthorne changed the spelling of his surname after graduating from Bowdoin College in 1825.

13. James (1879: 7-8) identifies the woman concerned as Anne Coleman.

to fashion the character of Hester Prynne. This is the charismatic leader Ann(e) Hutchinson (1591–1643),[14] who is mentioned several times in the course of *The Scarlet Letter*. There is some evidence to suggest that in the composition of the novel Hawthorne was consciously using details of the Puritan reaction to Anne Hutchinson, who was condemned for antinomianism and banished in 1638.[15] Understandably, the representation of Hester Prynne and of Anne Hutchinson has been the focal point for many feminist interpretations of *The Scarlet Letter*, although this is not without its own difficulties.[16] On slightly less contentious ground is the suggestion that the character of Hester Prynne was modelled in part upon Hawthorne's own mother, Elizabeth, who conceived her first child out of wedlock and was forced, for the most part, to raise her children on her own (Hawthorne's father was a sea captain and died of yellow fever when the author was only four years old).[17] This suggestion is given additional weight when we consider that his mother died in July 1849, and her death certainly served as a catalyst for Hawthorne to begin the novel.[18] In any event, it seems clear that Hester Prynne is a composite figure, created in Hawthorne's fertile imagination and shaped by the author's interest in his own family history and his investigations into the Puritan past of the Massachusetts Bay Colony.[19] In this respect, Hester Prynne perfectly expresses Hawthorne's description of his art in 'The Custom House'. There he speaks

14. Primary sources vary as to the spelling of her first name.

15. Colacurcio (1972); Bell (1971: 179-81); Davis (1984); and Martin (1994: 46-53, 370-71). For a helpful introduction to the theological controversy between Hutchinson and the Puritans of New England, see Adair (1982: 171-74); Koehler (1987); and Cooper (1988).

16. Colacurcio (1972: 460) argues that this is to fall into Hawthorne's deliberately set trap, the bait of which is a saint's legend. McWilliams (1984: 66) asserts that the interpretation of Hester Prynne as 'a prophetess of feminism' has little basis in the text of *The Scarlet Letter* itself (with only '13: Another View of Hester' and a single paragraph in '24: Conclusion' in support). For additional discussions of feminist interpretations of *The Scarlet Letter*, see Doubleday (1939); Cronin (1954); Baym (1982a); DeSalvo (1984); Lang (1987); Herbert (1988); Schwab (1989); Martin (1990); Benstock (1991); and Segal (1992).

17. Prompting Miller (1991: xvi) to remark about the scarlet letter 'A' at the centre of the story, 'The A signifies many things but perhaps chiefly Absence'.

18. On this point see Baym (1982b). Hoeltje (1954) also offers some important discussion.

19. Boewe and Murphey 1960–61.

of his office, where he did his writing, as the symbolically neutral ground 'where the Actual, and the Imaginary may meet'.[20]

The introductory essay 'The Custom House' is important not only in providing incidental facts of history which help to set the tone for the story,[21] but also in establishing a determined relationship between the author and his readership, one in which Hawthorne is able to keep authorial distance from the narrator of 'The Custom House' and yet draw his audience into the telling of the tale. He does this most effectively by creating the fiction of having the Custom House surveyor find within some old documents of the upper story of the Custom House a manuscript detailing the essence of Hester Prynne's story. This manuscript is bound in red tape (a very appropriate image of a soulless bureaucracy!) and consists of half a dozen foolscap sheets, gathered by a previous surveyor named Jonathan Pue 100 years or so earlier. It also contains the actual embroidered scarlet letter itself, a faded and worn letter 'A' made from scarlet fabric with a fine gold stitching around its edges. Just to round off the fiction of this discovery, and give an opening insight into the mysterious nature of the scarlet letter itself, Hawthorne writes, or rather, has the Custom House surveyor tell us:

> I happened to place it on my breast. It seemed to me,—the reader may smile, but must not doubt my word,—it seemed to me then, that I experienced a sensation not altogether physical, yet almost so, as of burning heat; and as if the letter were not of red cloth, but red-hot iron. I shuddered, and involuntarily let it fall upon the floor (*SL*: 32).[22]

The Custom House surveyor functions as the narrator of 'The Custom House' and clearly the reader is to identify him in some way with Hawthorne and his own life and thoughts.[23] Yet, the narrator of 'The Custom House' is not to be simply equated with the narrator of *The Scarlet Letter*; at times there are crucial differences of perspective

20. See Brodhead (1976); Rowe (1980); Bell (1985) and Martin (1994: 363-64), for more on this important passage.

21. Scholarly opinions vary as to how integral 'The Custom House' is to the story as a whole. For more on this topic, consult Ziff (1958); Baskett (1961); McShane (1962); McCall (1966–67); Eakin (1971–72); Fossum (1972); Baym (1973); and Berner (1979).

22. See Ringe (1982: 153-60) for a discussion of Hawthorne's use of Gothic elements within the story.

23. Deusen 1966–67; Stouck 1971; Hansen 1975; Cox 1975; Cottom 1982; Millington 1992; and Martin 1994: 35-46.

between the two narrative roles. Hawthorne cleverly veils himself behind his various narrators, and only occasionally do we get a glimpse of, or *think* we get a glimpse of, Hawthorne himself. The result is a work which is mysterious, tremendously enticing and, at the same time, disturbingly inscrutable. All of this serves to establish a bond between Hawthorne, his various narrators, and the reader who serves as part of an audience of co-conspirators. As co-conspirators we are invited not only to unravel the mysteries of the introductory essay and its precise relationship to the story that it introduces, but also to ponder what both reveal to us about the man who produced them. Only by a judicious balancing of these concerns do we begin to understand *The Scarlet Letter* and appreciate it as the literary masterpiece that it is.

2. *The Story and the Characters:* The Scarlet Letter *Summarized*

The Scarlet Letter relates the tragic story of a forbidden liaison between a married woman and an unmarried Puritan minister, and the effects it has upon the couple and the closed, religious society in which they live. There are four main characters in the novel: Hester Prynne (the young Puritan woman); Roger Chillingworth (her estranged husband); Reverend Arthur Dimmesdale[24] (Hester's lover and the father of her illegitimate child); and Pearl (the child of the illicit relationship).[25] From the vantage point of the reader, there is never any doubt as to the extramarital relationship between Hester Prynne and Reverend Dimmesdale. That liaison is something which took place some time in the past, at least as far as the narrative of the story is concerned, and it does not figure prominently within the narrative. Yet, within the story-line itself, although the relationship between Hester Prynne and Reverend Dimmesdale has been kept concealed from the community in which they

24. In '9: The Leech' Dimmesdale is presented as having graduated from the University of Oxford as a Church of England priest. We are never told how he came to be a Puritan minister, but no doubt Hawthorne intends us to detect something of a tortured religious history within the characterization of the man.

25. Many have sought to interpret the four main characters allegorically, an interpretative approach which works better for some characters than it does for others. For example, Abel (1951) argues that Pearl functions more as a symbol than a character within the novel, and that her characterization is weak and unbelievable as a result. For more on this controversial way of reading the story, see Winters (1966); Feidelson (1966); and Katz (1968–69). Garlitz (1957) surveys how Pearl has been interpreted over the years.

both live, there is great pressure for details of the adultery to be revealed. Precisely how and in what manner this revelation is to be achieved provides the story with its dramatic force. As within most of Hawthorne's fiction, we are not treated to an in-depth psychological analysis of any of the characters, although here he not infrequently invites his readership to search their own consciences and assess what lies within their own hearts. Hawthorne is not much interested in assigning blame, but on illustrating how past faults, and the secret sufferings which arise from them, can blossom into spiritual strength and demonstrate moral truth. Thus, *The Scarlet Letter* is not so much a story about a particular person, or a character, but rather it is the explication of a theme—the concealment of sin and the effects which such concealment has upon those involved.[26] There are three particular features of the storyline which are worth highlighting for the purposes of this study, the first focusing on a central theme of the novel and the other two concentrating on aspects of the highly refined literary structure of the work. Together these features will serve to set the stage for the more detailed analysis of the novel which I shall pursue below.

The first feature is the way in which an atmosphere of religious condemnation and judgment pervades throughout the story. This is most clearly evident from the way in which Hester is treated by the Puritan community, which in *The Scarlet Letter* symbolizes society in general.[27] As the tale commences the narrator paints us a dark and gloomy picture of the Puritans of Boston in 1642. The heroine of the story, Hester Prynne, stands under judgment by the townspeople with her

---

26. Given the nature of the complex interactions between the main characters, it is inevitable that the novel has been subjected to a number of psychological analyses. The concealment of sin motif, which is the mainspring of the storyline, readily lends itself to a Freudian interpretation which sees Hawthorne's presentation of the actions of Hester, Dimmesdale and Chillingworth as classic anticipations of Freud's idea that repressed desires inevitably manifest themselves as guilt and effect a crisis in the subject concerned. Thus, Dimmesdale cannot reconcile his libidinous desires with his conscience, and as a result he is at war with himself psychologically. The oft-cited study by Crews (1966) is a convenient starting point for this sort of approach to the interpretation of *The Scarlet Letter*. Also worth consulting, simply for the novelty of some of the psychological suggestions made, are Kushen (1972); Lefcowitz (1974); Franzosa (1978); and Diehl (1991).

27. This is brought out forcibly by Baym (1976: 141-42; 1986: xii-xxiv). Korobkin (1997) also provides some important discussion on the question of Hester Prynne's treatment by the legal authorities.

three-month-old baby Pearl, the irrefutable evidence of her sin, held close to her breast. She is condemned by the Puritan society of which she is a part, and is ordered to stand in the middle of the town on the scaffold of the pillory for three hours so that the townspeople might mock and ridicule her. The visible symbol of her condemnation is the scarlet letter 'A' which she is to wear on the bosom of her dress for the rest of her life.[28] The letter is richly embroidered with gold stitching and stands in stark contrast to the unadorned, sombre-hued clothing of the Puritan community. The scarlet letter testifies not only to Hester's judgment by others in the community, but throughout the novel it is a constant visual reminder of her smouldering sensuality. The fact that Hester sewed the scarlet letter, and wears it somewhat defiantly, means that it eventually becomes transformed from a badge of punishment into an emblem of pride. The object of shame and ridicule has become an object of reverence and respect, in much the same way that the cross of Christ undergoes a transformation of meaning—first it was a scandal; later it becomes sacred.[29] That Hawthorne intends us to pursue precisely this connection of thought appears indicated by a line that occurs in '13: Another View of Hester'. He writes of Hester's wearing the scarlet letter: 'the scarlet letter had the effect of the cross on a nun's bosom. It imparted to the wearer a kind of sacredness, which enabled her to walk securely amid all peril' (*SL*: 142).

The social judgment of Hester is also emphasized by the fact that she lives in a small, thatched-roof cottage on the outskirts of town, as if to symbolize that she is in the borderlands of the two worlds. Hester is neither a part of the town of Boston itself, nor of the wilderness beyond its boundaries; she lives in a twilight zone, caught between the repression of the market/town and the freedom of the wilderness/forest.[30] Against the backdrop of this symbolic geography both Hester and Dimmesdale struggle to find their place within society, attempting to find integration within the Puritan community but being faced with isolation because of their adultery. Hester cannot run away and start a new life elsewhere for she cannot leave the community in Boston without

28. Hester's scarlet letter is variously described in the course of the narrative. Negatively, it is 'her ignominious badge', her 'badge of shame', her 'mark of shame', her 'letter of infamy', the 'burning shame' upon her bosom, the 'token of her shame', the 'red symbol which sears her bosom'.

29. As Astrov (1942: 306) notes.

30. For more on the spatial metaphor in Hawthorne's fiction, see Ringe (1981).

destroying something precious within herself. Although isolation was anathema to the Puritans, it is even more destructive to Hester for it represents a denial of the human spirit and a renunciation of the things which she holds dear in her heart. Her conflict with society is one characterized by alienation from the essentially religious world of the Puritans, and is witnessed to by Hawthorne's suggestive description of the Puritan elders as wearing 'steeple-crowned hats'. This phrase occurs four times in the book and symbolizes the character of the elders through their dress, just as the scarlet letter is made to symbolize Hester's. It is the clash between the public expectations of a religious community and the private demands of a forbidden love between Hester and Dimmesdale which makes the story such a powerful, romantic tale.

At the same time, the drama of the story is maintained by the roles that Dimmesdale and Chillingworth have within it, and the reader is teased to consider how they will play their respective parts. How far will the condemnation and judgment of the Puritan community extend? Will the two men be included? Will Chillingworth discover the secret lover of his wife? Will Dimmesdale have the courage to admit his part in the affair and make a public confession of his involvement with Hester? How these affairs of the heart are to be resolved is one of the great 'hooks' of the story.

The second feature worth mentioning concerns the way in which the novel is structured as a whole. *The Scarlet Letter* contains 24 chapters in addition to the introductory essay 'The Custom House'. There has been considerable scholarly debate over the narrative structure of the novel.[31] Most agree, however, that in terms of overall storyline, the narrative is built around the three scaffold of the pillory scenes found in '2: The Market Place', '12: The Minister's Vigil' and '23: The Revelation of the Scarlet Letter'.[32] In each of these scenes all four of the central characters converge on the scaffold, the main structural device of the novel, and interact with one another, to great dramatic effect. There is a deliberate progression of what is publicly revealed by Hester and Dimmesdale in these scenes. The first scaffold scene presents us with a

---

31. The assessment of Gerber (1944) is a useful starting point for this matter, although it is not without its critics. See, e.g., Roper (1950–51); Haugh (1956); Abel (1956–57); Cowley (1958); and Tanselle (1962–63).

32. On this point, see Matthiessen (1941: 275); Schubert (1944: 138-39); Doren (1949: 164-65); Roper (1950–51: 78); Chase (1957: 70); Waggoner (1963: 128); Warren (1973); and Clark (1987).

powerful image of Hester's public humiliation and Dimmesdale's secret shame. In the second scaffold scene, Dimmesdale goes to the pillory under cover of darkness and confesses his guilt in the affair, but there is no one to hear him. He is soon joined on the scaffold by Hester and Pearl, with Chillingworth eventually coming to escort him away, unaware of the full implications of Dimmesdale's midnight visit to the scaffold. In the third scaffold scene, Dimmesdale publicly confesses to his part in the whole affair and dramatically reveals his own breast in the process, where there appears to be a scarlet letter like Hester's. He has Hester and Pearl beside him as he makes his public confession, and having made his peace with his God and his conscience, he slumps to the ground and dies.[33]

A third feature concerns the way in which the ending of the novel functions as a counterpart to the beginning, making a thematic closure which is quite satisfying. As I have noted above, *The Scarlet Letter* begins with a scene outside the prison of Boston as the crowds await Hester Prynne's release from her confinement, and it ends with an image of the burial-ground in which Hester and Dimmesdale are buried. Thus the ominous declaration which Hawthorne included as the opening line of the second paragraph of the novel serves to frame the overall story:

> The founders of a new colony, whatever Utopia of human virtue and happiness they might originally project, have invariably recognized it

---

33. The scaffold of the pillory might be said to be a parallel to Christ's cross, the scene of public judgment, ridicule and death. The second scaffold scene is exactly midway through the novel and the pace picks up considerably after it. In fact, the second 12 chapters cover only a few weeks, at most, within the narrative, whereas the first half of the novel covers a narrative span of some seven years. In terms of structure, this makes *The Scarlet Letter* look very much like the Gospel narratives which give roughly half of their narrative over to Jesus' ministry in Galilee and Judaea (traditionally a three-year period), and the second half concentrating on the last week of his life. Certainly in both the Gospel accounts and in *The Scarlet Letter* the pace of the narrative is accelerated and the timescale shortened at the midway point of the work. It is also worth noting the import of Dimmesdale's exclamation in '12: The Minister's Vigil', as he stands alone at midnight on the scaffold of the pillory. It is easy to see this as an echo of Jesus' final words during the crucifixion. Dimmesdale has revealed his breast under cover of darkness and expects the whole world to have seen it. He exclaims, 'It is done!', and in so doing reflects Jesus' cry of triumph recorded in Jn 19.30 as he dies on the cross.

among their earliest practical necessities to allot a portion of the virgin
soil as a cemetery, and another portion as the site of a prison (*SL*: 45).

Effectively, the prison symbolizes the place of judgment of sin on
earth, while the graveyard symbolizes the eternal place of judgment.
Life, or at least the life of the characters within the novel, is to be lived
between these two arenas of judgment.[34]

The story concludes with a brief chapter which opens by relating the
debate within the community of Boston about the significance of the
revelation of the scarlet letter on Dimmesdale's breast. The eventual
fate of Hester, Pearl and Chillingworth is also recounted in this chapter.
The vengeful and vindictive Chillingworth, having been robbed of his
reason for living when Dimmesdale dies, quickly withers away 'like an
uprooted weed that lies wilting in the sun'; he is dead within a year.
Chillingworth, who had allowed himself to become an instrument of
Satan, is assigned a place in hell where he receives the just rewards for
a life consumed with the desire for revenge. The only positive thing
said about him is that he leaves a substantial legacy of property, both in
England and in Massachusetts, for little Pearl. This leaves Pearl the
richest heiress in New England and she travels with her mother to
England where she marries into a noble family and lives happily. Hester
eventually returns to Boston, and to the cottage on the outskirts of town
which had been her home for the seven years of the storyline. Of her
own free will she continues to wear the scarlet letter until she dies. The
townspeople eventually come to respect, even revere, her—a change of
heart brought on by her years of selfless service among them. When she
passed away she was buried in the burial-ground near to Arthur Dimmesdale, and although they did not share a common grave since, as the
narrator explains, their souls have no right to mingle, they do share a
common headstone.

3. Hawthorne's Use of Biblical Imagery

Although the biblical story of the woman taken in adultery is never
mentioned within *The Scarlet Letter*, there are a number of places
within the novel where Hawthorne makes deliberate allusion to biblical
passages and images. Sometimes these are channelled through the

34. Waggoner (1948). Shulman (1984) offers an interesting discussion of how
the imprisonment motif influenced Hawthorne (and other novelists!) in their
writing.

works of other writers whom Hawthorne had read; he was familiar with Milton and Dante[35] and was inordinately fond of Bunyan's *The Pilgrim's Progress*, which is alluded to many times within his work.[36] At other times he alludes to biblical passages directly, showing himself to be quite conversant with the Christian scriptures as a whole.

For instance, in 'The Custom House' he pokes fun at the lassitude of his fellow customs officers by contrasting them with their New Testament counterpart, the tax collector Matthew, who receives an apostolic calling from Jesus in Mt. 9.9:

> These old gentlemen—seated, like Matthew at the receipt of custom, but not very liable to be summoned thence, like him, for apostolic errands— were Custom-House officers.

Another passage from Matthew is also used to great effect within the novel. This is the parable of Jesus recorded in 13.25-26, which likens the kingdom of heaven to a valuable pearl:

> Again, the kingdom of heaven is like a merchant in search of fine pearls, who, on finding one pearl of great value, went and sold all that he had and bought it.

Hawthorne clearly draws upon this parable when he gives the name of Pearl to the daughter of Hester and Dimmesdale; two passages are of special note in this regard. The first of these occurs in '6: Pearl', where we are provided with an extended description of the child:

> [Hester] named the infant 'Pearl', as being of great price,—purchased with all she had,—her mother's only treasure! (*SL*: 80).

The second of these occurs in '8: The Elf-Child and the Minister', where Governor Bellingham requests that Reverend Wilson question Pearl and attempt to determine Hester's fitness as a mother. He asks her what in essence is a theological question and seeks to determine if Hester has nurtured her daughter in a Christian atmosphere and instructed her properly in matters of catechism. The older minister asks:

> 'Pearl', said he, with great solemnity, 'thou must take heed to instruction, that so, in due season, thou mayest wear in thy bosom the pearl of great price. Canst thou tell me, my child, who made thee?' (*SL*: 98-99).

The close relationship between Hester and her daughter Pearl also

---

35. Matthews 1940.
36. Carpenter 1936; Johnson 1951a; and Stanton 1956.

provides the basis for one of the most debated passages within the novel. This occurs in '2: The Market-Place', where the narrator is describing the reaction of the hostile people of Boston to Hester's public humiliation on the scaffold of the pillory. He comments on the way that Hester clutches the child to her bosom and offers a remark about the crowd's reaction:

> Had there been a Papist among the crowd of Puritans, he might have seen in this beautiful woman, so picturesque in her attire and mien, and with the infant at her bosom, an object to remind him of the image of Divine Maternity, which so many illustrious painters have vied with one another to represent; something which should remind him, indeed, but only by contrast, of that sacred image of sinless motherhood, whose infant was to redeem the world (*SL*: 53).

In other words, the traditional imagery of Madonna and child, based on New Testament stories of Jesus' birth and infancy (Mt. 1–2 and Lk. 1–2), is used to make an exceedingly ironic comment about the Puritan on-lookers.[37] The fact that the Puritans were vehemently anti-Papist, and in large measure defined their own religious identity as over against the Roman Catholic Church, makes this passage one of the most interesting examples of Hawthorne's use of religious themes.[38] It has a counterpart at the end of the novel in '23: The Revelation of the Scarlet Letter', where Dimmesdale dies on the scaffold of the pillory with his head cradled in Hester's bosom. Several commentators have suggested that the picture painted here corresponds to the traditional imagery of the *pietá*, thus reinforcing the presentation of Hester as a Madonna figure.[39]

One might expect, given the underlying theme of adultery within *The Scarlet Letter*, that Hawthorne would refer to the most famous biblical

---

37. Lucke (1965) discusses the passage.

38. The traditional Madonna and child imagery is carried over into artistic representations of Hawthorne's *The Scarlet Letter*. A case in point is the painting by Hugues Merle entitled *The Scarlet Letter*, which is part of the collection housed at the Walters Art Gallery in Baltimore, Maryland. One could be excused for thinking at first glance that this painting is one of Madonna and child; a more detailed inspection will reveal the partially obscured scarlet 'A' on the mother's chest. The painting is used on the cover of the Penguin Classics edition (1986) of *The Scarlet Letter*.

39. See Newberry (1988: 235) on this point. Waggoner (1962: 37) suggests that the final scaffold scene is akin to Christ's death on the cross and likens the final scene in the novel to 'a kind of gloomy Good Friday'.

example of it, the story of David and Bathsheba (2 Sam. 11–12), at some point within the novel. He does this only once, in a beautifully nuanced sentence which comes in '9: The Leech'. The chapter describes the developing relationship between Dimmesdale and Chillingworth. The two men agree to share lodgings, and Hawthorne includes the David and Bathsheba reference as part of the description of their accommodation:

> The walls were hung round with tapestry, said to be from the Gobelin looms, and, at all events, representing the Scriptural story of David and Bathsheba, and Nathan the Prophet, in colors still unfaded, but which made the fair woman of the scene almost as grimly picturesque as the woe-denouncing seer (*SL*: 111).

This is a seemingly irrelevant detail, but it represents Hawthorne at his best as he uses image after image, patiently building up layer upon layer, to reinforce his central theme. The three named characters of the biblical story have their counterparts in *The Scarlet Letter*: the adulterers Dimmesdale and Hester play the roles of David and Bathsheba and Chillingworth the part of Nathan the accusing prophet.[40] Hawthorne reinforces his appropriation of the story by describing the colours of the tapestry as 'unfaded', suggesting that they are still vibrant and visible today. And yet an ominous note is injected as well, as the stories, both the biblical one and the Puritan one, are said to be 'grimly picturesque'.

Several other Old Testament stories are alluded to briefly in *The Scarlet Letter*. In '3: The Recognition', the mystery of who the father of Hester's child is being discussed by the townspeople, with one of them remarking that it is unlikely that the riddle will be solved since 'the Daniel who shall expound it is yet a-wanting' (*SL*: 58). This echoes the biblical tradition of the prophet Daniel as an interpreter of dreams and mysteries. There is also a brief mention of the story of Cain and Abel (Gen. 4.1-16). Hester's alienation and loneliness, reinforced by the

---

40. One can but speculate to what degree Hawthorne as author/narrator identified with the namesake prophet Nathan at this point, seeking to expose the hypocritical David/Dimmesdale. Lawrence (1964: 85) seems to suggest outright identification when he exclaims, 'The Scarlet Woman becomes a Sister of Mercy. Didn't she just, in the late war. *Oh, Prophet Nathaniel!*' (emphasis added). For more on the use of the Old Testament passage within the story, particularly as a way of Hawthorne expressing his anger about being ousted from his Custom House job, see Bronstein (1987).

social stigma of having to wear the scarlet letter in public, is likened to
the 'mark of Cain':

> it had set a mark upon her, more intolerable to a woman's heart than that
> which branded the brow of Cain (*SL*: 76).

The story of Pentecost in Acts 2.1-4 is used several times within the
novel. It appears in '11: The Interior of a Heart' as part of the description of clergymen who were devout and learned, but who somehow
never grasped the inner workings of the human heart:

> All that they lacked was the gift that descended upon the chosen disci-
> ples at Pentecost, in tongues of flame; symbolizing, it would seem, not
> the power of speech in foreign and unknown languages, but that of
> addressing the whole human brotherhood in the heart's native language.
> These fathers, otherwise so apostolic, lacked Heaven's last and rarest
> attestation of their office, the Tongue of Flame (*SL*: 124).

The passage from Acts also appears in '17: The Pastor and his
Parishioner', as Hester and Dimmesdale meet in the secrecy of the forest. Here the anguished Reverend gives voice to the struggle within him
to reconcile his public image of saintliness to his private knowledge of
sinfulness. He describes how his congregation expect his preaching to
be as inspired as one of the Spirit-filled disciples at Pentecost:

> Canst thou deem it, Hester, a consolation that I must stand up in my pul-
> pit, and meet so many eyes turned upward to my face, as if the light of
> heaven were beaming from it!—must see my flock hungry for the truth,
> and *listening to my words as if a tongue of Pentecost were speaking*!—
> and then look inward, and discern the black reality of what they idolize?
> I have laughed, in bitterness and agony of heart, at the contrast between
> what I seem and what I am! (*SL*: 167; emphasis added).

The motif is carried through in '23: The Revelation of the Scarlet
Letter', when Dimmesdale preaches the Election Day sermon, which is
itself associated with Whitsuntide holidays,[41] and through it inspires the
congregation as they have never been inspired before. The narrator of
the story offers an interpretative comment which builds not only on the
'tongues of flame' idea from Acts 2.3, but also hints at 'the mighty
rushing wind (or breath)' of the Spirit from Acts 2.2:

> [T]he crowd began to gush forth from the doors of the church. Now that
> there was an end, they needed other *breath*, more fit to support the gross

---

41. Newberry (1988: 242-44) gives details of this.

and earthly life into which they relapsed, than that *atmosphere which the preacher had converted into words of flame*, and had burdened with the rich fragrance of his thought (*SL*: 215; emphasis added).

The Pentecost imagery is continued as Dimmesdale moves from the church to the marketplace, thronged by a worshipping crowd of church members. The traditional idea of 'tongues of flame' resting on the first disciples' heads becomes modified into an image of Dimmesdale's saintliness, at least as far as the members of the congregation are concerned. The narrator tells us:

Were there not the brilliant particles of a halo in the air about his head? So etherealized by spirit as he was, and so apotheosized by worshipping admirers, did his footsteps in the procession really tread upon the dust of earth? (*SL*: 217).

Also worth noting is the way in which the Pentecost imagery of flaming tongues of fire is carried over and applied to Pearl. Insofar as she is the 'living hieroglyphic' of the secret relationship between Hester and Dimmesdale, the living result of transgressed law, she points powerfully, but obliquely, to both of her parents.[42] Thus, it is not surprising that Pearl is frequently presented as wearing bright red clothes, symbolically representing in another form the scarlet letter of her mother; her crimson dress also points to the colour of the Pentecost flame which her father strove to embody in his preaching.[43] In '7: The Governor's Hall' we have a good illustration of this interlocking of symbols:

Her mother, in contriving the child's garb, had allowed the gorgeous tendencies of her imagination their full play; arraying her in a crimson velvet tunic of a peculiar cut, abundantly embroidered with fantasies and flourishes of gold thread. So much strength of coloring, which must have given a wan and pallid aspect to cheeks of a fainter bloom, was admirably adapted to Pearl's beauty, and made her the very brightest little jet of flame that ever danced upon the earth (*SL*: 90).

Even more to the point, there is a paragraph in '19: The Child at the Brook-Side' which brings together the various interlocking symbols that Hawthorne was so adept at creating. Speaking of Pearl as the daughter of Hester and Dimmesdale he writes:

In her was visible the tie that united them. She had been offered to the world, these seven past years, as the living hieroglyphic, in which was

42. Irwin (1980: 239-84) offers a fascinating study of the image.
43. McNamara (1955–1956) discusses this at length.

revealed the secret they so darkly sought to hide,—all written in this
symbol,—all plainly manifest,—had there been a prophet or magician
skilled to read the character of flame! (*SL*: 180).

Perhaps the most important New Testament passage for this study of
The Scarlet Letter is one that is not quoted directly, but which nonetheless hovers in the background and sets the agenda for much of the
novel. This is Jesus' saying about adultery being a matter of the heart,
the second of the so-called six antitheses in which Jesus' teaching is set
alongside the traditional Mosaic commands (Mt. 5.21-48):

> You have heard that it was said, 'You shall not commit adultery'. But I
> say to you that every one who looks at a woman lustfully has already
> committed adultery with her in his heart (Mt. 5.27-28).

I move now to consider how the themes of sin, accusation and confession are handled within the novel. These themes strike at the central
point of Jesus' teaching and thus might be described as 'affairs of the
heart'.

4. *Sin, Accusation and Confession in* The Scarlet Letter

The temptation of every reader is to conclude that *The Scarlet Letter* is
a book preoccupied with human sinfulness and evil, one which is predi-
cated upon an act of adultery between two people who ought to have
known better. Yet, *The Scarlet Letter* is a much more theologically pro-
found book than this, for it grapples nobly and realistically with a number of other complex theological ideas.[44] For example, the story addresses traditional theological concepts of predestination and divine sov-
ereignty, offering penetrating challenges to the prevailing understandings of them.[45] Nowhere is this more sharply brought into focus than

---

44. Walcutt (1952) offers some helpful suggestions about the various theological readings of *The Scarlet Letter* which have been put forward by critics in recent
years (from his perspective he means the 1920s–1950s). Ultimately Walcutt suggests that Hawthorne was deeply influenced by a Calvinistic doctrine of sin which
saw it as permanently warping human nature, but that he reacted violently against a
divine providence which ordained this as the order of existence. For more on these
matters, which were a primary topic of interest a generation ago, see Mills (1948);
Schwartz (1963); Sachs (1980); and Kazin (1997: 24-39).

45. See Madsen (1996: 88-92) for some fresh comments along these lines. In
particular, Madsen offers some interesting thoughts about the passage in '12: The
Minister's Vigil' in which a celestial letter 'A' appears in the sky when Governor

when discussing the birth of Pearl, the 'love-child' of Hester and Reverend Dimmesdale. Thus, in '6: Pearl' the birth of the child is said to have come about by 'the inscrutable decree of Providence', and it is the operation of the hand of God in her conception and birth which forms the basis of Hester's argument in '8: The Elf-Child and the Minister'. Here Hester puts forward her case about why she should not have the child taken from her and raised by the Puritan community at large. She is resolute in her defence of her parental rights in this matter, as she appears before Governor Bellingham and his ministerial colleagues, including her secret lover Reverend Dimmesdale. We read:

> 'God gave me the child!' cried she. 'He gave her, in requital of all things else, which ye had taken from me. She is my happiness!—she is my torture, none the less! Pearl keeps me here in life! Pearl punishes me, too! See ye not, she is the scarlet letter, only capable of being loved, and so endowed with a million-fold the power of retribution for my sin? Ye shall not take her! I will die first!' (*SL*: 100).

Effectively she turns the theological tables on her antagonists, putting them in the awkward position of denying divine providence if they insist in taking Pearl from her. This is rightly recognized by Reverend Dimmesdale, who affirms that Hester has perceived God's hand in 'the solemn miracle' which the very existence of Pearl represents, and then proceeds to outline the theological dilemma at issue. He says:

> For, if we deem it otherwise, do we not hereby say that the Heavenly Father, the Creator of all flesh, hath lightly recognized a deed of sin, and made of no account the distinction between unhallowed lust and holy love? This child of its father's guilt and its mother's shame has come from the hand of God, to work in many ways upon her heart, who pleads so earnestly, and with such bitterness of spirit, the right to keep her (*SL*: 101).

This is a perfect illustration of an idea which Hawthorne evidently held as expressive of the paradox which is central to human existence: 'Man's accidents are God's purposes'.[46]

Winthrop dies. Dimmesdale interprets this to be a heavenly indictment of himself as an adulterer, whereas the people of Boston view it as an affirmation of the Governor's apotheosis.

46.   These words were incised in 1843 by Hawthorne and his wife Sophie in the west window of his study in the manse in Concord where they lived. It is difficult to think of a better paraphrase of the theological paradox contained in Rom. 8.28 in all

There is much theological insight that is to be gleaned from *The Scarlet Letter* about human sinfulness, about the social effects of sin and the accusations that arise in response to it, and about the role that confession plays in healing the breach caused by sin and bringing ultimate redemption to the repentant sinner. The ideas of sin, accusation and confession are important to any reading of the novel, particularly one which invites a close comparison with the woman taken in adultery. I shall deal with these three themes in turn, attempting to relate the discussion to the way in which they also figure within the parallel passage from Jn 7.53–8.11. In this way I shall demonstrate some of the points of similarity and contrast between the biblical story and Hawthorne's classic tale.

a. *Sin: Publicly Revealed and Privately Concealed*
The Scarlet Letter is perhaps the premier example in Hawthorne's fiction of what Herman Melville, with considerable prophetic insight, described, in a celebrated comment which was written as a review of Hawthorne's earlier publication of *Mosses from an Old Manse* (1846), as his 'great power of blackness'.[47] Yet we need not despair, for, as Henry James humorously remarked over a century ago, Hawthorne had a 'cat-like faculty of seeing in the dark'.[48] It is undoubtedly true that Hawthorne had a gift for being able to expose the darker side of human nature. Human existence for him was conceived as a bloody battleground, a terrible war between good and evil, between the spiritual and the carnal. He well understood that humankind embodies both good and evil, and that it provides tremendous raw material out of which a storyteller can practise his art. In Hawthorne's thought human sinfulness was not simply an inherited condition, as the Calvinistic theology of the Puritans would have us believe. On the contrary, for Hawthorne, sin

of literature! Pauly (1976–77) offers some discussion of Hawthorne's house in Concord.

47. The remark was made by Melville in a pseudonymous two-part essay published in *The Literary World* in August 1850. The full comment is: 'Certain it is, however, that this great power of blackness in him derives its force from its appeals to that Calvinistic sense of Innate Depravity and Original Sin, from whose visitations, in some shape or other, no deeply thinking mind is always and wholly free'. On the matter of Hawthorne's sense of the tragic evil inherent within humanity's nature, see Stewart (1957).

48. James 1879: 99.

was something generated by the conscious will, and thus it was not simply to be reduced to the sinful act itself. Neither was sinfulness to be encouraged, as if by committing acts of sin people assisted the divine cause by giving a reason for good to be made manifest. Rather, human sin was an occasion for good to be injected into the equation of life, through the power and agency of divine mercy and grace.

There is no doubt that *The Scarlet Letter* does indeed explore the dimensions of human sinfulness with considerable acumen. Most agree that Hawthorne demonstrates his indebtedness to a Calvinistic heritage in this regard.[49] This is true, even if he goes a considerable way towards breaking out of the theological straitjacket which might easily have been imposed upon him by a slavish adherence to those traditions. With the publication of *The Scarlet Letter* Hawthorne laid himself open to the vitriol of some clergymen of the day who felt that the book was an attack on Christian teaching concerning the sanctity of marriage.[50] The celebrated line which Hester says to Dimmesdale when they meet secretly in the forest and talk together about the love that they had for one another and the adultery which they committed, has been a focal point for such criticism. Hester says: 'What we did had a consecration of its own. We felt it so! We said so to each other' (*SL*: 170).

One of the most outspoken of these early critics describes *The Scarlet Letter* as 'the nauseous amour of a Puritan pastor' and castigates Hawthorne for 'having done not a little to degrade our literature, and to encourage social licentiousness'. He was afraid that the adultery of Hester Prynne and Reverend Arthur Dimmesdale was not dealt with harshly enough and that 'the whole tendency of their conversation is to suggest a certain sympathy for their sin'.[51] One cannot help but wonder if this stern reaction reveals more about the reviewer and his own preoccupations than it does about the novel or its author! Yet, there is

49. Johnson 1951b; Miller 1955; Fairbanks 1956; McCullen and Guilds 1960–61; Askew 1962–63; Downing 1979–80.

50. The concept of an ideal marriage has a central role in much of Hawthorne's fiction. He is at his most creative when he is exploring the difficulties that there are in living up to those ideals given the weaknesses and imperfections of human agents. On the place of marriage and family values as a backdrop to Hawthorne's fiction, see Erlich (1984); Young (1984); Person (1987); and Anderson (1990: 97-120).

51. Coxe (1851); see also Martin (1994: 381-412). In contrast, Doren (1966: 140) describes the scene as 'the high mark in American fiction'.

never any doubt that the relationship between Hester and Dimmesdale was 'sinful', and that they are both sinners. Hester describes her adultery as 'sin' on nine occasions, while the narrator of the novel (Hawthorne?) refers to her adultery as 'sin' in eight different passages. At the same time, there is little doubt that the way in which the adultery is presented within the story is somewhat ambiguous.[52] The story does seem in places to portray Hester as a romantic heroine willing to follow the passion of her heart at all costs. As a result *The Scarlet Letter* has been a focus of discussion about Hawthorne's views of love and romanticism ever since it appeared in print. Little wonder, then, that Hester's 'sin' has attracted such attention, for it illustrates the collision between private love and social responsibility, a clash that concerns every age.

Yet it is important to remember that the estranged husband, Roger Chillingworth, is not without his share of blame for the whole affair. Indeed, in '4: The Interview' there is an interesting conversation between him and Hester where he admits he was at fault as well as she.[53] He identifies several problem areas within their relationship: a considerable difference in age (implying his sexual inadequacy);[54] his physical deformity (one shoulder hunched higher than the other); not to mention an essential intellectual incompatibility. All of this means that their marriage was always one of convenience rather than love, and in this sense it was hypocrisy of the heart. Nevertheless, it is Hester's adultery which is the initial focal point of human sinfulness within the novel, even though we quickly discover that the infection of sin spreads far and wide.

Critics have long noted the narrative contrast between Hester's sin, which has been *publicly revealed*, and Dimmesdale's sin, which has been *privately concealed*. This is correct at one level, but somewhat misleading on another. Hester, too, has her private concealments, as her refusal to reveal either the identity of her lover to the Puritan community, or the identity of her husband to her lover, amply demonstrates. She is dually complicit, as indeed the woman taken in adultery apparently is within the New Testament story. This conspiracy of silence stands as one of the most intriguing points of contact between Hester

52. The influential article by Carpenter (1944) is well worth considering on this point.

53. Chillingworth is frequently vilified and presented as an evil figure, an agent of Satan. For more on this point, see: Abel (1953) and Vogel (1963).

54. A point made by Johnson (1993).

Prynne and the unnamed adulterous woman. Both women are caught
out in their sin; both women protect equally guilty partners. Within *The
Scarlet Letter* the refusal to reveal her partner is also one of the main
reasons why the Puritan townspeople are so hostile to Hester and hurl
harsh accusations against her. I move to consider the place that accusation has within the stories of the two adulterous women.

b. *Accusation: Invading Sacred Space and Violating the*
Sanctity of the Human Heart
There are several features of *The Scarlet Letter* which parallel the story
of the woman taken in adultery, particularly with regard to the place
that accusation has in the two stories. Both stories leave many questions
unanswered, as do *all* narratives insofar as they are, by their very
nature, mere snapshots of life (whether real or imagined instances). Yet
what is astonishing about the woman taken in adultery is the way in
which so many questions we might pose as readers are left completely
unaddressed.

   In the Gospel story the woman taken in adultery is brought before
Jesus, but nowhere in the account is there ever even the briefest mention of the man with whom she had committed adultery. Where is this
man? How is it that they were able to catch her 'in the very act of adultery' and yet somehow manage to lose him on the way to the Temple?
Likewise, one is left wondering how it was that the two were actually
caught in the very act of adultery. Who saw them and under what circumstances?[55] Who precisely are her accusers and why do they slink
away from the scene when Jesus invites the one who is without sin to
cast the first stone? And what is it that Jesus scribbles in the sand as he
waits for the first stone to fly? When he wrote with his finger on the
ground, did he make some secret sign, or compose some mysterious
symbol? Did he write some counter-accusations, or, as Jerome suggests
(*Dial. Pel.* 2.17), list some other sins of which others in the crowd knew
that they were guilty? Each of these open-ended questions has its counterpart in Hawthorne's *The Scarlet Letter*. It is in the investigation of
such questions that the narrative similarities and differences between
the novel and the woman taken in adultery can best be seen. I shall
attempt to address some of these unanswered questions by examining

---

55. Derrett (1963–64) thinks that the suspicious husband may have been
involved in arranging for two or three witnesses to be on hand to catch her in the act
of coitus.

four key motifs within the story. These all arise from a consideration of the accusations which are made against the adulteresses at the centre of the two works and the way those accusations are treated within the storyline.

1. *The Hostile Crowd*. One of the most striking features of the story of the woman taken in adultery is the way in which accusation is made against her by a hostile, on-looking crowd. In Jn 8.3-5 we read:

> The scribes and the Pharisees brought a woman who had been caught in adultery, and placing her in the midst they said to him, 'Teacher, this woman has been caught in the act of adultery. Now in the law Moses commanded us to stone such. What do you say about her?'

The hostility of the scribes and Pharisees should not be taken as historically accurate, as if to suggest that Jesus was in continual opposition to the Jewish religious leaders of his day. There is every indication that 'scribes and Pharisees' are representative opponents within the Gospel accounts, most particularly within the Gospel of John. As such they function in much the same way that the Puritans do within Hawthorne's narrative world. Just as it is unwise to assume that Hawthorne is presenting us with an accurate picture of seventeenth-century New England Puritanism,[56] so too it is unwise to assume that the woman taken in adultery is presenting us with an accurate picture of the antipathy of the scribes and Pharisees to Jesus in first-century Judaea. The writers of both stories employ figures of opposition within the course of their narrative, and both use them to assist their aim of addressing wider issues. We, as attentive readers, can appreciate that the writers have larger fish to fry, and attempt to see beyond the inaccuracies of the detail to the essential issues at hand.[57]

The scribes and Pharisees within the New Testament story probably have in mind Lev. 20.10 and Deut. 22.21-22 (which stipulate death by stoning for adulterers) when they approach Jesus and ask his opinion concerning the matter of adultery. In his cautious reply Jesus alludes to Deut. 13.9-10 and 17.6-7 (which require the witness of the trans-

---

56. On this point, see Baym (1970); Bell (1971); and Turner (1981).

57. It is increasingly clear that Hawthorne employed the Puritan past as a disguise for concerns which arose from his own time and social context. Recognition of this fact has been one of the focal points of New Historicist criticism of the novel. For example, note, Reynolds (1985); Railton (1993); and Bercovitch (1991a, 1991b).

gression to throw the first stone), saying, 'Let him who is without sin among you be the first to throw a stone at her'. At a stroke he cuts through the hypocrisy of the accusers, and reveals divine mercy in the process.

In *The Scarlet Letter* there is a much more developed scene of public accusation and revilement, but, interestingly, one in which religious traditions are also brought into the argument. In '2: The Market-Place', one of the Puritan women gives vent to her opinions as to the way that Hester Prynne should be handled:

> This woman has brought shame upon us all, and ought to die. Is there no law for it? Truly there is, both in the Scripture and the statute-book. Then let the magistrates, who have made it of no effect, thank themselves if their own wives and daughters go astray! (*SL*: 49).

In short, both the woman taken in adultery and *The Scarlet Letter* present us with an image of the condemnation of an offender by the religiously minded community of which they were a part. The judgment of the adulteresses by the crowd is an indictment of their lack of sympathy and understanding, illustrating what happens when mercy is sacrificed for inflexible law. In Hawthorne's novel the Puritans of Boston are an embodiment of this attitude in that they are:

> a people among whom religion and law were almost identical, and in whose character both were so thoroughly interfused, that the mildest and severest acts of public discipline were alike made venerable and awful (*SL*: 47).

2. *The Hidden Partner.* In '5: Hester at her Needle', the omniscient narrator of *The Scarlet Letter* asks the rhetorical question: 'Had Hester sinned alone?' The narrator's question is similar to one which lies unvoiced in the story recorded in Jn 7.53–8.11. Has either woman sinned alone? The answer in both the Gospel story and Hawthorne's novel is a resounding 'No!', and one could argue that the heartbeat of the drama of both narratives focuses on the exposure of the men involved with the two unfortunate women. Occasionally it is suggested by critics of *The Scarlet Letter* that the trail of the man should not be pursued at all, especially if he was seduced by the highly sexed Hester.[58] But this hardly seems fair, and most agree it is a misreading of the characterization of Hester intended by Hawthorne.

---

58. Lawrence (1964) first suggested that Hester seduced Dimmesdale.

In one very important respect *The Scarlet Letter* breaks with the woman taken in adultery in that it provides us with the identity of the man concerned. There is no named counterpart to Dimmesdale within the New Testament story, and in this sense at least, a blow has been struck for equality of the sexes in matters of adultery! Or so it would seem. But how central is the role of Arthur Dimmesdale to the storyline of *The Scarlet Letter*? As long ago as 1879 Henry James remarked that Hester Prynne is not the central character of the story but was merely 'an accessory figure'. Rather, James suggests, it is upon Arthur Dimmesdale that the drama depends:

> It is upon her guilty lover that the author projects most frequently the cold, thin rays of his fitfully-moving lantern.[59]

Many others have followed this line of interpretation, even to the point of suggesting that the essential plot of *The Scarlet Letter* consists of the 'struggle between God and the devil for the soul of Arthur Dimmesdale'.[60] Hester is regarded by many to be merely a supporting character in the drama which is *The Scarlet Letter*. In any event, whatever conclusion we come to about whether Hester or Dimmesdale should enjoy top billing as the central character, the key point is that the identity of the secret partner is revealed in the course of the story, first to us as readers and eventually to the stunned Puritans of Boston.

3. *The Secret Sign.* What was it that Jesus paused to write in the ground with his finger when the scribes and Pharisees brought the woman taken in adultery before him? This has been described as 'an unanswerable conundrum for exegetes of all time'.[61] Jesus' act of writing is obviously an important feature of the story, for it is mentioned twice (in 8.6 and 8.8). Is it possible for us to 'crack the code' on this, or at least to appreciate the significance of the action within the context of the story? Commentators have made a number of suggestions on this matter. Many commentators have pointed to Jer. 17.13 ('O Lord, the hope of Israel, all who forsake thee shall be put to shame; those who turn away from thee shall be written in the earth, for they have forsaken the Lord,

---

59. James 1879: 112.
60. Abel 1956–57: 82. For further discussion on the centrality of Dimmesdale as a character in the novel, see Granger (1964–65). Baym (1988) offers a powerful refutation of this way of reading the novel.
61. Abel 1956–57: 82.

the fountain of living water') as a scriptural basis for Jesus' curious actions. In other words, Jesus' writing on the ground functions as an enacted parable, challenging the onlookers to consider whether they have forsaken the Lord by pursuing their course of judging the woman. Although this interpretation has had many advocates (both ancient and modern) over the centuries,[62] it does assume that the crowd would have understood the significance of Jesus' actions.

But there are other characters who need to be accounted for, and in this regard we might well ask about the husband of the woman taken in adultery. How does he figure in the action at this point, and might the writing in the sand have something to do with him? J. Duncan M. Derrett puts forward the intriguing suggestion that the woman's husband is acting with duplicity in the whole matter and that Jesus first wrote on the ground the words of Exod. 23.1b ('You shall not join hands with a wicked man') as a warning to the crowd not to have anything to do with it. He follows this up when writing on the ground again, this time scribbling 23.7 ('Keep far from a false charge, and do not slay the innocent and righteous').[63]

Yet when we turn to Hawthorne's story we see that there is a much more elaborate equivalent for this mysterious 'scribbling in the sand' which is done by Jesus. The multivalent symbol which provides the title of Hawthorne's work tantalizes the reader from start to finish, niggling away in the back of one's mind. And what are we to make of this mysterious 'scarlet letter'?[64] What does it 'mean' and what is its signifi-

---

62. Beasley-Murray 1987: 146. Including Ambrose, Augustine, Jerome, Jeremias (1950–51: 148-50), and Schnackenburg (1980: 165-66).

63. Derrett 1963–64: 16-22.

64. The phrase 'scarlet letter' occurs 90 times within the body of the story itself. Hawthorne builds an elaborate colour scheme within the story, contrasting the brightness of the hues of red with the dark and gloomy world of the 'sad-coloured' Puritans who are clothed in grey and black. To this end, he frequently uses such words as 'red' (30 times), 'crimson' (8 times), and once, to great effect, the obscure heraldic line with which the story concludes 'THE LETTER A, GULES'. Similarly, in '15: Hester and Pearl', he has little Pearl use eel-grass to adorn herself with a *green* letter 'A', thus employing another vibrant colour associated with life and fertility to contrast with the drab world of community in Boston. Fiedler (1967: 434) relates the colour red to Hester's sexuality: 'red is the color of sexuality itself, the fear of which haunts the Puritan world like a bloody specter'. For more on the creative use of such a primary scheme, see Blair (1942); Waggoner (1963: 127-38); and Levy (1969).

cance in the story? These matters remain some of the most discussed within critical literature of *The Scarlet Letter*, a fact which in itself testifies to its character as a rich and powerful symbol within the novel. However, we must avoid what has been described as 'the Scylla and Charybdis of Hawthorne criticism'.[65] We must avoid the 'rock' of an exclusive and definitive interpretation, while at the same time steer clear of the 'whirlpool' of viewing the symbol as utterly indecipherable and collapse into a deconstructionist reading of it wherein the significance of the letter is found to lie in its ambiguity, its indecipherability.[66] This has always been the challenge of interpreting Hawthorne's story.

A number of focal points emerge within the critical discussion concerning the meaning of the scarlet letter; several of them are based upon hints which Hawthorne himself provides within the course of the story. The 'A' which Hester bears on her bosom immediately signifies the Adultery of which she is guilty. It could also signify *A*ble, *A*dmirable, *A*ngel, *A*lienation, *A*postle, *A*tonement, or even *A*rthur, thereby indicating her partner in sin and the one that she holds dearest to her heart. Each of these is suggested in its own way within the story.[67] But what of 'the scarlet letter' which Reverend Dimmesdale reveals to the crowd on the scaffold of the pillory in the climax of the book in '23: The Revelation of the Scarlet Letter'?[68] First of all, it is almost always assumed that the letter which he reveals is an 'A', corresponding to that

65. Kinkead-Weekes 1982: 81.

66. Bell (1982: 9) describes Hawthorne's novel as one whose theme is the 'indeterminacy of signs'. Bryson (1983) and Smith (1984: 9-30) are also worth consulting on this point. For more on the deconstructionist reading of *The Scarlet Letter*, see White (1982) and Ragussis (1991).

67. Madsen (1991) suggests that the 'A' may stand for 'Abolition' and that we are able to detect something of Hawthorne's attitudes towards the slavery issue through a close reading of the novel. In this sense, Toni Morrison's *Beloved* (1987) can be read as something of a creative re-writing of Hawthorne's novel in which the character Sethe is an Afro-American version of Hester Prynne. There are also important parallels between Morrison's novel and Harriet Beecher Stowe's *Uncle Tom's Cabin* (1852). See Arac (1986); Yellin (1989); Fleischner (1991); Askeland (1992); Wiodat (1993), and Robbins (1997), for more on these matters.

68. Hawthorne (1972: 618) has a note suggesting that the New Plymouth colony enacted a law in 1636 which required two letters on the adulterer's clothing, namely the letters 'AD'. It is possible that Hawthorne has the initials in mind when he names his character Reverend *A*rthur *D*immesdale.

worn by Hester. But is this correct? Nowhere does Hawthorne ever state that the letter which Dimmesdale bore in his flesh is an 'A'. In fact he goes out of his way to suggest that it was not recognizable, or even visible, to everyone; hence the various explanations provided in '24: Conclusion', from which the reader is encouraged to choose for himself or herself. Effectively this means that Hawthorne converts the revelation of the scarlet letter into a riddle which is impossible to interpret.

Assuming for the moment that there is some justification in saying that *one* of the symbolic meanings of the 'A' which Hester wears is indeed *A*rthur, the name of her lover, could we not say that the logic of this is that Arthur has a corresponding 'H' as his scarlet letter of the heart, symbolizing *H*ester? A certain symmetry is thereby injected into the symbolism of the story. This opens the door to a number of other meanings of Arthur's 'scarlet letter', which fit quite appropriately within the storyline. Arthur's scarlet letter 'H' could refer to the *H*eart itself, or to *H*oly, *H*eaven, *H*alo, *H*ell, or perhaps even to *H*awthorne given that the author obviously invested much of himself in the character of Arthur Dimmesdale.[69] All of these symbolic interpretations of the scarlet letter too have their anchor points within the story. Nor should we forget that there was great debate among those in the crowd who had witnessed the events on the scaffold about what was actually seen and what it all meant. Although Hawthorne does indeed write in '24: Conclusion' that 'Most of the spectators testified to having seen, on the breast of the unhappy minister, a scarlet letter ... imprinted in the flesh', he is careful to qualify this somewhat by adding that this scarlet letter was 'the very *semblance* of that worn by Hester Prynne'. One wonders what weight should be given to 'semblance' in this connection; could an 'H' be fairly described as a *semblance* of an 'A'? This also provides another way of reading the second scaffold scene where Hester, Arthur and Pearl are brought together, first in private and then in public. It is

---

69. A careful reading of 'The Custom House' suggests that Hawthorne is giving voice to his own artistic struggle as a writer. He is torn between his desire to follow the dictates of his heart and pursue his calling as a writer, and the various demands of the society in which he lives (his family, friends, work colleagues, etc.). This is reflected in Arthur Dimmesdale's struggle of spirit as to whether he should confess the nature of his relationship with Hester and thereby follow the dictates of his heart, or continue to conceal his sin and thereby serve the Boston community as a minister of the church, even at the cost of spiritual bankruptcy. O'Donnell (1959–60) and Porte (1969: 98-114) both contain some fine discussion along these lines.

frequently suggested that the trio form some sort of a symbolic 'A' with Hester and Arthur representing the two arms of the letter and Pearl representing the cross stroke. However, one could equally as well say that the three characters form a letter 'H', thereby avoiding the difficulty (at least in terms of the eye of the imagination) of how the two 'strokes' of the letter 'A' are joined' on the platform. Perhaps the strokes of the letter 'A' are meant to suggest that Hester and Dimmesdale are joined in a kiss.

4. *A Sacred Setting.* It is sometimes overlooked that the woman taken in adultery in Jn 7.53–8.11 is set within the precincts of the temple in Jerusalem. We read in 8.2, 'Early in the morning he [Jesus] came again *to the temple*; all the people came to him, and he sat down and taught them.'

Is the temple setting of any significance to the story? There is every reason to suggest that it is indeed significant, for it means that the accusations made against the woman by the Jewish leaders take place in a sacred setting.[70] This makes their hypocrisy and failure to exhibit divine compassion and mercy all the more ironic as a result. The way in which the woman is treated by the scribes and Pharisees not only represents a violation of sacred space, but it also dehumanizes her as a person, for she simply becomes a convenient means whereby they attempt to trap Jesus in religious debate. Little wonder, then, that Jesus turns the legislative tables upon her (and his!) accusers and rescues the situation by embodying God's grace in how he deals with the woman in the temple precincts.

The word 'temple' never occurs in *The Scarlet Letter*, although the parallel structure within the Puritan community, the word 'church', is used frequently. Yet Hawthorne chooses in the novel to focus not on the violation of *physical* sacred space as he does on the violation of *personal* sacred space. This is his equivalent to the accusation made in the temple, and it is a motif which is used to great effect within the novel. As mentioned above, *The Scarlet Letter* is much more concerned with the affairs of the heart, those things that lie buried deep within the thoughts and feelings of Hester Prynne, Roger Chillingworth and, above all, Reverend Dimmesdale, than it is with the act of adultery itself. The way in which Hawthorne uses the idea of the 'sanctity of the human heart' is crucial for any interpretation of *The Scarlet Letter*, for

70. Tanner (1979: 18-24) has a stimulating discussion along these lines.

it is in the exploration of Hawthorne's creative juxtaposition of the visible and the unseen, of the revelations of the flesh and the concealments of the heart, that the purpose of the story is to be found. In the evocative words of Nina Baym, 'The focus of Hawthorne's fiction is the heart, seen in its capacities for both good and evil'.[71]

A good indication of the centrality of this idea is the frequency with which terminology concerning 'the heart' appears in the novel. The terms 'heart' and 'hearts' occur 57 times within the novel, while 'bosom' is found 11 times, 'breast' and 'breasts' 11 times, and 'chest' once. Hawthorne describes the heart using a variety of other images, including a prison, a tomb, a cave and a mansion.[72] Generally he employs these as a means of illustrating the spiritual struggle which is going on inside his main characters. Indeed, the very first mention of 'heart' within the story hints at the inner turmoil which is raging inside the Reverend Dimmesdale. This occurs in '2: The Market-Place', as the Puritan women of Boston gather outside the prison door and await the public humiliation of Hester Prynne. One of the women comments:

> Reverend Master Dimmesdale, her godly pastor, takes it very grievously *to heart* that such a scandal should have come upon his congregation (*SL*: 48; emphasis added).

A large number of the references to 'heart' are connected with the description of Reverend Dimmesdale placing his hand over his heart as a sign of guilt concerning his concealed sin (the nervous gesture is mentioned over 20 times in the novel). In terms of the story, this is an extremely effective dramatic device which hints at the climactic moment in '23: The Revelation of the Scarlet Letter', where Reverend Dimmesdale reveals the hidden secrets of his heart before the stunned Puritan community and confesses his role as Hester's lover.

The first instance of Dimmesdale performing the gesture of lifting his hand to his heart, as if he is acknowledging and yet concealing his own complicity in Hester's situation, occurs in '3: The Recognition'. The scene involves Hester's humiliation before the town as she stands on the scaffold of the pillory. She is exhorted by the leaders of the community, including Reverend Wilson (the eldest clergyman in Boston) and Reverend Dimmesdale, who stand above her on a balcony over-

---

71. Baym 1967: 46. Mizener (1967: 9) similarly remarks: 'All Hawthorne's novels are what he once called a group of his short stories, "allegories of the heart".'

72. Shroeder (1950) and Waggoner (1963: 141-45).

looking the marketplace. She is asked to confess and identify her secret lover; this she refuses to do. Her silence elicits Dimmesdale's response:

> 'She will not speak!' murmured Mr. Dimmesdale, who, leaning over the balcony, *with his hand upon his heart*, had awaited the result of his appeal. He now drew back, with a long respiration. 'Wondrous strength and generosity of a woman's heart! She will not speak!' (*SL*: 63; emphasis added).

The next chapter, '4: The Interview', has a reciprocal gesture on the part of Hester. She is being interrogated by her estranged husband Roger Chillingworth, and places her hand over her heart, as if to mimic the guilt-ridden actions of her secret lover.

> The eyes of the wrinkled scholar glowed so intensely upon her, that *Hester Prynne clasped her hand over her heart*, dreading lest he should read the secret there at once (*SL*: 67; emphasis added).

Another of the most interesting uses of the motif occurs in '15: Hester and Pearl', where there is a long exchange between mother and daughter about the meaning of the scarlet letter which Hester wears on her bosom. Hester asks her daughter if she understands the meaning of the scarlet 'A'. Pearl replies in a way which hints at a connection between Hester and Dimmesdale:

> 'Dost thou know, child, wherefore thy mother wears this letter?'
> 'Truly do I!' answered Pearl, looking brightly into her mother's face. 'It is for the same reason that *the minister keeps his hand over his heart!*'
> ' And what reason is that?' asked Hester, half smiling at the absurd incongruity of the child's observation; but, on second thoughts, turning pale. 'What has the letter to do with any heart, save mine?'
> 'Nay, mother, I have told all I know', said Pearl, more seriously than she was wont to speak. 'Ask yonder old man whom thou hast been talking with! It may be he can tell. But in good earnest now, mother dear, what does this scarlet letter mean?—and why dost thou wear it on thy bosom?—and *why does the minister keep his hand over his heart?*' (*SL*: 156; emphasis added).

Hester is hesitant in answering, unsure if she had the right to inflict the terrible truth upon her young child. Pearl, persistent and unwilling to be deflected in her search for the truth of the matter, asks again. Hester is unable to speak the truth and lies to her daughter:

> 'What shall I say?' thought Hester to herself.—'No! If this be the price of the child's sympathy, I cannot pay it!'
> Then she spoke aloud.

'Silly Pearl', said she, 'what questions are these? There are many things in this world that a child must not ask about. What know I of the minister's heart? And as for the scarlet letter, I wear it for the sake of its gold thread!' (*SL*: 158).

The use of 'heart' imagery is also a key feature in the presentation of the cat-and-mouse relationship between Chillingworth and Dimmesdale. Indeed, the supreme example of human sinfulness in the story is the monomaniac Chillingworth, who is so driven by the thirst for revenge that he commits the unpardonable sin. Chillingworth's malevolent attempts to force a confession from the tormented Dimmesdale are summarized by Hawthorne in a memorable phrase, put on the lips of Dimmesdale, as the 'violation of the sanctity of the human heart'. Perhaps the prime example of such a violation comes in a celebrated passage at the end of '10: The Leech and his Patient' as Chillingworth attempts to discover the secret sin of Dimmesdale.[73] Dimmesdale is fast asleep in the chair in his room when the malicious Chillingworth slips into the room:

The physician advanced directly in front of his patient, laid his hand upon his bosom, and thrust aside the vestment, that, hitherto, had always covered it even from the professional eye. Then, indeed, Mr. Dimmesdale shuddered, and slightly stirred. After a brief pause, the physician turned away (*SL*: 121).

The point here is that the internal, spiritual struggle which is consuming the hapless Reverend Dimmesdale is given, or *appears* to be given, a physical expression, one that Chillingworth discovers when he pulls aside the ministerial vestments. At the same time it is important to note that Hawthorne provides no description of what it is that the monomaniac physician actually *sees*. We are left to infer that it was a physical scarlet letter, exactly as we are to infer that Dimmesdale's public confession and self-exposure in '23: The Revelation of the Scarlet Letter' revealed a physical stigma on his chest. Hawthorne is far too clever to leave the matter of Chillingworth's discovery clear and unambiguous, for that would be to reduce his central theme of exploring the human heart to something crassly physical. With the confidence of a master craftsman Hawthorne is able to maintain a dialectic between the literal and the symbolic, and there is no better example of it than the

---

73. Some recent readings of this celebrated passage have detected within it an underlying homoeroticism. For more on this, see Leverenz (1989: 227-58); Derrick (1995).

scarlet letter on one's chest (whether it be Hester's or Dimmesdale's). Indeed, it is surely no accident that the chapter immediately following Chillingworth's thrusting aside of Dimmesdale's ministerial vestments is entitled '11: The Interior of a Heart', for it is this inward reality of the heart which preoccupies Hawthorne and it is to this inward dimension of human existence that the outward symbol of the scarlet letter is intended to point.[74]

c. *Confession: Redemptive Actions and Ultimate Rewards*
Public confession plays a central role in much of Hawthorne's fiction, not least within *The Scarlet Letter*. Confession by its very nature involves an audience, someone to whom the confession is given and from whom absolution is sought. In this sense there is an all-important social dimension within public confession, inasmuch as it involves the healing of a social breach. As we read *The Scarlet Letter* we are intrigued not only about who is in need of confession, but about what will be confessed by whom, and how these confessions will be brought about. Hawthorne has the central characters Hester and Dimmesdale caught up in the moral dilemma about whether or not they should publicly confess the whole truth concerning their relationship. This is one of the ways in which he maintains a relationship between himself as the writer and his reader (or more precisely, between the story's narrator and his listener). By any reckoning, the confession motif is a powerful instrument in the hands of a writer as skilled as Hawthorne.[75]

It is interesting to note how Hester's confession is handled within the story. In one sense Hester does not need to confess her part in the affair, for Pearl is living proof of her guilt. Thus, a show of public repentance by Hester is conspicuously absent, and no more so than during the climactic scaffold scene in '23: The Revelation of the Scarlet Letter'. Here she remains silent, even defiant, in the face of Dimmesdale's admission of his liaison with her. This is not unlike the actions of the woman taken in adultery in Jn 7.53–8.11, for there is nothing within the story to suggest that she repented of her sin. Her only recorded words are a

74. Rogers (1991: 76-99) discusses the importance of this passage for the overall structure of the novel.

75. For more on the idea of confession in Hawthorne's fiction, see Stewart (1958: 73-88); Baughman (1967); Dillingham (1969); Hutner (1983); Foster (1987: 52-77); Fleischner (1989–90); Dreyer (1991); Swann (1991: 75-95); Pimple (1993); and Martin (1994: 46-48).

reply to Jesus' question about whether there is anyone left to accuse her. 'No one, Lord', she replies. Jesus' reply is to command her, 'Go and do not sin again'. We are never told in the New Testament story what happened to the woman, although she quickly became the subject of much speculation and legend. In contrast, Hawthorne provides us with a few additional details about the fate of his adulteress, and suggests that her actions following the death of Dimmesdale demonstrated in themselves something of her repentance. Thus she stays in Boston and cares for other sad and unhappy women within the community, thereby atoning, in part, for her sins. In '24: The Conclusion', we read:

> Here had been her sin; here, her sorrow; and here was yet to be her penitence. She had returned, therefore, and resumed,—of her own free will, for not the sternest magistrate of that iron period would have imposed it,—resumed the symbol of which we have related so dark a tale. Never afterwards did it quit her bosom. But, in the lapse of the toilsome, thoughtful, and self-devoted years that made up Hester's life, the scarlet letter ceased to be a stigma which attracted the world's scorn and bitterness, and became a type of something to be sorrowed over, and looked upon with awe, yet with reverence too. And, as Hester Prynne had no selfish ends, nor lived in any measure for her own profit and enjoyment, people brought all their sorrows and perplexities, and besought her counsel, as one who had herself gone through a mighty trouble. Women, more especially,—in the continually recurring trials of wounded, wasted, wronged, misplaced, or erring and sinful passion,—or with the dreary burden of a heart unyielded, because unvalued and unsought,—came to Hester's cottage, demanding why they were so wretched, and what the remedy! Hester comforted and counselled them, as best she might. (*SL*: 227).

To return to Hester's partner for a moment: what is it that motivates Dimmesdale to make his confession on the scaffold? He does, of course, take steps towards repentance earlier in the story, as the self-flagellation mentioned in '11: The Interior of a Heart' demonstrates.[76] He also includes veiled allusions to his sinful past within his sermons to the devout townspeople who attend worship on Sunday. But are these rather feeble attempts at public confession *genuine* acts of repentance, or do they merely demonstrate duplicity on his part? Does he *really* want the congregation to see through the facade of his innuendo, or is he content to allow them to perceive him as a saint all the while he decries himself to be the most wicked of sinners? And why does it take

---

76. Bensick (1993) discusses Dimmesdale's celibacy.

him so long to getting around to making his role in the whole affair clear? Is the guilt that he feels primarily sexual in nature, a sort of inability to face up to the fact of his sexuality? Or does he delay in making public confession because he fears the public exposure and scandal that would ensue, the fact that it will mean the loss of his vocation as a clergyman, if not the forfeiture of his own life? All of these interpretations have been put forward and they all have their anchor points within the text.

Let us consider for a moment to whom Dimmesdale might have offered his confession. An intriguing number of possible Father Confessors are to be found within the story, particularly in '12: The Minister's Vigil'. In the second scaffold scene Dimmesdale could confess to any one of the three people who happen to observe his midnight escapade on the pillory of the scaffold, namely Governor Bellingham, Mistress Hibbins (who dabbles in witchcraft), or Reverend John Wilson. These three represent the three realms of authority in the Puritan community in Boston, the secular, the satanic and the sacred respectively.[77] The complexity of the scene suggests that there is a deliberate layering by Hawthorne at this point, as if he wished to contrast the *potential* confession contained in this second scaffold scene with the *actual* confession we are given at the end of the novel in the third scaffold scene. However, Puritanism had no place for private confession such as might be offered to any of the three minor characters, even though they represent secular, satanic and sacred authority. A confession offered at midnight, under cover of darkness, to any one of these figures would simply not suffice. Confession was seen as a consequence of repentance, and as such it was very much an action which was made before the townspeople at large, given that the adultery was viewed as a sin against the whole of the Puritan community. Thus, a full public confession is demanded by the story-line—it is needed to resolve the dramatic tension which Hawthorne has creatively fashioned throughout the novel. For Dimmesdale, public confession is a matter of revealing the affairs of the heart, and this is accomplished by means of a physical gesture which speaks more powerfully than words alone ever could. Even Dimmesdale's spirit-inspired eloquence in the Election Day sermon is but a preparatory step for what takes place on the public scaffold.[78] Dimmesdale's revelation of his breast is as great a shock to the

---

77. Hoffmann 1961: 181-82.
78. Martin (1981) stresses the dramatic importance of the sermon as a prelude

Boston townspeople who are gathered around the scaffold as it is a relief for the readers of Hawthorne's story. Finally, the confession is made, and narrative resolution achieved. Yet there is at the same time an almost magical force within the story at this point which pulls us into it. It demands that we assess ourselves in light of the story and in this sense make it our own. To this end, Leslie A. Fiedler, in his seminal study *Love and Death in the American Novel* (1967), brings together the confession motif and an allusion to the story recorded in Jn 7.53–8.11. Speaking of Dimmesdale's public confession, and the revelation of the scarlet letter on his breast, he says: 'In his dumb flesh is confessed what his articulate mouth cannot avow, not his transgression alone but that of all men who have cast the first stone'.[79]

This brings us back full-circle to the saying of Jesus recorded in Mt. 5.27-28. It suggests that Dimmesdale represents all men who transgress and throw the first stone of hypocrisy whenever they condemn others and are guilty of adultery within the confines of their own hearts. This seems to be one of the main purposes of Hawthorne's fictional tale, and no doubt is one of the reasons why *The Scarlet Letter* continues to hold the fascination that it does for us today. We can readily find our place, and examine our own hearts, within it.

Given that part of Hawthorne's intention was to address his readership in this way, what can be said about the effects of Dimmesdale's public confession upon the characters of the novel? One of the most important things that such confession brings about is the liberation of little Pearl. Note how Hawthorne brings this to the fore in '23: The Revelation of the Scarlet Letter':

> Pearl kissed his lips. A spell was broken. The great scene of grief, in which the wild infant bore a part, had developed all her sympathies; and as her tears fell upon her father's cheek, they were the pledge that she would grow up amid human joy and sorrow, nor for ever do battle with the world, but be a woman in it. Towards her mother, too, Pearl's errand as a messenger of anguish was all fulfilled (*SL*: 222).

But does this liberation extend to Hester and Dimmesdale? Is there a sense in which the adulterous couple are in any way redeemed through their suffering and Dimmesdale's public confession? And what is it that Hester hopes will happen? Does she dream of a time when Dimmesdale

to Dimmesdale's public confession.

79. Fiedler 1967: 435.

will publicly acknowledge her and Pearl and whisk them off to a proverbial life of unending bliss on earth? Is she as romantic and ideal-istic as that? Or is she realistic enough to know that such an earthly existence is not possible and therefore will transfer her dreams else-where and hope for a reconciliation in which she and Dimmesdale will be forever in the heavenly realms?[80] Perhaps she is so astute that she knows the only place that she and Dimmesdale will ever be eternally together is in a Dante-like existence in the lower levels of hell.[81] Or does Hawthorne just not tell us, allowing the matter to stand open-ended in the text and us in the dark about the couple's eternal destiny?[82]

There is much to be said for the suggestion that Hawthorne is content to have Hester and Dimmesdale buried next to each other in the burial-ground beside the King's Chapel, Boston, and not comment on their future bliss or damnation. Effectively this is to leave their eternal fate as a matter to be decided by an otherworldly authority. And yet, tantaliz-ingly, Hawthorne leaves us with a closing image which threatens to re-open the theological can of worms all over again. In '24: Conclusion', we read:

> And, after many, many years, a new grave was delved, near an old and sunken one, in that burial-ground beside which King's Chapel has since been built. It was near that old and sunken grave, yet with a space between, as if the dust of the two sleepers had no right to mingle. Yet one tombstone served for both (*SL* 228).

The final image is of the *common* headstone for Hester and Dim-mesdale, into which is carved an heraldic emblem and a coat of arms. Could it be that this shared grave marker somehow signifies their joint redemption, that they share a blissful eternity together?[83] If so, then we have a romantic end to the story of two tragic lovers, or at least one that lends itself to such an interpretation by Hollywood. This leads me to consider briefly four cinematic treatments of Hawthorne's novel, each of which, in its own way, transforms the story. *The Scarlet Letter* thus becomes a tale of forbidden passion between a man and a woman who

80. So Brodhead (1976: 66) suggests.

81. As Leverenz (1982–83: 558-59) suggests on the basis of an obscure para-graph in '5: Hester at her Needle'. For further discussion of the ultimate fate of Hester and Dimmesdale, see: Waggoner (1962: 36-37); Davidson (1963); Nolte (1965); and Porte (1969: 109-112).

82. This is the position of Fogle (1964: 132-35).

83. On this, see Greenwood (1974–75).

are caught in difficult circumstances, but whose love manages somehow to sustain them.

5. *Some Film Interpretations of* The Scarlet Letter

There is certainly a sense in which *The Scarlet Letter* can legitimately be described as a 'love-story'.[84] Each of the three central characters of the forbidden love-tryst contributes to such a reading of the story. Hester Prynne can be interpreted as continuing to love Arthur Dimmesdale despite all that has happened to her, even in the face of his inability to reciprocate that love openly. In fact, one could argue that she endures the torture and shame of wearing the scarlet letter precisely because it serves as an emblem of her love for him. Her silence in not revealing him as her partner is frequently taken as another indication of the love which she has for him.[85] It is true that Reverend Dimmesdale is generally portrayed as a weak character, a sad and pathetic figure who cannot bring himself to confront the hypocrisy of his life. Yet here too there is a good case for interpreting his inability to feel penitent over his act of adultery with Hester as a sure-fire sign of his continuing love for her. The elf-child Pearl is also important within the novel in this regard. She is the 'living hieroglyphic', the 'scarlet letter endowed with life', which unites Hester Prynne and Arthur Dimmesdale and as such symbolizes their love for one another.[86]

Hollywood filmmakers are notorious for their freewheeling adaptation of classic works of literature, and *The Scarlet Letter* certainly is no exception on this score. Four film versions of *The Scarlet Letter* in particular are worth considering in this regard: the silent classic from 1926 directed by Victor Sjöström; a German version from 1972 directed by Wim Wenders; a made-for-television version from 1979 directed by Richard Hauser; and the recent big-budget release from 1995 directed by Roland Joffé. Each in its own way transforms the novel into a love story, and each in its own fashion presents an alternative vision of the

84. As Sandeen (1962) and Gross (1968) argue.

85. Although Person (1988–89) puts forward the suggestion that the silence motif is much more complicated within the novel and includes an element of vengeance on Hester's part for Dimmesdale not having stood by her.

86. The importance of Pearl within the storyline of *The Scarlet Letter* remains one of the most debated topics in critical discussion. For further discussion on this, see McNamara (1955–56); Male (1957: 95); and Whelan (1967–68).

relationship between Hester and Dimmesdale.[87] At the same time, the kind of romantic adaptations of the novel contained within the four films invite us once again to compare them with the woman taken in adultery from Jn 7.53–8.11. This is especially true when it comes to some of the key points of discussion noted above in the study of the biblical passage. The most important of these concerns the way in which the mysterious 'sign' of the scarlet letter is portrayed within the film adaptations, effectively functioning as a parallel to the enigmatic actions of Jesus within the story from Jn 7.53–8.11.

a. *Victor Sjöström's* The Scarlet Letter *(1926)*
The Metro-Goldwyn-Mayer (MGM) production of Hawthorne's novel is generally regarded as *the* classic treatment from the silent era.[88] It is perhaps the best-known film from the Swedish director Victor Sjöström and is based on the screenplay of Frances Marion, at the time one of Hollywood's most respected female writers. The film, which lasts approximately 90 minutes, stars Lillian Gish as Hester Prynne and Lars Hanson as Arthur Dimmesdale.[89] Many of the most important scenes

87. Not surprisingly, neither Sjöström's film from 1926 nor Wenders's film from 1973 includes anything of 'The Custom House' within its adaptation, although the voice-over by Pearl in the Joffé film from 1995 at least tips its hat in this direction. The only place that 'The Custom House' is given any substantial treatment is in Hauser's film from 1979. Dittmar (1983: 192) argues that this absence of 'The Custom House' is due to the fact that framing narratives (as represented by 'The Custom House') do not lend themselves readily to cinematic interpretation. Because, she suggests, they focus on 'telling and listening, they are verbal constructs which do not film well'. Hauser's treatment shows this to be a false assessment.

88. Several adaptations of *The Scarlet Letter* were made in the early days of film-making, including US versions from 1910, 1911, 1913, 1917, 1934, and a British version from 1922. In addition, *The Scarlet Letter* has been adapted many times for television, including a Westinghouse Studio One play aired live by the Columbia Broadcasting System (CBS) on 3 April 1950 as part of the celebrations marking the centenary of the writing of the novel. This adaptation was directed by Franklin Schaffner, directed by Joseph Liss and stars Mary Sinclair as Hester Prynne, John Baragrey as Arthur Dimmesdale, and Richard Purdy as Roger Chillingworth. The black-and-white adaptation lasts 52 minutes and is available on video from Video Yesteryear, Sandy Hook, Connecticut 06482, USA.

89. See Estrin (1974; 1977: 20-29); McFarlane (1996: 38-68). McFarlane's study contains a shot-by-shot analysis of the film within an appendix (pp. 203-238). The film is also discussed briefly in Gish (1969: 285-86). The book contains three still-photographs from the film, including one from the final scaffold scene in which

from the novel are given cinematic expression within this film, including Dimmesdale's nervous habit of placing his hand over his heart, a crowd hostile to the adulterous Hester, the attempt by the Puritan authorities to take Pearl away from Hester, and images of Hester and Dimmesdale on the scaffold of the pillory.

At the same time, the film is a rather freehanded interpretation of the novel and contains many extra-textual scenes which pander to standard Hollywood conventions and interests. Chillingworth, for instance, does appear at several key points in the film, but he becomes little more than a villain and there is no real development of his character in the story. He does confront Hester and Dimmesdale face to face at one point in Hester's cottage, where he deduces that the anguished minister is the father of Pearl. He reveals that he is Hester's husband before pointing his finger at Dimmesdale and pronouncing, in an enactment of the Old Testament story of Nathan confronting King David, 'Thou art the man!' (this appears in a title board, a standard feature to convey conversation in silent films). In a somewhat bizarre twist to the original storyline, *Chillingworth* then promises not to betray their guilty secret, wishing instead that his revenge might be private, and (thereby) prolonged for his pleasure.

Much is made of the romantic relationship between Hester and Dimmesdale, with nearly the first third of the film given over to detailing their courtship in scenes which are not found in the novel itself. By this means a suitable context is provided for the passion between Hester and Dimmesdale. Borrowing imagery from Hawthorne's short story 'Endicott and the Red Cross' (1838) which is intended to portray the stern, unforgiving character of the Puritan community, Hester is put in stocks 'For Running and Playing on Ye Sabbath'. Reverend Dimmesdale shows compassion on her, bringing her a cup of water, and, after she has drunk it, releases her from the stocks. This in itself is an unremarkable beginning to the love affair between the fated couple. However, intimacy between the pair is later conveyed in an extended segment in which Dimmesdale catches Hester washing her underwear in public (we are told that displaying undergarments where men could see them was condemned by the laws of the Puritan community). This leads to a sequence where the two walk in nearby woods, with signs of a growing affection in evidence. Eventually mutual declarations of love

Dimmesdale reveals his scarlet letter. Gish (1973: 145-50) also contains 13 still-photographs relating to the film.

are made, followed by their sexual liaison (or at least we presume so, since their lovemaking is only hinted at and never explicitly shown). Hester is presented as actively instigating the affair with Dimmesdale, pursuing him into the woods.[90]

The relationship between Hester and Dimmesdale is next advanced in a scene where Dimmesdale comes to Hester's cottage and proposes marriage. He is being sent to England on an ambassadorial mission and wishes Hester to go with him. At this point she reveals to Dimmesdale (and us!) that she is already married and shows him her wedding ring— there is anguish and recrimination all around. Hester begs his forgiveness, explaining that the marriage had been arranged by her father and that she had never loved the man, a wealthy surgeon. He forgives her and the two sit together in front of the flickering fire. We next see Dimmesdale as he returns from his trip to England. He is confronted by a commotion as the townspeople gather to punish Hester for having given birth to a child during his absence (finally we are at the point in the film where the novel commences). Dimmesdale is distraught, and goes to meet her in prison. He declares via a title board that she will not face the punishment alone:

> Thou shall not be branded alone. Together we must stand, thou and I. I am the guilty one, Hester. I must share thy punishment.

Hester replies that this would represent double suffering for her, since she would thus bring about *his* destruction. She says:

> Thou hast no right to tear down the ideals of thy followers who look to thee for guidance. I shall have comfort in beholding thy life of devotion and service. Atone! Atone for both of us with thy good works.

Hester is taken to the scaffold and is exhorted by the Governor, along with Dimmesdale, to reveal the identity of her lover. This she refuses to do, making an explicit declaration of love (which again is extra-textual):

> I will never betray him. I love him—and I will always love him. And would that I might endure his agony as well as my own.

Throughout the first half of the film Dimmesdale genuinely desires Hester to reveal his paternity, and virtually demands that he be allowed to take his place at her side. There is no sign of him as the weak-willed

90. Much along the lines of D.H. Lawrence's portrayal of her as the sexual predator (see above p. 163). This is discussed in Smith (1974: 105).

and spineless partner that he is presented as being in the novel. In fact, the remorse and incapacitating guilt which are so much a part of the characterization of Dimmesdale within the novel are suddenly inter-jected into the storyline about halfway through the film (the novel's second scaffold scene, the one which takes place at midnight and sym-bolizes his anguish of heart, is dropped altogether in the film). One of the most important ways that the minister's internal struggle is con-veyed is in a short segment which has no equivalent in the novel at all. It presents Dimmesdale in his private rooms in the church, seated before a stone fireplace in which a fire is burning. Dimmesdale places a poker within the fire and, when it is red-hot, he applies it to his breast. The title board which introduces the scene tells us: 'The tortured heart—doubly tortured by the love and veneration of his people.'

What is significant about this scene is that it completely removes any mystery as to the nature of the scarlet letter on Dimmesdale's breast, the enigmatic character of which Hawthorne skilfully sets forth in '24: Conclusion'. Within the film it is a literal letter 'A' which Dimmesdale has branded onto his own breast. Indeed, this is precisely what we see at the end of the film in the climactic scaffold scene, where Dimmesdale rips open his shirt to reveal his scarlet letter, his self-inflicted 'A' (see Figure 1).[91]

It is also interesting to note how Dimmesdale's scarlet letter and Hester's are brought together in the final sequence of the film. As Dimmesdale lies dying in Hester's arms on the scaffold we are given several close-up shots of both his branded 'A' and the embroidered let-ter on her bodice. Dimmesdale then reaches up and tears the scarlet let-ter from Hester's dress, placing it on his own self-inflicted 'A'. Looking

---

91. Arthur Dimmesdale is also presented as having a literal 'A' on his breast in the Westinghouse Studio One television adaptation of *The Scarlet Letter* (see n. 85 above for details of this film). This is most clearly seen in the final scaffold scene, which is remarkably similar to the concluding scene of Sjöström's film. However, there is no suggestion that the Dimmesdale has *branded* the 'A' upon himself within this version. This television adaptation does have a scene wherein the evil physician Roger Chillingworth gives a sleeping-draught to Arthur Dimmesdale so that, when the troubled minister falls asleep under the effect of the drink, he can remove his shirt and reveal the literal 'A'. In short, there are *two* scenes within the Westinghouse Studio One adaptation in which the viewing audience clearly is able to see Dimmesdale's equivalent of the scarlet letter which Hester Prynne bears upon her bosom.

Figure 1. Dimmesdale reveals his self-inflicted 'A' in
Victor Sjöström's *The Scarlet Letter* (1926).

up into Hester's face he asks: 'Is not this a better freedom than any we have dreamed of?'

He then dies in her arms. Several brief scenes of the mourning crowd are provided, included one of the Governor looking on sadly. The crowd take off their hats as a sign of respect for the departed minister, and the film is over.

One other brief scene from the film is worth mentioning in that it provides an interesting link to the woman taken in adultery. It is a scene which is not contained in the novel and comes as part of the depiction of the life that Hester and Pearl share in their cottage on the edge of town. We are given an image of Pearl drawing in the sand in the path leading up to the cottage; she draws an 'A'. Hester, who is sewing, looks on as her daughter finishes and laughs with delight, seeking approval. Hester's own scarlet letter is clearly visible as she beholds her daughter's handiwork; a look of sadness passes over Hester's face. It is not difficult to see this as a parallel to Jesus' mysterious writing of ciphers in the sand as he takes on the Jewish authorities who accuse the unnamed woman. Thus, both the New Testament story and Sjöström's film contain a common image, one which suggests the indecipherability of symbols and demands that a deeper search for what lies at the centre of the two stories be undertaken.

b. *Wim Wenders's* Der Scharlachrote Buchstabe *(1972)*

Wim Wenders is perhaps best known in the English-speaking world for his film *Paris, Texas* (1984), which won the coveted Palme d'Or at the Cannes Film Festival. His version of Hawthorne's classic novel was made in 1972. The film was originally made in German, but subtitled versions of it in English and Spanish were also released the following year.[92] The film stars Senta Berger as Hester Prynne, Hans Christian Blech as Roger Chillingworth, and Lou Castel as Reverend Dimmesdale. The Hawthorne storyline is adapted within a screenplay written by Tankred Dorst, Ursula Ehler, Bernardo Fernández, and Wim Wenders himself. The cinematography is by Robby Müller and employs scenery of a beautiful, but rugged, coastline to portray the town of Salem which is carved out of the wilderness that was seventeenth-century New England.

Much of the film is presented in such a way that Roger Chillingworth

92. Within this essay I shall use the English subtitles rather than the German dialogue.

is the main character, although the relationship between Hester Prynne and Reverend Dimmesdale (his first name is never mentioned) builds steadily towards its fateful denouement. Wenders's film has several stylistic touches which make it a most interesting adaptation of Hawthorne's novel, not least of which is the transferral of the setting of the story from the port city of Boston (as it was in the novel) to the coastal village of Salem. No doubt this shift of location was done in part because it meant that fewer buildings were required for the on-site locations, an effect which helps contribute to the impression of Salem as a stark and lifeless place. The altered setting also builds upon popular associations between Salem and the so-called witch trials of 1692. In fact, the film makes several references (both in dialogue and within visual shots) to witches and witchcraft, effectively presenting the confrontation between the city of Salem and witchcraft as a parallel for its treatment of Hester and little Pearl. Wenders also has Hester live not on the edge of the community, on the borderland with the forest (as is the case in Hawthorne's novel), but on an nearby island off the coast. This serves to heighten the element of rejection which Hester feels at the hands of the townspeople of Salem; she is physically cut off from civilization (such as it is). Her enforced isolation is even further emphasized by the fact that the townspeople are forbidden to visit her at her home (several scenes mention this town law).

The indecipherability of the scarlet letter is conveyed in two ways within the film which are quite unusual; the first concerns the difficulty of translating a cipher such as the scarlet letter into another language (in this case German); the second is a variation of the complex alliteration which we have noted several times arises from a reading of the novel. I shall briefly discuss these two points in turn. First, we have to take into account the fact that in German the word for adultery ('Ehebruch') means that the natural association of the scarlet letter 'A' which Hester wears with her condemnation by the townspeople as an adulteress is lost. One wonders why Wenders chose consistently to retain the letter 'A' within the film and not substitute a scarlet 'E' in its place. Apparently Hawthorne's novel is so well known internationally that the scarlet 'A' could be retained without difficulty, with the audience readily making the necessary translations in their mind. In any event, the meaning of the 'A' within the storyline of the film takes on another level of meaning when we pause to consider the implications raised by a foreign-language production of Hawthorne's novel.

Second, there is an intriguing exchange of dialogue between Pearl and one of the sailors of the ship *Providence* which has arrived in Salem from Liverpool (the ship upon which Hester plans to make her escape with Dimmesdale from the harsh and forbidding territory of New England). The sailor is playing a flute and Pearl approaches him wrapped up in curiosity; Hester looks on bemused as the sailor allows Pearl to try to play his flute. After a moment of this, the sailor notices the scarlet letter 'A' embroidered on Hester's dress and asks Pearl, 'What does the letter mean?' Pearl hesitates momentarily before replying mischievously, 'America!' Her answer is all the more ironic when it is remembered that Hester views the community of Salem in which she lives as a cruel and unforgiving outpost in the new America. In the end she chooses to leave this new frontier of America in favour of the cities of the Old World and she persuades Dimmesdale that this is indeed what is best for the three of them (Hester, Dimmesdale and Pearl) as a family. It is surely not without significance that the final scenes of Wenders's film show Hester and Pearl being rowed out in a small boat to board the *Providence* and set sail to England. She leaves this America which has forced her to wear the symbolic 'A' on her breast for seven long years, with only the living symbol of her shame, the daughter Pearl, alongside her (more on this below). On the shore stands Chillingworth, foiled in his attempt to gain passage with her on the ship and disrupt Hester's plans to start a new life with her daughter in England.

But what of Reverend Dimmesdale? Where does he fit within this rendition of the story? And how does Wenders portray the love story between the tortured minister and the valiant woman who, despite extreme pressure from the Salem community, refuses to name him as the father of her child? The love affair between Hester and Dimmesdale is not explicitly portrayed within the film and there is little if anything said about the pre-history of Hester's life (the story begins, and ends, with Pearl as a seven-year-old child). Much of the feeling that the two lovers have for each other is conveyed through doubtful glances and agonized lowering of eyes so as to avoid giving anything away to surrounding people. Yet even here there is certainly not a brooding passion between Hester and Dimmesdale; if anything Dimmesdale is presented as something of a self-obsessed and spineless man and we cannot help but feel that Hester would be better off without him. As to the sense of guilt that Dimesdale feels for his part in the fated love affair, many of the features noted above in the 1926 film by Victor Sjöström are found here, including scenes in which he covers his heart with his hands, and a scene in which he collapses on the scaffold.

Interestingly, Wenders's film presents Dimmesdale as making his public confession to the townsfolk of Salem about his part in the Hester Prynne affair as taking place *in the church*, rather than on the scaffold outside following the worship service (as it is within the novel and in the 1926 film). Dimmesdale is driven to this by the demands of his own conscience, although he is sorely tempted by Hester to avoid the public exposure and simply slip away quietly. As he tells Hester following a meeting with him on the cliffs overlooking the sea (the film's equivalent of the forest scene in '17: The Pastor and his Parishioner' in which she persuades him to leave with her and go back to Europe):

> Dimmesdale *(noticing that Pearl is hesitant to come to him)*: Hester, our child knows very well that something or other is wrong. Listen, you two go to the ship and I'll go back. I must tell them in my sermon that I was the one responsible.
>
> *(Hester looks at him with mild astonishment which quickly gives way to anger and then leaves his side to go to Pearl.)*
>
> Dimmesdale *(pleading to her)*: I have to, Hester!
>
> Hester: Go then!
>
> Dimmesdale: Hester, listen to me! I can't just run away. I'll go with you afterwards. I must preach my sermon first.

The confession scene within the church is one of the most interesting in the film and brings together the three protagonists of the drama (Prynne, Chillingworth and Dimmesdale), effectively compressing much of chapters 21–23 of the novel into one dramatic episode. From the pulpit Dimmesdale makes his confession as part of his Election Day sermon on the nature of the Salem community as a 'city set on a hill' within New England. The confession sequence is intercut with shots of the congregation, including a bewildered Hester Prynne and a judgmental Roger Chillingworth. Dimmesdale says to the assembled church-members:

> Like Jesus, we were led into the wilderness to be tempted by Satan. And to resist Satan in the name of God. God reckons on us. If we do not resist Satan in this wilderness, wilderness will descend upon us, and the city on the hill will be a city accursed of God, and our children, and their children will be accursed. *(He begins to unbutton his shirt.)* I did not resist

Satan. I am the most dishonourable of you all. I have sinned more greatly and fallen lower than you all. And I cannot repent. Beneath the mask of your minister I have deceived you all. I was Hester Prynne's lover. I am little Pearl's father. I should be punished ten thousand times more than she, and I am a vile coward. I said nothing. Punish me with the same just severity that you punished her with.

As he finishes his confession Dimmesdale rips open his shirt and reveals the scarlet 'A' on his breast. He then collapses to the floor and Hester pushes her way out of the church with Pearl in tow, heading for the waiting rowboat which will take her to a new future. Meanwhile, Dimmesdale is helped to the vestry and is laid on a bench where he is attended by Reverend Wilson and Governor Fuller (who has succeeded the deceased Governor Bellingham). Dimmesdale recovers and begins to sit up, saying: 'Now I can go on board'. However, the Governor presses him back down upon the bench and strangles him, thereby ending any hopes of him ever meeting Hester and starting a new life in England. We can only assume that Hester somehow instinctively knows that the act of preaching the sermon will kill Dimmesdale. Certainly she does not wait for Dimmesdale to come to the boat on the shore following the confession in the church and there isn't any way that she could anticipate the murderous actions of Governor Fuller. It is as if Hester, at this point, finally moves beyond the need for Dimmesdale and strikes out for a new life without him, fulfilling her destiny as a follower of Anne Hutchinson.[93] The final words of the film are placed on the lips of

93. At one point in the film Hester has the following conversation with Pearl about Anne Hutchinson as mother and daughter walk along a barren beach:

Hester:	Did I tell you about Anne Hutchinson?
Pearl:	She is a witch.
Hester:	Who says so?
Pearl:	The children. They play 'Burning Anne Hutchinson'.
Hester:	She was banished, but she wasn't a witch. She was a wise woman.
Pearl:	Just like you…
Hester:	No, not like me.
Pearl:	Where was she chased to?
Hester:	She fled to Providence.
Pearl:	Where is Providence?
Hester:	Three days by ship from here. They have a different government there.

Pearl as she is in the rowboat with Hester, her head in her mother's lap. She sings softly, 'My father is dead, I'm living instead'.[94]

Two final notes about the film are also worth noting, both of which have to do with the way that the scarlet letter 'A' itself is presented. The first is to note that Wenders has chosen to include a depiction of the incident in '10: The Leech and his Patient' in which Roger Chillingworth creeps up upon the sleeping Dimmesdale and opens his shirt in order to view the minister's bare breast. Within this scene (which takes place at the bedside of the deceased Governor Bellingham) Wenders follows the lead given by Victor Sjöström in the 1926 version of the novel and has the camera clearly show the audience a bright red 'A' marked out on his breast. Once again, the subtlety of Hawthorne's open-ended description of the incident gets lost in the rush to make explicit to the viewer what is left to the imagination of the reader.

The second note concerns a scene which is not found within Hawthorne's book, but one which is added within the film to help fill out the character of Mistress Hibbins, played by Yelena Samarina. Mistress Hibbins, Governor Bellingham's sister, is presented as a deeply troubled woman, one who is involved in witchcraft, but someone who had identified Hester Prynne as a kindred spirit who is under persecution by the community. In one particular scene which highlights the effects of such persection, Hibbins goes so far as mounting the scaffold of the pillory in the town square and setting her dress on fire. More importantly for our consideration is another scene which demonstrates the extent of Hibbins's identification with Hester Prynne; the persecuted witch wears a scarlet letter on her dress as she goes to church on Sunday, much to the dismay and disapproval of her brother, Governor Bellingham. A solidarity between the two despised and rejected women of Salem is given expression as they are united through the badge of the scarlet 'A'.

c. *Richard Hauser's* The Scarlet Letter *(1979)*
This made-for-television version of *The Scarlet Letter i*s a WGBH/ Boston Production made possible by grants from the National Endowment for the Humanities, the Corporation for Public Broadcasting, the Exxon Corporation, the Andrew W. Mellon Foundation, and the Arthur Vining Davis Foundations. It stars Meg Foster as Hester Prynne, John

---

94. The subtitle attempts to reproduce a rhyme within the German dialogue: 'Mein Vater ist gestorben, es freue mich erfolgen'.

Heard as Arthur Dimmesdale, and Kevin Conway as Roger Chilling-worth. The role of Nathaniel Hawthorne, in what is in effect a cameo role for the author (a feature unique among film adaptations of the novel), was played by Josef Sommer. The screenplay is by Allan Knee and Alvin Sapinsley, with a moving musical score being provided by John Morris. The film is in four one-hour segments and is available from WGBH Boston Video. Much of it was filmed at Fort Adams State Park in Newport, Rhode island, which adds greatly to the sense of realism in portraying a harsh seventeenth-century New England environment, a realism which pervades throughout the production. There are two short excurses within the boxed set, which explain some of the considerations for presenting a realistic seventeenth-century feel for the film. The producer/director Rick Hauser is shown walking the cast and extras through various scenes, most notably the crowd scenes surrounding the Election Day celebrations. Interestingly, many of the production crew are shown wearing T-shirts which contain the elaborately drawn scarlet 'A' on them. Obviously this was a production logo, but it in itself is a symbol of the timeless quality which pervades Hawthorne's story.

Perhaps the oddest thing about this creative adaptation of Hawthorne's classic novel is that the letter which Hester wears throughout film is not a *scarlet* letter at all, but a gold 'A' stitched upon a scrap of scarlet cloth. True, Hester is often portrayed as wearing a scarlet dress with this golden letter prominently placed on her bosom, but the fact remains that a description of the film as one about 'the *scarlet* letter' is something of a misnomer. In fact, the only time that a literal scarlet letter (as opposed to one conjured up in the imagination of Hester or the townspeople of Boston, as we shall see below) is portrayed is in the very last shot of the film, one which remains on screen as the final film credits roll by. This final image is of a stark, black post which marks the joint grave of Hester Prynne and Arthur Dimmesdale; upon the wooden marker is painted an elaborately scripted letter 'A'. Having noted this rather curious feature of the production, there are several distinctive features of the film which make it worth our consideration.

First, we note that the film begins with a four-minute portrayal of Hawthorne's introductory essay to the novel proper, 'The Custom House'. This opening sequence sets the tone for the film that follows; it includes the discovery of the 'scarlet letter' whose story is then narrated. Nathaniel Hawthorne is identified explicitly as the discoverer of a folded piece of parchment, bound in red ribbon, in which was contained a scrap of scarlet cloth onto which is embroidered the golden letter 'A'. There is no confusion of narrator and authorial voice here; in fact a narrator's voice is heard explaining the discovery, but it is interspersed with words spoken to the audience by the actor playing Hawthorne (when we hear him speak we also recognize that his is the voice of the narrator). We watch Hawthorne enter an unfinished room of the Custom House and rummage through some old papers until he finds the letters and parchment. The voice of the narrator is interspersed with two sections in which the actor playing Hawthorne speaks directly to the camera. The opening narration, including the words spoken to camera (here placed in brackets and given in capitals) are:

> I chanced upon a mysterious package, an official record of some period long past. It might be that a treasure would here be brought to light. The object that most drew my attention was a certain affair of fine, red cloth upon which was wrought with wonderful skill of needlework the semblance of the letter 'A'. *(Hawthorne places the piece of scarlet cloth on his breast.)* It seemed to me (YOU MAY SMILE, BUT YOU MUST NOT DOUBT MY WORD!) that I experienced a sensation not altogether physical, yet almost so, as of burning heat, as if the letter were not of red cloth, but red-hot iron. *(Hawthorne then reads from the parchment sheet.)* HERE IS SKETCHED THE STORY OF HESTER PRYNNE, WHO LIVED IN MASSACHUSETTS 200 YEARS AGO. YOU MUST NOT THINK THAT IN DRESSING UP THE TALE OF HESTER PRYNNE, AND IMAGINING THE MOTIVES AND MODES OF PASSION THAT INFLUENCE THE CHARACTERS THAT FIGURE IN IT, I HAVE CONFINED MYSELF TO WHAT IS WRITTEN HERE. ON THE CONTRARY, I HAVE ALLOWED MYSELF NEARLY, OR ALTOGETHER, AS MUCH LICENSE, AS IF THE FACTS WERE ENTIRELY OF MY INVENTION. WHAT I CONTEND FOR IS THE AUTHENTICITY OF THE OUTLINE.

The same introductory scene of Hawthorne in the Salem Custom House (or at least a shortened version of it) introduces each of the further three one-hour segments.

Second, we note that the film follows the storyline of the novel quite faithfully, with rich costuming and realistic sets for a seventeenth-century Boston adding to the overall impact of this beautifully presented production. Even the dialogue of the film draws heavily upon the phrasing of Hawthorne's novel, with great attention being paid to the key words and phrases which have helped to make the literary work so memorable. Most of the major episodes of the novel are portrayed within the film, including the three main scaffold scenes, a sensitive and moving depiction of the famous meeting in the forest where Hester and Dimmesdale rediscover and declare their love for one another and where Dimmesdale is persuaded by Hester to leave the iron men of Boston, and a concluding depiction of the graveyard in which Hester Prynne and Arthur Dimmesdale are interred, their graves separated by an empty space but sharing a common grave marker. The dialogue between Hester and Pearl about the meaning of the scarlet letter and her persistent questioning as to the reason for the minister placing his hand over his heart are well presented. This includes Pearl's attempt to fashion out of moss a green letter 'A' for her own bosom (although the scene is placed at the seashore rather than at the brook).

In addition, many scenes not commonly included within film adaptations of the novel are portrayed here. Thus we have depictions of Hester's visit to Governor Bellingham's mansion to plead for the care of her daughter, Reverend Dimmesdale's quasi-confessional sermons from the pulpit to his adoring congregation, Dimmesdale's self-flagellation with a whip of leather. The film also has a depiction of Chillingworth's viewing of the bosom of Dimmesdale as the troubled minister sleeps, although, to its credit, the film avoids showing us what Chillingworth discovers as he unbuttons the vestments (in contrast to the films by Sjöström and Wenders discussed above). Instead, we see the effects of the discovery upon Chillingworth, a scene which is thus much more in keeping with the way that Hawthorne relates the incident. The same reserve in portraying the actual scarlet letter on the breast of Arthur Dimmesdale is maintained in the portrayal of the climactic third scaffold scene. Hester helps Dimmesdale ascend the scaffold of the pillory where the weak and emaciated minister stands alongside Hester and Pearl and faces the assembled townspeople of Boston. He makes his anguished confession and moves to open his vestments and reveal his chest. However, the camera work is such that at the critical moment of revelation we are given a reverse angle shot which affords us a view of the effect of Dimmesdale's actions upon the crowd rather than on the Reverend's scarlet letter.

More importantly for our considerations within this study, there are several scenes in which the inscrutability of the scarlet letter 'A' is conveyed. For example, as Hester is forced to stand in the public pillory, the narrator explains:

> So forcibly did the Reverend Mr Wilson dwell upon the scarlet letter
> stitched by Hester Prynne, that it assumed new terrors in the imagination
> of the people. She meanwhile kept her place upon the pedestal of shame,
> having borne that day all that nature could endure. *(A guard comes to*
> *escort her from the pillory.)* And so Hester Prynne was led back to
> prison and vanished from the public gaze. It was whispered by those who
> peered after her, that the scarlet letter threw a lurid gleam along the pas-
> sageway.

Similarly, in attempting to answer to Hester's own satisfaction the
origins of little Pearl's ever-growing wild nature, the narrator offers
additional information about how the scarlet letter was understood by
the townspeople. The narrator relates to us Hester's thoughts about the
origins of her 'strange and elfish child':

> But Hester Prynne could not resolve the query, being herself in a dismal
> labyrinth of doubt. She remembered the talk of the townspeople, who
> had given out that poor, little Pearl was a demon offspring. They had a
> story about the scarlet letter. They averred that the symbol was not mere
> scarlet cloth tinged in an earthly dye-pot, but was red-hot with infernal
> fire and could be seen glowing all alight whenever Hester Prynne walked
> abroad in the night-time. And we must need say, it seared Hester's
> bosom so deeply, that perhaps there was more truth in the rumour than
> our modern incredulity would be inclined to admit.

Perhaps the best example of the enigmatic nature of the scarlet letter
occurs in connection with the various interpretations of the crowd following Dimmesdale's revelation of his breast on the scaffold of the
pillory. This scene is presented in such a way that closely follows Hawthorne's description in the novel. A variety of explanations of what the
crowd saw, or thought they saw, are enumerated. As a montage of
images of the principal characters appear and fade on the screen, the
narrator tells us:

> After many days, after people had time to think, there was more than one
> account of what had happened on the scaffold. Most, but by no means
> everyone, saw the semblance of the scarlet letter imprinted in the minis-
> ter's flesh. Some said when Hester put the letter on, so did he. Or did old
> Roger Chillingworth cause it to appear by magic and poisonous drugs?
> Or did heaven show forth its judgment in a lurid 'A' gnawing from the
> minister's innermost heart? We put only this moral into a sentence: Be
> true! Be true! Be true!

At the same time, there are a couple of scenes in which the subtlety
of Hawthorne's description of the scarlet letter is forsaken in favour of

cinematic special effects. These make the scarlet 'A' visually explicit, whereas Hawthorne's description leaves what is seen much more to the realm of the reader's imagination. The best example of this occurs in connection with the second scaffold scene in which Dimmesdale, Hester and Pearl all stand together on the scaffold of the pillory. Hester has just come from the deathbed of the Governor Winthrop and as she and Pearl join Dimmesdale upon the scaffold, they look up towards the heavens. A comet crossing the sky fades into a cloud-like 'A', brilliantly lit up for all to see. In accordance with the novel, the incident is mentioned again by a churchman who returns Dimmesdale's glove, lost on the scaffold the night before. The sexton mentions the portent of the redletter 'A' which had appeared in the sky the night before. This he explains as referring to 'Angel', thereby relating it to the passing of the beloved Governor Winthrop.

In addition, there is a scene in which Hester is shown at her cottage on the edge of the town, with little Pearl asleep in her bed. Hester is cooking over an open fire, stirring a large kettle. She gazes in the fire and a scarlet letter 'A' appears flickering among the burning logs. Hester places her hand over the letter on her breast and sees a number of faces fade in and out of the fire, replacing the scarlet 'A'. They are the faces of other adulterers within the town of Boston, men and women alike. Speaking of the letter on her breast, Hester says to herself:

> I felt it move, as though in sympathy. Do sinners walk among us then unknown, because they wear no scarlet letter? Why then does God visit the fullness of his wrath upon me? If others walk in the town with equal guilt and are not punished for it ...? He would not! Therefore, none have sinned, save I.

The womanly strength and sympathy that Hester's scarlet letter brings to her in her dealings with the townspeople of Boston is brought out in another scene alluded to, but not explicitly described in, the book. At one point Hester assists one of the women in the town to give birth to a child. It is a difficult birth and when the child is safely handed over to another assistant, the exhausted mother asks Hester if she can touch her scarlet letter. 'Please, Hester,' she pleads, 'I want my baby to be strong.' The woman places her hand on the letter displayed on Hester's bosom and Hester's expression intimates that power goes out from her.

The subsequent assessment of the meaning of the letter by the townspeople is nicely brought out in a scene in which a young man, newly arrived in the town, asks his uncle the meaning of the 'A' on her bosom. He is told that it stands for 'Able', although it used to mean something else. The legend that the scarlet letter also stopped an Indian's arrow is also mentioned briefly in this scene (see 13: 'Another View of Hester').

All in all, Hauser's film is an imaginative and full-bodied attempt to place Hawthorne's novel on the movie/television screen, one that strives to convey the richness of expression and imagery that characterizes the original novel. The love affair between Hester and Dimmesdale is certainly an important feature within the film, but it doesn't overpower the storyline and, if anything, lies simmering in the background. Rather, it is the mysterious nature of the scarlet (!) letter, with its superhuman power and ability to transform human lives, that dominates throughout.

d. *Roland Joffé's* The Scarlet Letter *(1995)*

Director Roland Joffé has made himself something of a reputation as a filmmaker whose work is given over to the exposé of historical injustices, often with a strong religious theme at their core. His films *The Killing Fields* (1984), *The Mission* (1986) and *City of Joy* (1992) all testify to such an interest on his part, and *The Scarlet Letter* certainly continues in this vein. The film is a Cinergi Moving Picture production which lasts 129 minutes and is readily available on video. It has a big-name cast including Demi Moore as Hester Prynne, Gary Oldman as Arthur Dimmesdale and Robert Duvall as Roger Chillingworth. It also had a considerable amount of publicity hype, focusing on the obvious physical beauty of Demi Moore and the teasing promise of steamy sex as evidenced by the words contained on the film's publicity posters: 'When intimacy is forbidden and passion is a sin, love is the most defiant crime of all' (see Figure 2). The opening credits declare that the screenplay (which was written by Douglas Day Stewart) is 'Freely adapted from the novel by Nathaniel Hawthorne', and the film certainly does play fast and loose with the original novel's storyline.

The film was not a box-office success and was slated by most critics. For example, *Halliwell's Film and Video Guide* describes it as: 'Hilariously bad period drama, loosely based on Hawthorne's original, with little sense of history or decorum; it represents Hollywood at its most crass and unthinking.'[95] Moreover, *Variety Movie Guide '97* declares

---

95. Walker 1996: 656.

Figure 2. The promotional poster for Roland Joffé's
The Scarlet Letter (1995).

that the film's 'borderline campy look at the Puritans is politically correct melodrama with sex on the brain'.[96]

Why has the reaction been so negative? Much of it has to do with the film's perceived infidelity to Hawthorne's classic tale and its anachronistic pandering to modern concerns. To illustrate: the screenplay subtly but crucially alters the historical setting of the novel, placing the story in the Massachusetts Bay Colony of the 1670s. The setting of Hawthorne's story is 1642–49 (as we noted above). Why the change? It is in part to accommodate three different historical events popularly associated in the imagination with Puritan New England and weave them together into a narrative whole. These are the trial of Anne Hutchinson (1630s), the Indian uprising led by Metacomet (1670s), and the witchcraft trials of Salem (1690s).[97] All of these historical happenings are integrated into the film's storyline; indeed, they even threaten to overtake Hawthorne's original focal point in the novel. As far as the film is concerned this means that a range of fresh characters and new dramatic possibilities are interjected into the action. Thus we see the inclusion of such characters as Mituba (Hester's mute Caribbean slave-girl), Running Moose (Arthur Dimmesdale's faithful Indian convert and ministerial colleague), and Reverend Horace Stonehall (one of the more oppressive leaders of the Puritan community), as key figures in the story. Hawthorne's character Mistress Hibbins is significantly expanded to become Mistress Hibbons (played by Joan Plowright), a sympathetic figure who is eventually embroiled in controversy over witchcraft. As a result, the film becomes a forum where a number of contemporary social issues are addressed, under the safe guise of denouncing the excesses of a Puritan community which existed over 300 years ago. The rights of indigenous Indian peoples in the face of religious proselytism, the oppression of the indentured workers by greedy property speculators, the freedom of individual religious expression over against the state church, and above all, the sexual liberation of women in an essentially male-dominated Puritan society,[95] are all matters handled within the film.

96. Ellery 1996: 824.

97. Bercovitch (1996) discusses the historical background of the film and the way in which the Puritans have been used as a symbol of national origins by both Hawthorne and the filmmakers.

98. Bromley (1999) offers an excellent study of how the film deals with the question of Hester Prynne's individuality as a sexual being in a manner which is

To return to my main consideration: what are we to make of the transformation of the novel into a cinematic love story? The film clearly follows the trail blazed by the 1926 version by Sjöström and turns the tale into a love story involving Hester and Dimmesdale. The first hour or so chronicles for us the growing affection and attraction between the two, both of whom (for obvious reasons!) are rather unsure about how to proceed with their relationship. We get the first declaration of their love for one another in a scene where Dimmesdale visits Hester's cottage and returns some books she has lent him. Dimmesdale is nervous and awkwardly blurts out his feelings; Hester replies in similar vein. The following exchange takes place between them:

Dimmesdale:	Hester, I'm…I am not the man I seem. I've lived in this township my whole life, my purpose clear. But now I would risk everything, my life, my ministry, my soul, just to spend a few moments alone with you. God help me, Hester. I love thee.
Hester:	God help me I love thee too.
Dimmesdale:	Oh God! Have we lost our way?
Hester:	No! I have dreamed of thee speaking thy heart. I have prayed for it even as I have dreamt it. Was I alive before I laid eyes on thee?
Dimmesdale:	What shall we do?
Hester:	I know not.
Dimmesdale:	Say something to end it, for I… I've not the power.
Hester:	Nor I.

However, this is a love story with a happy ending, at least as far as the two central characters are concerned, for in this version they survive all of the hate and prejudice that is directed at them. To be fair, their last-minute escape from hanging on the scaffold is only facilitated by the Indian uprising, with rebellious warriors sweeping through the settlement in an ironic reversal of the proverbial cavalry rescue. Thus, romantic sentimentality carries the day and the nuclear family is allowed to remain intact, free to conquer new worlds. Indeed, in the final scenes of the film, we see Hester and Dimmesdale riding off into the sunset in a horse-drawn wagon with their little Pearl who unceremoniously

quite different from how Hawthorne did so in the novel. He notes that the film 'seems designed to provoke contemporary fundamentalism by conferring on Hester and Dimmesdale an ongoing sexual relationship and an autonomy which are both at the core of bourgeois ideology, but take no account of the Puritan context of an authoritarian theocracy' (1999: 72).

throws her mother's scarlet 'A' into the mud where it is run over by the wagon wheels, a discarded emblem evacuated of its power. A voice-over is provided by Pearl who explains that her parents were taking her far away from Boston to start a new life in the (presumably) less repressive Carolinas.

Several key images of the novel are not given cinematic expression in this adaptation, notably Dimmesdale's nervous gesture of placing his hand over his heart. Yet we are alerted to the importance of Dimmesdale's inward heart in one of the opening scenes of the film where the Indian chief Metacomet acknowledges that Dimmesdale is different from most white men and declares, 'You are the only one who comes to us with an open heart'. No doubt the declaration is intended to be somewhat ironical given the secrecy with which Dimmesdale has to conduct himself among his fellow Puritans. In contrast, Hester's equivalent of the concealed heart, the scarlet 'A' which she has to wear as an emblem of shame, is prominently displayed in the film. Yet even here its centrality is somewhat secondary within the storyline in that the compulsory wearing of it in public is suggested in passing by the hateful and vindictive wife of Reverend Stonehall as the self-righteous couple are preparing for bed. This is a community punishment which, in the words of Reverend Stonehall, is 'cunningly contrived'.

Nevertheless, most of the themes I have been concentrating on in this study of Hawthorne's novel are given expression within the film. Images of sin, accusation and confession are all to be found, although in suitably altered forms. For example, the 'sin' of the film is essentially that of the repression of the love between Hester and Dimmesdale by the cold, 'iron men' of the Puritan community. The fact of Hester and Dimmesdale's adultery which triggers the tragic events in the novel is all but forgotten, or at least severely downplayed. Even the sexual liaison between the two is carefully plotted to occur only *after* the news of Chillingworth's (probable) death has been conveyed to Hester. The very notion of their adultery as a heinous sin against the rules of society is rationalized in favour of the romantic love they have for one another. Hester and Dimmesdale are portrayed as more sinned against than sinning; it is the Puritan community which is caught in the trap of sin and hypocrisy. Nowhere is this tendency to decriminalize their adultery more clearly seen than in the final voice-over by Pearl as she relates the fate of her parents and asks the key rhetorical question: 'Who is to say what is a sin in God's eyes?'

The film has an interesting confession scene which serves as the equivalent of the meeting of Hester and Dimmesdale in the forest, an encounter so beautifully set out in Hawthorne's novel in '16: A Forest Walk' and '17: The Pastor and his Parishioner'. Here we have Dimmesdale gather his beloved Hester and the child of their union, Pearl, into his arms. The trio are centrally framed by the camera in an evocative image of the family. Dimmesdale embraces the two, raises his eyes toward the heavens, and prayerfully confesses to God:

> Lord God, we stood before Thee naked once. And now we stand before Thee naked again, as a family. God! Thou hast given me this as a gift. And I will not, *not*, give it up. Not while I have the strength!

However, this confession is not only to God above, for unbeknown to Dimmesdale, the hate-filled Roger Chillingworth is observing the scene from the bushes. The confession galvanizes the malevolent husband of Hester into action and he attempts to murder Dimmesdale. His actions wreak havoc in the community and eventually culminate in Dimmesdale's declaration on the scaffold, a scene which is interrupted by the Indian attack and moves the narrative to its conclusion.

What about the central structural feature of the novel, the three scaffold scenes? This too has undergone considerable alteration within the screenplay, particularly with regard to the second midnight visit to the scaffold which is missing altogether (although there are two brief glimpses of Dimmesdale's secret visits to the scaffold of the pillory as he agonizes over his part in the whole affair). Moreover, there is no final revelation of the scarlet letter by Dimmesdale on the scaffold; in this sense, the novel's climactic episode is missing within the film. Rather, Dimmesdale does make a final appearance on the scaffold, but it is to declare openly before all assembled his love for the much maligned Hester. She has fallen foul of the superstitious Puritans and, together with some other women from the community, is about to be hanged as a witch. Dimmesdale ascends the scaffold and declares:

> There is no witchcraft here! If we hang these women then what have we become? Who are we, to condemn on God's behalf? *(removing the noose from Hester's neck and drawing his gagged and bound lover to his side)* I love this woman! I am the father of her child. And in God's eyes I am her husband. Now if you must hang someone to appease your anger and your fear, then hang me!

Interestingly, there is an exchange between Hester and Chillingworth which highlights the metaphorical nature of the scarlet letter which

Dimmesdale carries on his heart. It comes as Chillingworth visits Hester's cottage and demands to know who her lover is:

Chillingworth:	I do not expect your heart to return to me quickly. But I hope one day you will draw me again into your heart's innermost chambers.
Hester:	God help me, love has forced my heart to open to another.
Chillingworth	*(angrily)*: Watch your tongue, woman! It is this phantom lover who puts these words into your mouth. Where is he, woman? Is his kiss still wet on your lips? On your breast? I demand to know!
Hester:	If I could spend six months in a cold jail and not tell those iron men, what makes you think I will tell you now? I have grown strong through these trials, sir, and I am not the child you married. Why not announce yourself openly and cast me off at once?
Chillingworth:	No, no. I seek no vengeance against you, child, but the man lives who has wronged us both. He bears no letter of infamy wrought into his garment, but I shall read it *(stabbing his finger aggressively at the scarlet letter on her bosom)* on *his* heart!

Similarly, at another point in the film we see Hester going through the town with the baby Pearl in her arms. She is shopping and is being followed by a drummer boy who beats loudly on his drum to signal to all her progress through the market. The scarlet 'A' is boldly emblazoned on her dress and many of the people mock her and point derisively at her. The camera then pans to a shot of Dimmesdale at the window in his study, watching the humiliation of Hester taking place below. The voice-over of Pearl tells us:

> Although he wore no outward symbol of his shame, my father bore his own scarlet letter on the very bosom of his soul.

One final visual image involving colour is worth mentioning. The film uses a red bird, no doubt picking up a motif which Hawthorne uses once in '8: The Elf-Child and the Minister' with reference to little Pearl. The chapter is given over to a discussion between Hester and the 'powers that be' about Hester's suitability as a parent. As part of Governor Bellingham's entourage, Reverend Wilson catches sight of the young child in the hallway and engages her in conversation (without yet recognizing that she is Hester's daughter). He says:

What little bird of scarlet plumage may this be? Methinks I have seen
just such figures, when the sun has been shining through a richly painted
window, and tracing out the golden and crimson images across the floor
(*SL*: 97).

Hawthorne's deliberate association of Pearl with a scarlet bird is well
brought out in the film, with most of the scenes of the little girl in the
second half of the film showing her dressed in bright red costume. The
red bird itself appears at several points in the film to support precisely
this association. Hester follows the bird into the woods and catches her
first glimpse of Dimmesdale swimming in the nude; a red bird flies into
Hester's cottage and becomes the object of attention of the slave-girl
Mituba, functioning as a symbol of sexual passion as we see the inter-
cutting of scenes of Hester and Dimmesdale making love in the barn
with Mituba taking a masturbatory bath in the cottage; and it is equated
with Mistress Harriet Hibbons as she is said to have cast her witch's
spell over the township. This last association is especially important in
that Mistress Hibbons is accused of leaving a witch's mark on little
Pearl when she helped deliver the baby during Hester's confinement in
prison. This is brought out forcefully in a courtroom scene in which
Chillingworth examines Pearl and calls attention to a red birthmark that
the little girl has on her stomach. He declares this to be 'the witch's
mark', and pandemonium breaks out in the courtroom. The superstitious Puritans panic, and moves to hang all suspected of involvement
with sorcery are set in motion.

What is most intriguing about this image of Pearl bearing 'the witch's
mark' is the way in which it could be said to function as the equivalent
of Dimmesdale's scarlet letter, which, as we have already noted, is not
revealed on the clinactic scaffold scene as it is in the novel. On the
other hand, the image of Pearl carrying her own bodily mark is *not*
found within the novel and was, no doubt, brought into the film's narrative to help fill out the witchcraft dimension of the storyline. Yet the use
of the scarlet 'witch's mark' remains an intriguing development of an
essential feature within Hawthorne's original story. The enigmatic scarlet cipher, which is missing in the person of Dimmesdale, is discovered
on the person of Pearl his daughter. In this sense, the film has its own
way of declaring Pearl to be the 'living hieroglyphic', revealing in the
strange scarlet sign the identity of her father.

6. *Conclusion*

Within this study I have been examining one of the classics of Western literature, Nathaniel Hawthorne's *The Scarlet Letter*, and attempting to demonstrate some of the parallels in thought, theme and expression between it and the New Testament story of the woman taken in adultery (Jn 7.53–8.11). Although the biblical story is never explicitly cited within Hawthorne's novel, the way in which he handles the tale of the adulteress Hester Prynne hints at more than just a passing familiarity with the New Testament account. One astonishing feature of the story of the woman taken in adultery which cries out for an explanation is the absence of the woman's adulterous partner. In his own way Hawthorne addresses precisely this question. He has chosen within *The Scarlet Letter* to offer his own version of the age-old story of an adulterous relationship, and in so doing he focuses the narrative on the quest for the identity of the missing partner. In this sense a bond is forged between the biblical text and Hawthorne's novel, one which we have seen was well worth examining. The ideas of sin, accusation and confession, which are so central to the storyline in *The Scarlet Letter*, have been especially important points of discussion as I compared Hawthorne's novel with the biblical story. Thus, the study of Hawthorne's masterpiece itself, together with an examination of several of the available film adaptations of it, has provided us with an intriguing interpretative window through which we have been able to consider afresh more of the meaning and significance of the New Testament story.

It is hardly surprising that *The Scarlet Letter* remains a work which continues to inspire readers (and filmmakers!) over 150 years after it was written. As readers we instinctively feel that we are swimming in deep waters within the novel, touching matters of ultimate concern for women and men in every society as we seek to live out our lives with integrity. No doubt the same was true in Jesus' day when he offered a message of mercy and grace to a woman confronted by a hostile and accusing crowd. Perhaps, at its most basic level, such compassion in the face of condemnation, is what unites these two enduring stories.

BIBLIOGRAPHY

Abel, Darrel
    1951   'Hawthorne's Pearl: Symbol and Character', *ELH* 18: 50-66.
    1953   'The Devil in Boston', *PQ* 32: 366-81.
    1956–57   'Hawthorne's Dimmesdale: Fugitive from Wrath', *NCF* 11: 81-105.
    1988   'Hawthorne's Hester', in Seymour Gross, Sculley Bradley, Richard
                Croom Beatty and E. Hudson Long (eds.), *The Scarlet Letter* (Norton
                Critical Edition; New York: W.W. Norton): 300-308.

Adair, John
    1982   *Founding Fathers: The Puritans in England and America* (London: J.M.
                Dent).

Anderson, Douglas
    1990   *A House Undivided: Domesticity and Community in American Culture*
                (Cambridge: Cambridge University Press).

Arac, Jonathan
    1986   'The Politics of *The Scarlet Letter*', in Sacvan Berkovitch and Myra
                Jehlen (eds.), *Ideology and Classic American Literature* (Cambridge:
                Cambridge University Press): 247-66.

Armstrong, Judith
    1976   *The Novel of Adultery* (London: Macmillan).

Askeland, Lori
    1992   'Remodeling the Model Home in *Uncle Tom's Cabin* and *Beloved*', *AL*
                64: 785-805.

Askew, Melvin W.
    1962–63   'Hawthorne, the Fall, and the Psychology of Maturity', *AL* 34: 335-43.

Astrov, Vladimir
    1942   'Hawthorne and Dostoevski as Explorers of the Human Conscience',
                NEQ 15: 296-319.

Baskett, Sam S.
    1961   '*The* (Complete) *Scarlet Letter*', *College English* 22: 321-28.

Baughman, Ernest W.
    1967   'Public Confessions and *The Scarlet Letter*', *NEQ* 40: 532-50.

Bayer, John G.
    1980–81   'Narrative Techniques and the Oral Tradition in *The Scarlet Letter*', *AL*
                52: 250-63.

Baym, Nina
    1967   'The Head, the Heart, and the Unpardonable Sin', *NEQ* 40: 31-47.
    1970   'Passion and Authority in *The Scarlet Letter*', *NEQ* 43: 209-230.
    1973   'The Romantic *Malgré Lui*: Hawthorne in "The Custom-House"', *ESQ*
                19: 14-25.
    1976   *The Shape of Hawthorne's Career* (Ithaca, NY: Cornell University Press).
    1982a   'Thwarted Nature: Nathaniel Hawthorne as Feminist', in Fritz Fleishmann
                (ed.), *American Novelists Revisited: Essays in Feminist Criticism* (Boston:
                G.K. Hall): 58-77.
    1982b   'Nathaniel Hawthorne and his Mother: A Biographical Speculation', *AL*
                54: 1-27.

1986   'Introduction' to Nathaniel Hawthorne's *The Scarlet Letter* (London: Penguin Books): vii-xxix.

1988   'Plot in *The Scarlet Letter*', in Seymour Gross, Sculley Bradley, Beatty Richard Croom and E. Hudson Long (eds.) *The Scarlet Letter* (Norton Critical Edition; New York: W.W. Norton): 402-407.

Beasley-Murray, George R.

1987   *John* (WBC, 36; Waco, TX: Texas: Word Books).

Bell, Michael Davitt

1971   *Hawthorne and the Historical Romance of New England* (Princeton, NJ: Princeton University Press).

1985   'Arts of Deception: Hawthorne, "Romance", and *The Scarlet Letter*', in Michael J. Colacurcio (ed.), *New Essays on The Scarlet Letter* (Cambridge: Cambridge University Press): 29-56.

Bell, Millicent

1982   'The Obliquity of Signs: *The Scarlet Letter*', *The Massachusetts Review* 23: 9-26.

Bensick, Carol M.

1993   'Dimmesdale and his Bachelorhood: "Priestly Celibacy" in *The Scarlet Letter*', *SAF* 21: 103-110.

Benstock, Shari

1991   '*The Scarlet Letter* (a)dorée, or the Female Body Embroidered', in Ross C. Murfin (ed.), *The Scarlet Letter* (Case Studies in Contemporary Criticism; Boston: Bedford Books of St Martin's Press): 288-303.

Bercovitch, Sacvan

1991a   'Hawthorne's A-Morality of Compromise', in Ross C. Murfin (ed.), *The Scarlet Letter* (Case Studies in Contemporary Criticism; Boston: Bedford Books of St. Martin's Press): 344-58.

1991b   *The Office of the Scarlet Letter* (Baltimore: The Johns Hopkins University Press).

1996   '*The Scarlet Letter*: A Twice-Told Tale', *NHR* 22: 1-20.

Berner, Robert L.

1979   'A Key to "The Custom-House" ', *ATQ* 41: 33-43.

Bigsby, Christopher

1992   'Introduction' to Nathaniel Hawthorne's *The Scarlet Letter* (Everyman Library; London: J.M. Dent): xx-xxviii.

Blair, Walter

1942   'Color, Light, and Shadow in Hawthorne's Fiction', *NEQ* 15: 74-94.

Boewe, Charles, and Murray G. Murphey

1960–61   'Hester Prynne in History', *AL* 32: 202-204.

Brodhead, Richard H.

1976   *Hawthorne, Melville, and the Novel* (Chicago: University of Chicago Press).

Bromley, Roger

1999   'Imaging the Puritan Body: The 1995 Cinematic Version of Nathaniel Hawthorne's *The Scarlet Letter*', in Deborah Cartmell and Imelda Whelehan (eds.), *Adaptions from Text to Screen, Screen to Text* (London: Routledge): 63-80.

Bronstein, Zelda
    1987   'The Parabolic Ploys of *The Scarlet Letter*', *AQ* 39: 193-210.
Bryson, Norman
    1983   'Hawthorne's Illegible Letter', in Susanne Kappeler and Norman Bryson (eds.), *Teaching the Text* (London: Routledge & Kegan Paul): 92-108.
Carpenter, Frederic I.
    1936   'Puritans Preferred Blondes: The Heroines of Melville and Hawthorne', *NEQ* 9: 253-72.
    1944   'Scarlet A Minus', *College English* 5: 173-80.
Chase, Richard
    1957   *The American Novel and its Tradition* (Garden City, NY: Doubleday).
Clark, Michael
    1987   'Another Look at the Scaffold Scenes in Hawthorne's *The Scarlet Letter*', *ATQ* 1: 135-44.
Colacurcio, Michael J.
    1972   'Footsteps of Ann Hutchinson: The Context of *The Scarlet Letter*', *ELH* 39: 459-94.
Cooper, James F., Jr
    1988   'Anne Hutchinson and the "Lay Rebellion" against the Clergy', *NEQ* 61: 381-97.
Cottom, Daniel
    1982   'Hawthorne versus Hester: The Ghostly Dialectic of Romance in *The Scarlet Letter*', *Texas Studies in Literature and Language* 24: 47-67.
Cowley, Malcolm
    1958   'Five Acts of the Scarlet Letter', in Charles Shapiro (ed.), *Twelve Original Essays on Great American Novels* (Detroit: Wayne State University Press): 23-43.
Cox, James M.
    1975   'The Scarlet Letter: Through the Old Manse and the Custom House', *Virginia Quarterly Review* 51: 432-47.
Coxe, Arthur Cleveland
    1851   'The Writings of Hawthorne', *Church Review and Ecclesiastical Register* 3: 506-507.
Crews, Frederick
    1966   *The Sins of the Fathers: Hawthorne's Psychological Themes* (Oxford: Oxford University Press).
Cronin, Morton
    1954   'Hawthorne on Romantic Love and the Status of Women', *PMLA* 69: 89-98.
Davidson, Edward H.
    1963   'Dimmesdale's Fall', *NEQ* 36: 358-70.
Davis, Sarah I.
    1984   'Another View of Hester and the Antinomians', *SAF* 12: 189-98.
Decter, Midge
    1997   'The Witches of Arthur Miller', *Commentary* 103: 54-56.
Derrett, J. Duncan M.
    1963–64 'Law in the New Testament: The Story of the Woman Taken in Adultery', *NTS* 10: 1-26.

Derrick, Scott S.
  1995   ' "A Curious Subject of Observation and Inquiry": Homoeroticism, the
            Body, and Authorship in Hawthorne's *The Scarlet Letter*', *Novel* 28: 308-
            326.
DeSalvo, Louise
  1984   *Nathaniel Hawthorne* (Brighton: The Harvester Press).
Deusen, Marshall van
  1966–67   'Narrative Tone in "The Custom House" and *The Scarlet Letter*', *NCF*
            21: 61-71.
Diehl, Joanne Feit
  1991   'Re-Reading the Letter: Hawthorne, the Fetish, and the (Family
            Romance)', in Ross C. Murfin (ed.), *The Scarlet Letter* (Case Studies in
            Contemporary Criticism; Boston: Bedford Books of St Martin's Press):
            235-51.
Dillingham, William B.
  1969   'Arthur Dimmesdale's Confession', *Studies in the Literary Imagination* 2:
            21-26.
Dittmar, Linda
  1983   'Fashioning and Re-fashioning: Framing Narratives in the Novel and
            Film', *Mosaic* 16: 189-203.
Doren, Mark van
  1949   *Nathaniel Hawthorne* (New York: William Sloane).
  1966   '*The Scarlet Letter*', in A.N. Kaul (ed.), *Hawthorne: A Collection of Crit-
            ical Essays* (Englewood Cliffs, NJ: Prentice–Hall): 129-40.
Doubleday, Neal Frank
  1939   'Hawthorne's Hester and Feminism', *PMLA* 54: 825-28.
Downing, David
  1979–80   'Beyond Convention: The Dynamics of Imagery and Response in
            Hawthorne's Early Sense of Evil', *AL* 51: 463-76.
Dreyer, Eileen
  1991   ' "Confession" in *The Scarlet Letter*', *JAS* 25: 78-81.
Eakin, Paul John
  1971–72   'Hawthorne's Imagination and the Structure of 'The Custom House'', *AL*
            43: 346-58.
Ellery, Derek (ed.)
  1996   *Variety Movie Guide '97* (London: Hamlyn).
Erlich, Gloria Chasson
  1968   'Deadly Innocence: Hawthorne's Dark Women', *NEQ* 41: 163-79.
  1984   *Family Themes and Hawthorne's Fiction: The Tenacious Web* (New
            Brunswick, NJ: Rutgers University Press).
Estrin, Mark W.
  1974   ' "Triumphant Ignomity": *The Scarlet Letter* on Screen', *LFQ* 2: 110-22.
  1977   ' "Triumphant Ignomity" on the Screen', in Gerald Peary and Roger
            Shatzkin (eds.), *The Classic American Novel and the Movies* (New York:
            Frederick Ungar Publishing): 20-29.
Fairbanks, Henry G.
  1956   'Sin, Free Will, and "Pessimism" in Hawthorne', *PMLA* 71: 975-89.

Feidelson, Charles, Jr
    1966   'Hawthorne as Symbolist', in A.N. Kaul (ed.), *Hawthorne: A Collection of Critical Essays* (Englewood Cliffs, NJ: Prentice–Hall): 64-71.

Fiedler, Leslie A.
    1967   *Love and Death in the American Novel* (London: Jonathan Cape).

Fleischner, Jennifer
    1989–90   'Female Eroticism, Confession, and Interpretation in Nathaniel Hawthorne', *NCF* 44: 514-33.
    1991   'Hawthorne and the Politics of Slavery', *SN* 23: 96-106.

Fogle, Richard H.
    1964   *Hawthorne's Fiction: The Light and the Dark* (Norman, OK: University of Oklahoma Press).

Fossum, Robert H.
    1972   *Hawthorne's Inviolable Circle: The Problem of Time* (Deland, Florida: Everett/Edwards Incorporated).

Foster, Dennis A.
    1987   *Confession and Complicity in Narrative* (Cambridge: Cambridge University Press).

Franzosa, John
    1978   ' "The Custom House", *The Scarlet Letter*, and Hawthorne's Separation from Salem', *ESQ* 24: 57-71.

Garlitz, Barbara
    1957   'Pearl: 1850–1955', *PMLA* 72: 689-99.

Gerber, John C.
    1944   'Form and Content in *The Scarlet Letter*', *NEQ* 17: 25-55.

Girgus, Sam B.
    1990   *Desire and the Political Unconscious in American Literature* (London: Macmillan).

Gish, Lillian
    1969   *The Movies, Mr. Griffith and Me* (London: W.H. Allen).
    1973   *Dorothy and Lillian Gish* (London: Macmillan).

Granger, Bruce Ingham
    1964–65   'Arthur Dimmesdale as Tragic Hero', *NCF* 19: 197-203.

Green, Carlandra
    1980   'The Custom-House: Hawthorne's Dark Wood of Error', *NEQ* 53: 184-95.

Greenwood, Douglas
    1974–75   'The Heraldic Device in *The Scarlet Letter*: Hawthorne's Symbolical Use of the Past', *AL* 46: 207-210.

Greiner, Donald J.
    1985   *Adultery in the American Novel* (Columbia: University of South Carolina Press).

Gross, Seymour
    1968   ' "Solitude, and Love, and Anguish": The Tragic Design of *The Scarlet Letter*', *College Language Association Journal* 3: 164-74.

Hansen, Elaine Tuttle
    1975   'Ambiguity and the Narrator in *The Scarlet Letter*', *The Journal of Narrative Technique* 5: 147-63.

Haugh, Robert F.
1956   'The Second Secret in *The Scarlet Letter*', *College English* 17: 269-71.
Hawthorne, Nathaniel
1972   *The American Notebooks* (ed. Claude M. Simpson; Centenary Edition, 7 ; Columbus: Ohio State University Press).
1986   *The Scarlet Letter* (with an Introduction by Nina Baym; London: Penguin Books).
1992   *The Scarlet Letter* (with an Introduction by Christopher Bigsby; Everyman Library; London: J.M. Dent).
1994   *The Scarlet Letter* (edited and with an Introduction by John Stephen Martin; Peterborough, Ontario: Broadview Press).
Herbert, T. Walter, Jr
1988   'Nathaniel Hawthorne, Una Hawthorne, and *The Scarlet Letter*: Interactive Selfhoods and the Cultural Construction of Gender', *PMLA* 103: 285-97.
Hoeltje, Hubert H.
1954   'The Writing of *The Scarlet Letter*', *NEQ* 27: 326-46.
Hoffman, Daniel
1961   *Form and Fable in American Fiction* (Oxford: Oxford University Press).
Hutner, Gordon
1983   'Secrets and Sympathy in *The Scarlet Letter*', *Mosaic* 16: 113-24.
Irwin, John T.
1980   *American Hieroglyphics: The Symbol of the Egyptian Hieroglyphics in the American Renaissance* (New Haven: Yale University Press).
James, Henry
1879   *Hawthorne* (London: Macmillan).
Jeremias, Joachim
1950–51   'Zur Geschichtlichkeit des Verhörs Jesu vor dem hohen Rat', *ZNW* 43: 148-50.
Johnson, Claudio Durst
1993   'Impotence and Omnipotence in *The Scarlet Letter*', *NEQ* 66: 594-612.
Johnson, W. Stacy
1951a   'Hawthorne and *The Pilgrim's Progress*', *Journal of English and Germanic Philology* 50: 156-66.
1951b   'Sin and Salvation in Hawthorne', *Hibbert Journal* 50: 39-47.
Katz, Seymour
1968–69   '"Character", "Nature"' and Allegory in *The Scarlet Letter*', *NCF* 23: 3-17.
Kazin, Alfred
1997   *God and the American Writer* (New York: Alfred A. Knopf).
Keil, James C.
1992   'Reading, Writing and Recycling: Literary Archeology and the Shape of Hawthorne's Career', *NEQ* 65: 238-64.
Kinkead-Weekes, Mark
1982 '   The Letter, the Picture, and the Mirror: Hawthorne's Framing of *The Scarlet Letter*', in A. Robert Lee (ed.), *Nathaniel Hawthorne: New Critical Essays* (London: Vision Press): 68-87.

Koehler, Lyle
    1987   'The Case of the American Jezebels: Anne Hutchinson and Female
                Agitation during the Years of Antinomian Turmoil, 1636–1640', in Linda
                K. Kerber and Jane De Hart-Mathews (eds.), *Women's America: Refo-
                cusing the Past* (Oxford: Oxford University Press, 2nd edn, 1987): 52-65.
Korobkin, Laura Hanft
    1997   '*The Scarlet Letter* of the Law: Hawthorne and Criminal Justice', *Novel*
                30: 193-217.
Kushen, Betty
    1972   'Love's Martyrs: *The Scarlet Letter* as Secular Cross', *LP* 22: 109-120.
Lang, Amy Schrager
    1987   *Prophetic Women: Anne Hutchinson and the Problem of Dissent in the
                Literature of New England* (Berkeley: University of California Press).
Lawrence, D.H.
    1964   *Studies in Classic American Literature* (London: Heinemann [1923]).
Lee, A. Robert
    1982   ' "Like a Dream Behind Me": Hawthorne's "The Custom House" and *The
                Scarlet Letter*', in A. Robert Lee (ed.), *Nathaniel Hawthorne: New Criti-
                cal Essays* (London: Vision Press): 48-67.
Lefcowitz, Allan
    1974   'Apologia Pro Roger Prynne: A Psychological Study', *LP* 24: 34-43.
Leverenz, David
    1982–83   'Mrs. Hawthorne's Headache: Reading *The Scarlet Letter*', *NCF* 37: 552-
                75.
    1989   *Manhood and the American Renaissance* (Ithaca, NY: Cornell University
                Press).
Levy, Leo B.
    1969   'The Landscape Modes of *The Scarlet Letter*', *NCF* 23: 377-92.
Lucke, Jessie Ryon
    1965   'Hawthorne's Madonna Image in *The Scarlet Letter*', *NEQ* 38: 391-92.
Madsen, Deborah L.
    1991   ' "A for Abolition": Hawthorne's Bond-servant and the Shadow of Slav-
                ery', *JAS* 25: 255-59.
    1996   *Allegory in America: From Puritanism to Postmodernism* (London: Rout-
                ledge).
Male, Roy R.
    1957   *Hawthorne's Tragic Vision* (Austin, TX: University of Texas Press).
Martin, John Stephen
    1994   'Introduction' and 'Appendices' to Nathaniel Hawthorne, *The Scarlet Let-
                ter* (Peterborough, Ontario: Broadview Press): 11-62, 311-415.
Martin, Robert K.
    1990   'Hester Prynne, *C'est Moi*: Nathaniel Hawthorne and the Anxieties of
                Gender', in Joseph A. Boone and Michael Cadden (eds.), *Engendering
                Men: The Question of Male Feminist Criticism* (London: Routledge):
                122-39.
Martin, Terence
    1981   'Dimmesdale's Ultimate Sermon', *Arizona Quarterly* 27: 230-40.

Matthews, J. Chelsey
    1940   'Hawthorne's Knowledge of Dante', *University of Texas Studies in Eng-
                lish* 4026: 157-65.
Matthiessen, F.O.
    1941   *American Renaissance* (New York: Oxford University Press).
McCall, Dan
    1966–67   'The Design of Hawthorne's "The Custom House" ', *NCF* 21: 349-58.
McCullen, Joseph T., and Joseph C. Guilds
    1960–61   'The Unpardonable Sin in Hawthorne: a Re-examination', *NCF* 15: 221-
                37.
McFarlane, Brian
    1996   *Novel to Film: An Introduction to the Theory of Adaptation* (Oxford:
                Clarendon Press).
McNamara, Anne Maria
    1955–56   'The Character of Flame: The Function of Pearl in *The Scarlet Lette*r', *AL*
                27: 537-53.
McShane, Frank
    1962   'The House of the Dead: Hawthorne's Custom House and *The Scarlet
                Letter*', *NEQ* 35: 93-101.
McWilliams, John P., Jr
    1984   *Hawthorne, Melville, and the American Character: A Looking-glass
                Business* (Cambridge: Cambridge University Press).
Miller, Edwin Haviland
    1991   *Salem Is my Dwelling Place: A Life of Nathaniel Hawthorne* (London:
                Gerald Duckworth).
Miller, James E., Jr
    1955   'Hawthorne and Melville: The Unpardonable Sin', *PMLA* 70: 91-114.
Millington, Richard H.
    1992   *Practicing Romance: Narrative Form and Cultural Engagement in Haw-
                thorne's Fiction* (Princeton, NJ: Princeton University Press).
Mills, Barriss
    1948   'Hawthorne and Puritanism', *NEQ* 21: 78-101.
Mizener, Arthur
    1967   *Twelve Great American Novels* (London: The Bodley Head).
Newberry, Frederick
    1988   'Tradition and Disinheritance in *The Scarlet Letter*', in Seymour Gross,
                Sculley Bradley, Richard Croom Beatty and E. Hudson Long (eds.), *The
                Scarlet Letter* (Norton Critical Edition; New York: W.W. Norton): 231-
                48.
Nolte, William H.
    1965   'Hawthorne's Dimmesdale: A Small Man Gone Wrong', *NEQ* 38: 168-
                86.
O'Donnell, Charles R.
    1959–60   'Hawthorne and Dimmesdale: The Search for the Realm of Quiet', *NCF*
                14: 317-32.
Pauly, Thomas H.
    1976–77   'Hawthorne's Houses of Fiction', *AL* 48: 271-91.

Person, Leland S., Jr
      1987   'Hawthorne's Love Letters: Writing and Relationship', *AL* 59: 211-27.
      1988–89   'Hester's Revenge: The Power of Silence in *The Scarlet Letter*', *NCF* 43: 465-83.
Pimple, Kenneth D.
      1993   '"Subtle, But Remorseful Hypocrite": Dimmesdale's Moral Character', *SN* 25: 257-71.
Porte, Joel
      1969   *The Romance in America: Studies in Cooper, Poe, Hawthorne, Melville, and James* (Middletown, CT: Wesleyan University Press).
Ragussis, Michael
      1991   'Silence, Family Discourse, and Fiction in *The Scarlet Letter*', in Ross C. Murfin (ed.), *The Scarlet Letter* (Case Studies in Contemporary Criticism; Boston: Bedford Books of St Martin's Press): 316-29.
Railton, Stephen
      1993   'The Address of *The Scarlet Letter*', in James L. Machor (ed.), *Readers in History: Nineteenth-Century American Literature and the Contexts of Response* (Baltimore: The Johns Hopkins University Press): 138-63.
Reynolds, Larry J.
      1985   '*The Scarlet Letter* and Revolutions Abroad', *AL* 57: 44-67.
Ringe, Donald A.
      1981   'Romantic Iconology in *The Scarlet Letter* and *The Blithedale Romance*', in G.R. Thompson and Virgil L. Lokke (eds.), *Ruined Eden of the Present: Critical Essays in Honor of Darrel Abel* (West Lafayette, IN: Purdue University Press): 93-107.
      1982   *American Gothic: Imagination and Reason in Nineteenth-Century Fiction* (Lexington: The University Press of Kentucky).
Robbins, Sarah
      1997   'Gendering the History of the Antislavery Narrative: Juxtaposing *Uncle Tom's Cabin* and *Benito Cereno*, *Beloved* and *Middle Passage*', *AQ* 49: 531-73.
Rogers, Franklin R.
      1991   *Occidental Ideographs: Image, Sequence, and Literary History* (London: Associated University Presses).
Roper, Gordon
      1950–51   'The Originality of Hawthorne's *The Scarlet Letter*', *The Dalhousie Review* 30: 63-79.
Rowe, John Carlos
      1980   'The Internal Conflict of Romantic Narrative: Hegel's Phenomenology and Hawthorne's *The Scarlet Letter*', *MLN* 95: 1203-1231.
Sachs, Viola
      1980   'The Gnosis of Hawthorne and Melville: An Interpretation of *The Scarlet Letter* and *Moby Dick*', *AQ* 32: 123-43.
Sandeen, Ernest
      1962   'The Scarlet Letter as a Love Story', *PMLA* 77: 425-35.
Schnackenburg, Rudolf
      1980   *The Gospel According to St. John*, II (London: Burns & Oates).

Schubert, Leland
    1944   *Hawthorne, the Artist: Fine Art Devices in Fiction* (Chapel Hill, NC: University of North Carolina Press).

Schwab, Gabriele
    1989   'Seduced by Witches: Nathaniel Hawthorne's *The Scarlet Letter* in the Context of New England Witchcraft Fictions', in Dianne Hunter (ed.), *Seduction and Theory: Reading of Gender, Representation and Rhetoric* (Champaign-Urbana, IL: Illinois University Press): 170-91.

Schwartz, Joseph
    1963   'Three Aspects of Hawthorne's Puritanism', *NEQ* 36: 192-208.

Segal, Naomi
    1992   *The Adulteress's Child: Authorship and Desire in the Nineteenth-Century Novel* (Cambridge, MA: Polity Press).

Shroeder, John W.
    1950   ' "That Inward Sphere": Notes on Hawthorne's Heart Imagery and Symbolism', *PMLA* 65: 106-119.

Shulman, Robert
    1984   'The Artist in the Slammer: Hawthorne, Melville, Poe and the Prison of their Times', *MLS* 14: 79-88.

Smith, Allan Gardner Lloyd
    1984   *Eve Tempted: Writing and Sexuality in Hawthorne's Fiction* (Beckenham, Kent: Croom Helm).

Smith, Julian
    1974   'Hester, Sweet Hester Prynne: *The Scarlet Letter* in the Movie Market Place', *LFQ* 2: 99-109.

Stanton, Robert
    1956   'Hawthorne, Bunyan, and the American Romances', *PMLA* 71: 155-65.

Stewart, Randall
    1957   'The Vision of Evil in Hawthorne and Melville', in Nathan A. Scott, Jr (ed.), *The Tragic Vision and the Christian Faith* (New York: Association Press): 238-63.

    1958   *American Literature and Christian Doctrine* (Baton Rouge: Louisiana State University Press).

Stouck, David
    1971   'The Surveyor of the Custom House: A Narrator for *The Scarlet Letter*', *Centennial Review* 15: 309-329.

Swann, Charles
    1991   *Nathaniel Hawthorne: Tradition and Revolution* (Cambridge: Cambridge University Press).

Tanner, Tony
    1979   *Adultery in the Novel: Contract and Transgression* (Baltimore: The Johns Hopkins University Press).

Tanselle, G. Thomas
    1962–63   'A Note on the Structure of *The Scarlet Letter*', *NCF* 17: 283-85.

Turner, Arlin
    1981   'Nathaniel Hawthorne: Questioning Observer and Interpreter of America', in William L. Andrews (ed.), *Literary Romanticism in America* (Baton Rouge: Louisiana State University Press): 19-37.

Vogel, Dan
  1963   'Roger Chillingworth: The Satanic Paradox in "The Scarlet Letter"',
          Criticism 5: 272-80.
Waggoner, Hyatt H.
  1948   'Nathaniel Hawthorne: The Cemetery, the Prison, and the Rose', *University of Kansas City Review* 14: 175-90.
  1962   *Nathaniel Hawthorne* (Minneapolis: University of Minnesota Press).
  1963   *Hawthorne: A Critical Study* (Cambridge, MA: The Bellknap Press of Harvard University).
Walcutt, Charles Child
  1952   ' "The Scarlet Letter" and its Modern Critics', *NCF* 7: 251-64.
Walker, John (ed.)
  1996   *Halliwell's Film and Video Guide* (London: HarperCollins, 12 edn).
Wall, Kathleen
  1988   *The Callisto Myth from Ovid to Atwood: Initiation and Rape in Literature* (Montreal: McGill-Queen's University Press).
Warren, Austin
  1935   'Hawthorne's Reading', *NEQ* 8: 480-97.
Warren, Robert Penn
  1973   'Hawthorne Revisited: Some Remarks on Hellfiredness', *SR* 81: 95-111.
Weber, Alfred
  1992   'The Framing Functions of Hawthorne's "The Custom House"', *NHR* 18: 5-8.
Whelan, Robert Emmet, Jr
  1967–88 'Hester Prynne's Little Pearl: Sacred and Profane Love', *AL* 39: 488-505.
White, Nichola, and Naomi Segal (eds.)
  1997   *Scarlet Letters: Fictions of Adultery from Antiquity to the 1990s* (London: Macmillan).
White, Paula
  1982   ' "Original Signification": Post-structuralism and *The Scarlet Letter*', *Kentucky Philological Association Bulletin*: 41-54.
Winters, Yvor
  1966   'Maule's Curse, or Hawthorne and the Problem of Allegory', in A.N. Kaul (ed.), *Hawthorne: A Collection of Critical Essays* (Englewood Cliffs, NJ: Prentice–Hall): 11-24.
Wiodat, Caroline M.
  1993   'Talking Back to Schoolteacher: Morrison's Confrontation with Hawthorne in *Beloved*', *MFS* 39: 527-46.
Yellin, Jean Fagan
  1989   'Hawthorne and the American National Sin', in H. Daniel Peck (ed.), *The Green American Tradition: Essays and Poems for Sherman Paul* (Baton Rouge: Louisiana State University Press): 75-97.
Young, Philip
  1984   *Young Hawthorne's Secret: The Untold Tale* (Boston: Godine).
Ziff, Larzer
  1958   'The Ethical Dimension of "The Custom-House"', *MLN* 73: 338-44.

THE ONE THAT GOT AWAY

Jayne Scott

Once upon a time there was a rich, powerful baron who owned a very large castle surrounded by a moat. As so often happens in these stories, the baron fell in love with a young woman who soon became his baroness. Together they shared residence in the castle and the two of them created a life based around the castle which served them well. One day, however, the baron announced that he was to leave the castle for a while, to go on a visit to some of his far-flung territories.

The baron was to be away for a long time and, on his departure, issued these instructions to the baroness: 'You are to have a completely free run of the castle while I'm away, but there is one thing you must not do. You must not leave the castle. If you do so, I will kill you.' And so, having shared such fond farewells, the baron left on his journey.

Near to the castle there was a small hamlet where, unknown to the baron, the baroness had a secret lover. One afternoon, not long after the baron had left, the baroness received a note from her lover asking that she meet with him that night. Should she fail to do so, he would not want to see her again. With the words of warning from the baron still ringing in her ears, the baroness nevertheless decided to go to her lover that night. How would the baron ever find out anyway? She could easily buy the silence of her maid and the boatman. So it was that, when night fell, she told her maid of her plans and asked her to agree to keep silent about the event and to ensure that, on her return, the maid would let the baroness into the castle again.

The maid pleaded with the baroness not to go. As a servant with many years' of working in the castle behind her, her fear of the baron's revenge was rooted in experience and the threat to the baroness was very real in the maid's eyes. The need to go was too great for the baroness, however, and she left with only the boatman remaining between her and her lover. With a payment made to the boatman to buy not only his services but also his silence, the baroness went to her lover and returned to the castle as planned.

When the baron returned from his travels, he asked the baroness, the boatman and the maid whether or not the baroness had complied with his demands. From the inconsistencies in the stories which nurtured his own suspicions, the baron found out that the baroness had disobeyed his instructions. Carrying out what he had said he would do, and in anger, he killed the baroness for her disobedience.

Who was to blame for the death of the baroness? Attempts to respond to such a story and the ensuing question about blame lead to the uncovering of the value systems to which we ascribe. The allocation of blame does not resolve the sense of abhorrence at the act of one person taking the life of another purely on the grounds of disobedience of the accuser's self-made rules and self-assigned authority. The baroness in the story above becomes a legitimate target of the baron's action when the value system within which he is functioning is followed through to its logical conclusion. Honour is at stake. If rules are flaunted and broken with no regard, then there have to be consequences. Otherwise anarchy gains a foothold, or so the argument goes. The baroness must know that the rules were put in place for her own good. They were intended to protect her.

This is not simply a mythical story on a par with fables or fairy-tales—grim or otherwise. This is a story which resonates with women's real stories throughout the ages and speaks of responsibility, authority and blame. All three are located within our social and religious systems and there appears to be an inevitability about who will come off worst in such a scenario.

Here I will consider the story in Jn 7.53–8.11 and will arrange the discussion into three parts. First, I address the fact that almost every line of its telling is a condensed history of how women have carried the consequences of abusive value systems in every generation and, in contrast, how men have somehow escaped through the back door over and over again.

Second, I will outline how violence has been used as a means of furthering control and dominance over women. The extent to which this is accepted as an appropriate way of relating to women will be examined especially in the light of the story from John's Gospel about the woman allegedly caught in the act of adultery.

Finally, I will offer some observations on what might be thought of as 'sin' in this scene where a person's life is threatened by others in the name of God. Popular perceptions and 'groupthink behaviour'[1] are not reliable sources for drafting anything other than a superficial notion of

1.   Jarvis (1972) sets this out.

that which is a much more deeply entrenched and systematic human failing. This in itself urges us to re-examine how the term 'sin' is used, and to offer some critique from the women's rights perspective, bearing in mind that the scene depicted in Jn 7.53–8.11 has been repeated and rehearsed many times even in our present day.[2]

1. *The Game of Consequences*

Games have rules. They don't work if the rules are not followed. Should this happen, the players who renege on the rules are branded as 'cheats'; they are despised and, in the Wild West of the past, for example, were shot. Some games have more serious consequences than others. Some games are not just for the confines of the rather more sedate evening activities of the parlour, but have risk factors which serve to heighten the thrill of playing the game. As the stakes are increased, so the gains for the winner accumulate. From the underside (i.e. the perspective of the one who loses) the stakes may have been similar but the consequences are much greater.

Such are the rules of the game of patriarchy.[3] There are consequences for all concerned, and as the game progresses the winners accumulate greater gains, thus increasing their power and stake in the game. Meanwhile, from the underside, those who lose as a consequence of the game continue on the downward spiral towards oblivion. The game depends on this pattern; there are identifiable winners and losers, the important and the insignificant players, those who are dominant and those who are subordinate. Global economies, policies and social practice are constructed around this same pattern.[4] Whether it be in the games of

2.   An article in *The Guardian* (27 May 1999) tells of the murder of Rukshana Naz, a young woman (aged 19) from Derby, who was accused of adultery. Her mother and brother were convicted of murder on 25 May 1999 and jailed for life at Nottingham Crown Court.

3.   The term 'patriarchy' here is used to refer to the sociopolitical systems which develop when men refuse to share power with women. This results in power becoming a sought-after commodity which is only made available to a select grouping. Men are usually the beneficiaries of these systems, but it would be neither accurate nor appropriate to conclude that all men subscribe to the values which patriarchy promotes. Equally, it cannot be maintained that all women would speak out against patriarchal power. For a summary and description of the comprehensive nature of patriarchy, see Hearn (1998: 31-33).

4.   See Mies (1986); Gnanadason (1992); Elson (1995).

business or leisure, the boards may vary in design but the rules remain the same.

For women the consequences of this game, and of its rules, can be seen manifest in some of the statistics of our world at the end of the twentieth century. According to a report issued by the United Nations in 1980: 'Women constitute *half* the world's population, perform nearly *two-thirds* of its work hours, receive *one-tenth* of the world's income and own less than *one-hundredth* of the world's property' (emphasis added).

It is obvious that the amount of investment of women's selves into the well-being of humanity is disproportionately high in comparison to the benefits they accrue as a result. On this alone the rules of the game can be seen to be quite effective. It is a game of consequences—one consequence for those who continue to benefit, and another for those who are required to put in a stake much greater than the rewards they are given. It is a game which plays with people's lives as if they are expendable.

To maintain the pattern the rules are exploited to their limit and certain behaviour becomes expected almost to the point where it is accepted as an inevitable feature of life. Wave after wave of statistics reinforce the idea that men are in control and women are to be controlled. Data collected from the lives of women in Britain alone is sufficient to confirm this. One in two girls experiences some form of sexual abuse (from flashing to rape) before their eighteenth birthday (Child Abuse Studies Unit 1991). One in seven women is raped in marriage (Painter 1991). The acquittal rate in rape trials is 78% (Brown, Burman and Jamieson 1992). On average, one woman dies every three days as a result of domestic violence[5] (the baroness from our opening parable is certainly not an exception to the rule).

Continuous reminders to women abound that they are not afforded the freedom to be self-determining human beings to the same degree as men. While violence to women is a particular component of the maintenance of control,[6] there are characteristics of our value systems which hinge on an acceptance that this is the way things are. Whether it be those in a dominant or subordinate role, an inherent acceptance of the

---

5.   Statistics taken from 'World in Action' TV production on domestic violence, aired on 9 March 1998.

6.   I will look at this in more detail in the Section 2, below.

status quo is necessary to allow it to continue. In the words of one recent writer:

> [T]he maintenance of a dominant/subordinate social structure depends on the belief by subordinates in the rightness of, not so much their own position, but that of the dominants. The subordinates focus most of their energy on learning as much as possible about the dominants and providing them with what they require (Bohn 1989: 108).

For patriarchal values to hold, it is essential that those who are on the underside continue to believe that those in control have the right to be in the position they are in. If this belief structure is in place, then the dominants need not fret themselves over the security of their position.

This is the point of concern for many women's rights activists because this sentiment often forms the basis for placing even more blame on women for their so-called 'compliance' with the violence, rather than naming the perpetrator as the one actually responsible. In other contexts, such as the torture of prisoners, it would be unthinkable to suggest that the victim was responsible for her or his own suffering. This is no less the case for women who experience violence directed against them.

There are at least three further reasons, however, which also show why the suggestion of women's compliance is untenable. First, to argue that women collude with or are compliant in the face of violence is to reinforce the institutionalized domination of men over women. It is assumed that because women are silent, they do not want to change the situation or take responsibility for themselves. This is not an argument applied in relation to situations where violence is directed against men or children. There is no reason why it should be applied to women when they are the violated ones.

Secondly, the risks for women when they try to break the cycle of violence increase dramatically. There are more reasons to stay silent than to speak out. The silence is not compliance—it is a question of survival, something of which women in violent situations are particularly aware.

Thirdly, women will often take the blows believing that by doing so, they are protecting someone else—such as the children in the home or another relative. Again, this *might* be interpreted as a highly honourable thing to do. A woman, however, is more likely to be considered 'weak' for taking this course of action. This in itself is a reflection of the reluctance of society to acknowledge women's choices in such matters, as reasoned decisions which are far from simple compliance, collusion or weakness.

The complex web of legal and cultural practices and financial resources upon which men can draw are entirely different from those actually available to women. This comprehensive reinforcement of male power, combined with the continual neglect of women's rights, provides a dominant position for men in societal structures.

There are many ways in which such an unassailable stance can be, and has been, created. Terror is one of the methods which best catches media attention—particularly in circumstances where tyrannical figures control people through fear. This is apparent in both international political and familial domestic relationships alike. There is another much more widespread and insidious method, however, which has also proved effective for hundreds of years. It is to be found embedded in ideological principles which feed on the belief that biological differences validate blatantly unjust sociological constructs.

> Social power inequalities become occasions for the abuse of power. Those who are powerful can organise societies in such a way that those who are vulnerable are denied the full resources that life has to offer. Abuse of power relies on institutions and ideologies (Poling 1991: 29).

Christianity has much to answer for in its perpetuation of these methods and inequalities. This has not been restricted to judgment on aspects of behaviour, but is far more penetrative than this. Women have been roundly condemned by prominent men who have played a significant part in shaping the teaching of the Church. Thus, the Latin church father Tertullian (c. 150–222) pronounces judgment on all women when he declares in *De Cult. Fem.* 1.1.1-2:

> Do you not believe that you are [each] an Eve? The sentence of God on this sex of yours lives on even in our times and so it is necessary that the guilt should live on, also. You are the one who opened the door to the Devil, you are the one who first plucked the fruit of the forbidden tree, you are the first who deserted the divine law; you are the one who persuaded him whom the Devil was not strong enough to attack.

Similarly, in the fifteenth century Heinrich Institoris (1430–1505) wrote in the *Malleus Maleficarum* (Part 1, Question 6: 'Why Superstition is chiefly found in Women'):

> When a woman thinks alone, she thinks evil... I have found a woman more bitter than death, and a good woman subject to carnal lust...women

are naturally more impressionable, and more ready to receive the influence of a disembodied spirit…they have slippery tongues…they are fee-
bler both in mind and body…as regards intellect, or the understanding of
spiritual things, they seem to be of a different nature from men…
Terence says: Women are intellectually like children… And it should be
noted that there was a defect in the formation of the first woman, since
she was formed from a bent rib, that is, a rib of the breast, which is bent
as it were in a contrary direction to a man… And indeed, just as through
the first defect in their intelligence, they are more prone to abjure the
faith; so through their second defect of inordinate affections and passions
they search for, brood over, and inflict various vengeances… Women
also have weak memories; and it is a natural vice in them not to be
disciplined, but to follow their own impulses without any sense of what
is due…she is a liar by nature…woman is a wheedling and secret
enemy… All witchcraft comes from carnal lust, which is in women
insatiable… Wherefore for the sake of fulfilling their lusts they consort
even with devils (Summers 1928: 43-47).

It is a casting of women as being more existentially sinful than men
that is the essential point here. The inequalities relate to the core of our
being human—male or female. The former, while 'sinful', has a more
readily recognized route to salvation through saying 'sorry'. The latter,
on the other hand, has somehow to work continually for forgiveness
and salvation on account of two main factors: first, the belief that a
woman (Eve) was responsible for bringing sin into the realm of human
existence in the first place; and, second, as a biological definition, being
female is considered synonymous with 'weak', requiring more toler-
ance and, by implication, more forgiveness.

We can see from these examples that historical Christianity defined
women as inferior, subordinate, and prone to the demonic. These images
justified almost limitless violence against them whenever they crossed
the male will at home or in society. Woman as victim is the underside of
patriarchal history, seldom given respect or concern from agents of
morality or law enforcement. Women particularly have been subjected to
the double bind of blaming the victim in innumerable and convoluted
ways that women even today have a difficult time refuting. The assumption of patriarchal society is that when women are victims of either verbal abuse or physical violence, ranging from beating to rape, they themselves are responsible for it. They have 'asked for it' and therefore can
receive no sympathy, compensation, or restraint of their violators, but
only insult added to injury (Ruether 1989: 37).

Using the story of Eve in the Genesis 2–3 account of creation as
justification for treating women as suspect is a familiar line of argument

to everyone. The hold which it has over ecclesiological discourse is disturbing, but it is a myth which is gripping simply because it strengthens the status quo.

> [T]he Genesis 2-3 narrative may in fact be understood as a foundational myth of patriarchy, one which legitimates both the subordination of the female and male violence against her as a chaos agent who threatens the hierarchy of male dominance (Ess 1996: 112).

Similarly, a widespread popular view is that women are prone to making poor decisions. Their capacity for making wise choices is severely impaired—because they are women and God ordained it that way (so the patter goes). Even if we would like to dismiss this with no further comment, we do have to reckon with the strength of emotions which it rouses, regardless of our own stance. People are convinced by, and damaged by, the consequences of such systematic degradation of women. A recent sample illustrates the point:

> Adam was not deceived, whereas Eve was (1 Tim.2:14). This *might* mean that Eve was less culpable (she thought she was doing right, whereas Adam *knew* he was doing wrong) but it more probably means that Eve was more vulnerable to being seduced in mind. The context is Paul's practice of prohibiting instruction by women; however uncomfortable we may feel with his line of thought, he seems to be saying: Eve, as typical woman, was more liable to be misled and therefore more likely to mislead (Pawson 1989: 23).

Is it surprising that, with a prevailing perception of women as consistently faulty in their critical analysis of situations (the implication being that men seldom are) and with an 'unfortunate' burden of responsibility for introducing sin into the world, women have difficulty trusting their own judgment? Where could their views be heard, let alone accepted? Dominance and subordination are dressed up as 'protecting women from themselves' and 'making sure things don't become chaotic'.

Men are perceived to be the rightful carriers of responsibility with the unenviable task of dealing with women who are thought, by their nature, to bring instability, sinful seduction, temptation and chaos—all the elements most feared by organized religious institutions. Keeping women in order requires a steady hand—one which will punish in a manner which demonstrates to those with the 'weaker' mind what the consequences of their behaviour are. The administrators of the rule(s) are to be sympathized with because they have such a difficult task.

While they may make mistakes now and again, they are the guardians of righteousness.

Herein lies the hidden dynamic for why it is that, in the stories akin to that of Jn 7.53–8.11, the woman stands condemned and the man in question is the one who gets away. Men can ask for forgiveness almost at their leisure and it is assumed that it will be granted. Women, by way of contrast, often find their destiny in the hands of others and are not granted pardon, except through punishment and humiliation.[7]

For the woman charged with being caught in the very act of adultery in Jn 7.53–8.11, the rules of the game are being followed to the letter. The consequences would seem to be obvious, bearing in mind the level of awareness in the community of what the law stipulates is to be the accepted response to such an act. One of the reasons why the story in John is so remarkable is that Jesus' behaviour takes all concerned by surprise. It is a tragic comment on attitudes towards women of his day that the position in which this particular woman finds herself is not the remarkable feature in any respect.

This 'game of consequences', the rules of which are not far from our consciousness at any given time, gives rise to questions in at least three areas of societal behaviour and norms. It is in the manifestation of how a community organizes itself in matters of order and punishment where we can best observe the extent to which abusive patterns are tolerated. Many key questions arise.

Can capital punishment be justified as a suitable means of reinforcing societal norms? It is usually argued that to kill a person in order to maintain social order is allowed for two main reasons. First, that person will no longer be able to do what he or she was doing. Second, it serves as a deterrent for others who might consider doing something similar.

How can a less abusive system be developed when those who question the validity of the manner of punishment place themselves in danger simply by becoming associated with the one who has contravened the rules? Such a precarious position could result in them also standing condemned for allegedly promoting behaviour that is considered harmful.

How can it be suggested that God's laws and human moral codes can combine to result in an abusive outcome? Distinctions between divine imperative and group psychology become blurred at the point when a

---

7.   See Daly (1984: 178-222) for more on this point.

crowd becomes energetic in its desire to kill someone for daring to break the rules.

As if in a game of chess, the woman in the story from Jn 7.53–8.11 has become a pawn—an expendable piece in the hope of catching a valued prize. Indeed, one of the reasons why it is thought that this narrative found its way into the canon eventually is because the more 'valued player' in this game of consequences (Jesus) is seen to be the central character with the religious leaders playing a secondary role as a foil against which Jesus' wits are tested. The woman, whose life hangs in the balance, is peripheral to the 'real' plot. The 'game of consequences' which patriarchy plays could not be more clearly displayed.

The lines between what is right and wrong become very indistinct once the extent of the violence proposed is realized. The impetus to throw stones at a person in order to break the skull or limbs and to make her breathe her last comes not only from a momentary, spontaneous outburst of anger, but also from the deep-seated belief that such an act is somehow legitimate. Although describing how men's ways of accounting for their violence in the twentieth century, the words of Jeff Hearn are equally applicable to the biblical narrative found in Jn 7.53–8.11:

> When men account for their violence, they usually refer to specific incidents rather than some general social relation of violence. Incidents are, however, usually placed within more extended narratives. Violence is both specifically described and told through its location within stories—'this is what happened' (1998: 105-106).

Jesus' actions in the situation demonstrate his refusal to accept the validity of the violence—both the specific and more general social relation of violence represented here. His behaviour is to be noted and applauded, just as the commentators would want. But this is not enough. On its own this is an inadequate response to the game which is played out on this stage. Jesus' response to the situation was a brief respite for this particular woman, but the practice of stoning, punching and killing women who are accused of adultery has not stopped. Levelling the accusation of adultery against a woman is still considered sufficient in many men's eyes to justify their violence to their partners. Women still stand accused with little or no defence, dependent on the whim of their male partner or a chance encounter with another who might be able to secure them some safety. It is admirable what Jesus did—it is no mean feat for a man to challenge the rule of patriarchy. But he did have a voice in the situation. He was listened to. He was treated with regard even if the situation was a set-up. He had some power which he used to maximum effect. The woman, in contrast, had no voice, was not listened to, was treated with no regard whatsoever—her life did not matter at all to the religious leaders: it was neither here nor there whether she was killed or not. They wanted to trap Jesus. The woman was rendered utterly power-less. This reality has yet to dawn on our consciousness, nor has its impact as yet been properly felt. However, as these things begin to hap-pen they will hopefully result in women and men resolving to work together to dismantle this brutal game of consequences which runs according to the rules of patriarchy.

2. *The Rule of the Iron Fist*

Towards the close of the World Council of Churches' 'Ecumenical Decade for Churches in Solidarity with Women' (1988–98), several groups were commissioned to visit a wide variety of countries to find out what progress had been made and what issues still needed to be addressed by the churches if women's stories were to be heard and responded to appropriately. As a result of these visits there were partic-ular themes which emerged time and again. One of the themes was the impact of violence on women's lives.

> During our time with the churches we noted with sadness and anger that violence is an experience that binds women together across every region and tradition. The phenomenon is so pervasive that many women expect violence to be a part of their lives and are surprised if it is not. Often, girls are brought up to expect violence, perhaps at the hands of a loved one. Almost everywhere we went, this reality was acknowledged...we are convinced that violence against women is not only being more openly reported, at least by women, but is also escalating (World Council of Churches 1997: 23).

The catalogue of stories which women can, and do, tell is so exten-sive that it is impossible to hear it all. The scale of violence against women is so great that, on hearing but a small part of it, the listener may be tempted to respond by using language to minimize the signifi-cance of it, shutting off when facts and figures are too much to handle, or resigning oneself to accepting it as an inevitable ingredient of everyday living.

None of these responses seems to reflect Jesus' own behaviour in Jn

7.53–8.11. He shows a more developed understanding than others in the crowd. He directly challenges the 'rule' which suggests that violence is an appropriate method to employ to carry out God's will. He also takes issue with the shared common practice of ensuring that women are reminded of their secondary position in societal structure. Recent research shows that this formula which reinforces the 'rule of the iron fist' is still used today.

> Despite and perhaps because of many men's separation of sex and violence, sexual infidelity by the woman can be seen by some men as justification for their violence. In this view, the woman is not maintaining her self as the man presumes she should be...violence is then justified to 'make good' this gap/lack, either as a corrective of the particular instance or as punishment, even if that is not likely to be 'effective' in changing the situation (Hearn 1998: 150).

Jesus seems to know full well that, by confronting the accusers with the implications of their actions, he is in fact challenging this central characteristic of the 'rule' on which abusive systems depend.

Data gathered from our contemporary situation[8] serve as reminders that the 'rule of the iron fist' as faced by the woman in the story in John's Gospel, the women of Tertullian's day, mediaeval times and across the globe today are to be found in every generational, cultural and religious context.[9] We note the following facts:

- In Costa Rica, one in every two women can expect to be a victim of violence at some point in her life.
- In Canada, one in four women can expect to be assaulted at some point in their lives, half of them before the age of 17.
- In Peru, one in every four girls will be the victim of sexual abuse before she reaches 16.
- In the USA, every day four women are killed by their batterers and every six minutes a rape occurs.
- In France, 95% of the victims of violence are women.
- In Papua New Guinea, 60% of the persons murdered in 1981 were women.
- In South Africa, one woman out of every six is assaulted regularly by her mate.

8.   See Hester, Kelly and Radford (1996) and Hearn (1998).
9.   Gnanadason (1993: 2-3, 9-10, 14-16) discusses this.

These statistics tell us not that women are the only victims of violence, but that in all contexts they are the *primary* victims. We also have to contend with the facts which tell us of the use of violence to women as part of a strategic plan to secure control and power in the hands of oppressors. In the words of Aruna Gnanadason: 'Mass rape has frequently been used as a political or military weapon either to punish or to intimidate those who rebel. The logic here is to hurt the women in order to teach the men a lesson' (1993: 15).

Even in this, the women themselves are expected to bear the violence as if it has little effect on them, while it is hoped that the greatest impact will be felt by their male counterparts. What seems to matter is not the damage done to the women in terms of personhood and dignity, but how effectively the men have been dishonoured.

It has only been fairly recently that women who were used as sex slaves during World War II (1939–45) have been able to find their voice and express in public what happened to them. In the last decade the world press alerted us to how rape was used as part of the weaponry by all sides in the conflict in the former Yugoslavia. In an editorial feature in the *International Herald Tribune* dated 8 December 1992 and entitled 'The Rape of Bosnia', an interview with a Serbian fighter revealed that he and his companions had been told by their commanders that raping Muslim women was 'good for raising the fighter's morale'. He spoke of them following this advice on several occasions but added the claim that they routinely killed the women afterwards.

Women political prisoners are frequently subjected to rape and sexual assault as part of their torture. Amnesty International reports that this has happened in India, the Philippines, Bangladesh, Pakistan, Liberia, Mauritius, Uganda, Senegal, Peru, Guatemala, Mexico, Turkey, Greece, Ireland and Palestine. In a recent report Amnesty International states that

> many governments clearly regard rape and sexual assault as less serious
> offences than other human rights violations. This is a particularly fright-
> ening prospect when the perpetrators of these rapes are the same police-
> men and military personnel charged with the protection of the public
> (1991).

With such a backdrop and script of violence to them, it is easy to see why women find it hard to believe that there could be another way of living. Equally, it should come as no surprise to us that girls grow up expecting to receive the same treatment as their mothers and grandmothers. For the woman in the Gospel story, the anticipation of death by stoning once accused of adultery is unlikely to have been a surprise to her. Jesus' behaviour, on the other hand, as significantly different, is one of the core reasons for the story's eventual inclusion in the canon.

Once confronted with the statistics about violence to women, it is often the case that men (and women too afraid to challenge the 'rule') will offer at least one of two responses in the main (Miedzian 1992: 5-12). The first is an attempt to change the subject. By transferring the focus the responsibility for the violence is deflected elsewhere (Hearn 1998: 105-45). Often this is done by attributing the causes to social pressure, provocation, cultural expectations or even by claiming 'it couldn't be helped'. In other instances, the subject may be changed in a rather more subtle way—by diminishing the seriousness with which these statistics would be addressed should it be other than the issue of violence by men against women.

The second response frequently offered is related to the first, but employs a different strategy. It is the sentiment that 'women can be just as violent as men, given half the chance'. Sometimes it is stated in an even stronger tone, saying, 'Women can be *even more* vicious than men'. While both statements occasionally may well be true, they are not statements which can ever achieve a 'balancing up' of that which is the predominant scenario. In 1989, of those arrested for violent crimes in the USA, 88.6% were men (which means 11.4% were women) (Miedzian 1992: 6). At no stage in our considerations here is it the intention to suggest either that all men are violent or that women are not violent. Such a view would merely oversimplify the complexity of a system of relationships which displays a level of sophistication which can only be transformed or challenged should there be a committed and concerted effort by men and women alike.

In many matters of health, employment and economic trends such data would usually lead to a considered and committed response and strategy being developed. Should an epidemic break out, medical teams swing into action to respond both to the immediate needs of the situation and to discover how such an outbreak could be prevented in the future. Employment figures are watched very closely as an indicator of how well a government is performing in fulfilling its promises. Fluctuations in the global economy are so sensitive that a seemingly insignificant event in one country can jeopardize the stability in another. Data about these matters are provided with unfailing regularity through the media and we do not consider it melodramatic or obsessive behaviour when communities or governments collectively strive to address the concerns that they raise.

Why is it, then, that when it comes to matters related to violence to women and the statistics are made known, the primary responses revolve around wanting to diminish, decry, deny and destroy the evidence?[10] Like health, employment and economic issues, we hear of violence to women almost every day in the West through the media. For the most part, though, it is presented as a localized, personal issue between a few individuals. A woman's body is found at the bottom of a lake and the husband is the main suspect; a mother and her daughter are killed by an unknown man while walking down a country lane; a young woman is found beaten to death in her own home—her partner is charged with murder. A prostitute is beaten and raped by her pimp and customers alike; a wife is punched by her husband because she spoke to another man and he is jealous. A man who kills his wife because she was having an affair is treated with leniency by the male judge because somehow his violence is regarded as justified on account of his wife's actions. These are no imaginary tales. These are the people who make up the startling statistics.

On the one hand, women have been visible inasmuch as they are noted as the recipients of violence or as those who 'cause trouble' by protesting against the violence. On the other hand, women have been made invisible through persistent and consistent negation of what is

10. One very surprising attempt to do just this came from Erin Pizzey in the BBC 2 TV programme '*Counterblast: Who's Failing the Family?*' aired on 30 March 1999. Pizzey argued that the focus by women's groups and feminists on violence by men to women tears families apart and that sometimes the women are 'no angels' and should really accept the responsibility for having provoked the situation. This is a view which is not tenable for many of the reasons already stated in this essay, but is argued against fairly conclusively in many other places. These counter-arguments revolve around three central points. First, where it is men who are violent to women it is precisely that—the men are being violent and for that they are responsible and therefore should be held accountable. Secondly, it is the act of violence which destroys family relationships, not the protest against the violence. Thirdly, the 'private intimacy' of violence in the home (as the programme describes it) is a public issue because it is both endorsed and unquestioned by institutional policies, thus generating a public structural violence to women and their families. See Hearn (1998); Hester, Kelly and Radford (1996); Brown and Bohn (1989).

actually violence to them and denial that the majority of perpetrators are men.

Men, however, are present in every strata of society in prominent and dominant positions. The power that they hold simply by being there contributes to their all-pervading visibility. As Jeff Hearn perceptively comments, 'Men have been all too visible yet invisible to critical analysis and change' (Hearn 1998: 3). Self-analysis and change have been applied and demanded of women because it is expected that they will both absorb and adapt to the violence inflicted upon them. This has been the status quo. Challenging this assumption involves men becoming visible not for the violence they are capable of, but rather their capacity to embrace critical analysis and change as part of the process for constructive community-building.

Jesus, it seems, was attempting to make visible the need for men to do just this. In a scene which is the climactic moment of a very familiar story where there would appear to be no possibility of an alternative ending, he creates one. Left to their own devices, men have continued to develop systems of law and order, religious codes, cultural practices and governmental policies which inevitably bring men and women to this point. All the weaponry necessary to inflict as much violence as they want is in the hands of the leaders—men who are well known in the community and to the woman. As Susan Dowell and Linda Hurcombe put it, 'Female life it seems, was very cheap, and stones handy' (1987: 29). The woman stands accused, silent and, even if she were able to offer a defence of herself, is unlikely to be heard or believed. Honour is at stake and under no circumstances must the 'rule' be dishonoured or diminished in its strength. Violence—indeed murder—is the only possible outcome, or so it seems.

Abusive systems have an insatiable appetite for opportunities to demonstrate power over others. Power, according to this view, cannot be shared for it would then be diminished. It is to be exercised over others and the accumulation of more power depends on the subjugation of others. The desire to control matters of life and death combined with the fear that someone might take that control away is the basis of abusive structural patterns.

> Abuse of power for the individual is motivated by fear and the resulting desire to control the power of life. This fear and arrogance are then used to create societies in which structures of domination create special possibilities for the privileged at the expense of shared power for all persons (Poling 1991: 27).

Those who are dominant in the structures enjoy the benefits of their position but are only able to do so as long as those without power do not question their position. As for those who are marginalized, they need to be subdued in order to maintain the status quo for at least three reasons. First, power of this kind can only be retained when matters of life and death become a public demonstration of the power which can be wielded by those who 'have it'. Such manifestations of abusive power can only happen if no one stands in the way. Second, in order to maintain a position of power of this kind, the dominant person or group relies on the marginalized for their labour and compliance. This can only be achieved by exercising absolute power over their choices in life so that the dominated will eventually believe that they are 'in their rightful place'. Third, those who dare to question the authority structure are a threat to the continuance of this power. These people need to be silenced, and that silence needs to be absolute.

Violence finds a ready home within abusive systems because it is a necessary feature of keeping power in the hands of the few. Patriarchal values thus promote the possibilities for violence to permeate every aspect of life—personal and interpersonal, local and global, individual and institutional.

> Women in patriarchy find themselves on the downside of power hierarchies… The masculine and feminine views of power remain split into two sides of a dualism as polarized opposites. The two views of power depend on each other in a gender-stratified system of dominance and submission. Exploiter male and exploited female go hand in hand, just as powerful, controlling parent and abused child fit a system of hierarchical power… Both dominance and compliance confuse personal power with positional power. Positional power has to do with our status in social relationships and the extent to which our interpersonal world has emphasized control (Brock 1988: 30-33).

The 'rule of the iron fist' is proving not to be healthy for women, men or children. It results in abusive patterns being manifest in many different places. In itself it cannot be reformed, nor should it even be considered possible to do so. An alternative needs to be found. It is in Jesus' action in the face of the accusers on that day when the woman stood to lose her life that we find a suggestion for a way ahead. Probably it begins with a complete re-think on what has been viewed as either honourable or sinful in this story.

3. *Naughty and Nasty*

It was in the middle of a 'teaching session' that the scribes and Pharisees brought the woman before Jesus (Jn 8.2-4). A crowd was already gathered—a significant fact because it provided the scribes and Pharisees with a ready audience for the trap which they planned to set. The group already assembled were there with the intention of learning and hearing the things Jesus was about to say. In contrast, the scribes and Pharisees were much more interested in using a confrontational method to set a trap. Their approach displays a level of aggression which sets up a 'win/lose' scenario. The woman who stands accused was never likely to be a winner in the situation, but stood to lose her life. The best that could happen for her would be that she still be alive at the end of this confrontation. Winning and/or losing here was dependent upon the way in which honour and integrity were interpreted. Whose honour would be preserved and how could integrity in the eyes of the law be maintained? To set the standard, a clear decision needed to be made and publicly recognized. This is why the scribes and Pharisees wanted successfully to discredit Jesus and his teachings while at the same time increasing their own credibility as suitable guardians of the law. In other words, they want Jesus to be proved to be the 'loser' and themselves to be the undisputed 'winners' in the contest.

This approach and the values on which it rests result in destruction and humiliation. Credibility, honour and power are thought to be found through this route, and only this route. The nastiness of a value system of this kind lies in its inability to allow alternative interpretations to be recognized as valid perspectives. It is the heartbeat of fundamentalism. It is a fierce defence of positional power and it costs lives. This scenario is as old as the hills. It is the unadulterated manifestation of the spirit of destruction. Creative energy is not nurtured here, it is extinguished.

Consider this excerpt from a report in *The Observer* dated 18 April 1999:

> Lal Jamilla Mandokhel never stood a chance. The 16 year old was raped a month ago near her home in the mountains of Pakistan's northwest frontier. For bringing shame on her village, she was publicly executed...
>
> Her 'crime' occurred in a dirty hotel in the Pakistani frontier town of Parachinar, a short trek along a mountain track from Afghanistan. Over two nights, Lal Jamilla was repeatedly raped by a junior clerk in the local government's department of agriculture. When her ordeal ended and she returned to her village, elders in the traditional council or *jirga*

decided only her death would restore the honour of the tribe. She was
dragged from her home and shot in front of a large crowd. The government is keeping her rapist in custody 'for his own protection'.

Lal Jamilla's case hardly made the local press. Such deaths are not
uncommon. Hundreds of women and scores of men found guilty of adultery are shot in similar circumstances every year.

Let the issues be clear here. It is not only women who suffer at the
hands of these men. Nor is it a matter of holding a particular religion
more responsible than another. We know that this violation of humanity
crosses all known boundaries. The strength to resist requires an immea-
surable amount of courage and the ability to take untold risks.

In her biography, Sultana (her pseudonym), a Saudi Arabian princess
of the Al Sa'ud family, tells of her fear of being under threat for telling
her own story. Once her biography was written by Jean Sasson it was
agreed that the two should never meet again in order to avoid putting
the princess at any greater risk.

> At our final meeting, in August 1991, a feeling of perverse futility mired
> my joy, while I marvelled at Sultana's wave of optimism. She felt joyous
> hope at the outcome of our endeavour and declared that she would rather
> perish than live as one conquered. Her words gave me strength for the
> approaching storm: 'Until these despicable facts are made public, there
> can be no help; this book is like the first steps of a baby who could never
> run without the first brave attempt to stand on its own. Jean, you and I
> will stir the ashes and start a fire. Tell me, how can the world come to
> our aid if it does not hear our cry? I feel it deep in my soul; this is the
> beginning of change for our women' (Sasson 1997: 294-95).

Sultana's life is one which presents us with a contemporary situation
where the fate of women is completely in the hands of a legal, political
and religious system which seeks to draw a cover over the destructive
impact of treating women as expendable. Such comprehensive control
of the lives of human beings is widely condemned by many international human rights organizations, the United Nations and Amnesty
International being but two of them. So why is it that as humans we
seem incapable of being specific and clear in our recognition of the
value systems which we repeatedly develop and which, in turn, destroy
the human body and fragment the soul?

Are some sins greater than others? If so, which ones? Who decides?
Is being different or making choices different to the majority a sin? This
story in John's Gospel does beg some response to these questions, even
if the responses can only be partial.

For Tertullian, there would appear to be no hesitation in declaring that there are some sins which are greater than others and, yes, they can be identified. He would seem to suggest that it is the Bible itself which tells us of this distinction and the consequences.

> There are certain sins of daily occurrence to which we are all liable. For who escapes such sins as unjustified anger...or physical violence, or thoughtless slander, or heedless swearing, or breaking promises, or lying...? ...So that if there were no pardon for such faults, no one would attain salvation. But for these there will be pardon through the intercession of Christ with the Father. But there are other sins very different from these, as being too serious and ruinous to receive pardon. Such are murder, idolatry, fraud, denial (of Christ), blasphemy and, of course, adultery and fornication, and any other violation of the 'temple of God' (*De Pud.* 19.23-25).[11]

In Tertullian's understanding, the seven sins listed as most serious are in the realm of the unforgivable. In *De Pud.* 21.15 he argues, 'Since offences against man are forgiven, it is implied that sins against God are not to be remitted'.[12] In *Adv. Marc.* 4.9 he names these same seven sins as meriting punishment by death. It could be argued, however, that Tertullian is merely reinforcing existing social practice rather than offering any insight which might open up a new perspective. In this, he would stand much more easily with the scribes and Pharisees in our story than with Jesus and the woman.

More recent understandings of sin have brought a new perspective and result in a more humane response to human failings. Feminist thought, particularly, has contributed considerably to the gaining of a more developed method of interpreting sociopolitical behaviour. Lucy Tatman explains that common to most feminist theorists' work is the belief that sin is a constructed condition. She places the emergence of sin in the context of how relationships are built and shaped.

> Because right relations are those which are mutually empowering, sin occurs whenever a person or group use or abuse an individual, group or natural resource for their own purposes, thereby disempowering, degrading and all too often destroying who or what was used (1996: 217).

She calls for everyone to be accountable both for their own personal actions and for collective actions taken as members of social, political, economic and religious groups.

---

11. Cited in Bettenson (1956: 154).
12. Cited in Bettenson (1956: 155).

As the narrative of women's experiences is increasingly being listened to, descriptions of sin, such as Tertullian's, are cast in a very different light. Walter Wink, in his book *Engaging the Powers*, addresses many of the issues regarding the oppression of people through a comprehensive web of domination. He explores how social, religious and political systems manifest and reinforce their own rules of domination. Recognizing that power is not exercised only between individuals but also to be found in collective and institutional behaviours, Wink names these as the 'Powers':

> The Powers possess an outer, physical manifestation…and an inner spirituality, or corporate culture or collective personality. The Powers are the simultaneity of an outer, visible structure and an inner spiritual reality. The Powers, properly speaking, are not just the spirituality of institutions, but their manifestations as well (1992: 3).

His argument about the dominating 'Powers' is that they do not express the intention of God. Additionally, in Christian terms, they do not remain true to Jesus' life and death.

This recognition of institutionalized power as a phenomenon far greater than a collection of individuals is a fairly recent thing. The MacPherson Report on the Stephen Lawrence Inquiry (1999) marked a significant point in British legal history by naming 'institutional racism'. By doing so, it became possible to speak of how the triangulation of social, political and legal structures collude to reinforce and enforce unjust behaviours. In a not dissimilar way, violence to women has emerged as another aspect of human behaviour which is permitted, reinforced and often encouraged by the same social, political and legal structures. Here I mention but two of the underlying principles which have served for thousands of years as the accepted reasons for this having continued from one generation to the next.

First, justice has not been considered a right for all human beings. The parallels found between the struggle for racial justice and human rights for women are significant here. Race and gender have been used for centuries as the basis upon which power has been established or withheld. To be black and/or a woman has been thought to be sufficient to justify others' neglect of a person's human rights. Justice has been denied because it has not been regarded as a right. For the dominant race (usually white), class (usually landowning) and sex (male), justice has been unquestioned as a right. For everyone else it has been treated as a privilege which may or may not be granted—depending on the whims of those in power and the machinations of institutions. Struggles for justice have always centred on this point. Justice is for all, regardless of race, class or gender. Otherwise it is not justice. Equally, it is a basic human right and should not be handled as a commodity available only to the privileged. This is just as true for women whatever their circumstances, but it is even more so in situations where violence to them is endorsed by almost every context of their existence.

Second, issues relating to ownership are also among the shared themes for race and gender justice concerns. Social systems which have endorsed ownership of other human beings as property include principles which portray certain people as being dispensable. Slaves, bought and sold, controlled and confined, are an example of those who, at the disposal of their owners, become an integral feature of currency. Wealth is measured by how many are owned. Power is measured by the level of control over these human 'possessions'. Prostitutes, owned, only for a short time and for a specific purpose—but owned nonetheless—are someone else's property. Their bodies and personhood are so integrated into the prevailing patriarchal value system that they become almost invisible as people.

Women have fallen into the category of being among 'the owned'. Even in the public ceremony of marriage in Britain in the twentieth century there is still the common practice of a father 'giving his daughter away'. Whose is she to give? The notion of ownership in this context could be argued to be but a harmless custom. However, customs such as this reflect a deeper, accepted understanding which means they are not considered out of place. It is worth noting that, increasingly as women have established more rights for themselves, this custom is often not incorporated into weddings now.

Christianity has made use of ownership as a tool for securing power over nations, groups and individuals. 'This theology of ownership is pervasive and foundational to much of Christian thought and practice, though it is rarely named directly and most of its practitioners are unaware of it' (Bohn 1989: 106).

The creation stories in Genesis 2 and 3 have been thought to offer the blueprint for how God intends the relationship between men and women to be (i.e. the woman as essentially the property of the man). As a result, the stories have been used to secure the ownership of women by men.

Most biblical exegetes consider the Genesis creation accounts etiological stories; in other words, one might postulate that the attribution of man's

ownership of woman to God's intent was a way of explaining, justifying
and preserving what was already an accepted social behaviour (Bohn
1989: 106).

So it is that I return to our story in Jn 7.53–8.11 and ask of our contemporary context how we respond now with the more developed
understanding of human rights at our disposal. Winning and/or losing
here relies on the way in which honour and integrity are interpreted.
Whose honour will be preserved and how can integrity in the eyes of
the law be maintained? To set the standard, a clear decision needs to be
made and publicly recognized. What honour or integrity is to be found
in religious systems which fragment, destroy or violate human beings?
There certainly appears to be no shortage of examples to show that this
happens in any of our organized religious systems. Girard goes as far as
to portray religion as 'organized violence in the service of social tran-
quility' (Wink 1992: 146).

On the face of it, yet another story of a woman allegedly caught in
the act of adultery and the baying of the authorities for her murder
serves but to provide another addition to the already full collection of
such narratives. But here we have a plot with an alternative ending.
Jesus, in his behaviour, exposes sinful actions for what they really are
and shows who exactly is more accountable in the situation. The effect
of this is not at all agreeable to those who see themselves as being in
authority. Refusal to comply with the rules and consequences of the
games of violence is to expose sin in its most destructive forms. Those
'caught out' by this exposure are shamed by their own dishonourable
deeds. They are shown to be lacking the very integrity which they claim
to uphold.

By way of contrast and in contradiction to these guardians of
hypocrisy, Jesus' behaviour highlights the destructive nature of collective (or institutionalized) abuse by those in power of one who is given
no possibility of justice.

> In Jesus there is a total absence of positive or negative complicity in vio-
> lence. In his arraignment, trial, crucifixion, and death, the scapegoating
> mechanism is at last, categorically, revealed for all the world to see.
> Insofar as other deaths reveal the truth revealed in his dying, they share
> its integrity and continue its revelation (Wink 1992: 148).

This is not heartening for those who live their lives according to the
'rule of the iron fist'. This is not good news, for it means the potential
collapse of existing power systems. The last resort for those who are

most worried by the implications of a new order based not on privileges and violence but on rights and shared power, is to claim that they would *like* it to be possible, but it simply cannot be—human nature will not permit it. Is this not precisely the point?

> The reign of God means the complete and definitive elimination of every form of violence between individuals and nations. This is a realm and a possibility of which those imprisoned by their own espousal of violence cannot conceive (Wink 1992: 149).

Integrity and honour cannot be found in institutions or individuals who settle for unthinking repetition of destructive patterns of behaviour. It is to be found, however, where, without violating another, the 'Powers' are exposed and discredited. All too often and readily this has been designated as an issue for the privacy of home life. This results in untold manifestations of abuse, particularly to women and children, and dresses it up as an 'honourable way' of respecting intimate human relationships. To fail to recognize violences to women as a public, institutionalized issue is to ignore how matters of justice, honour and integrity, as commonly understood, repeatedly fail women.

Little did the scribes and Pharisees realize that by bringing the woman out into the open, believing they were exposing her sinfulness, they themselves were about to be the ones exposed as sinful in their collective enthusiasm for her murder. Jesus was the one who revealed to them the extent of their own hatred and just how destructive it can be. While claiming the need for God, the law and the honour of the community to be appeased, they discovered it was their own destructive intentions which called for closer inspection. At this point, sin and hatred are synonymous and are not evident in the woman facing execution. They are most clearly to be seen, however, in those whose hands are clenched around the stones. 'It is not God who must be appeased, but humans who must be delivered from their hatred' (Schwager 1987: 209).

In this story in John's Gospel, it is the accusers who are indeed found to be both naughty and nasty, not the woman.

BIBLIOGRAPHY

Adams, Carol J. Marie M. Fortune and Mary M. Fortune, (eds.)
 1996 *Violence against Women and Children* (New York: Continuum).
Amnesty International
 1991 'Rape and Sexual Abuse: Torture and Ill-Treatment of Women in Deten-
  tion', *ACT* 77.
Bettenson, Henry (ed.)
 1956 *The Early Christian Fathers* (Oxford: Oxford University Press).
Bohn, Carole R.
 1989 'Dominion to Rule: The Roots and Consequences of a Theology of
  Ownership', in Brown and Bohn (1989): 105-116.
Brock, Rita N.
 1988 *Journeys by Heart* (New York: Crossroad).
Brown, Beverly, with Michle Burman, and Lynne Jamieson
 1992 *Sexual History and Sexual Character Evidence in Scottish Sexual Offence
  Trials: A Study of Scottish Court Practice* (Edinburgh: Scottish Office).
Brown, Joanne Carlson , and Carole R. Bohn (eds.)
 1989 *Christianity, Patriarchy and Abuse: A Feminist Critique* (New York:
  Pilgrim Press).
Child Abuse Studies Unit
 1991 *An Exploratory Study of the Prevalence of Sexual Abuse in a Sample of
  16–21 Year Olds* (London: Child Abuse Studies Unit, North London
  Polytechnic).
Daly, Mary
 1984 *Gyn/Ecology: The Metaethics of Radical Feminism* (London: Women's
  Press).
Dowell, Susan, and Linda Hurcombe
 1987 *Dispossessed Daughters of Eve* (London: SPCK).
Elson, Diane (ed.)
 1995 *Male Bias in the Development Process* (Manchester: Manchester University Press).
Ess, C.
 1996 'Reading Adam and Eve: Re-visions of the Myth of Women's Subordination to Man', in Adams, Fortune and Fortune (1996): 92-120.
Gnanadason, Aruna
 1992 'Challenge from the South: Towards a New World Order', in Grant and
  Patel (1991): 51-62.
 1993 *No Longer a Secret: The Church and Violence against Women* (Geneva:
  World Council of Churches).
Grant, P., and R. Patel (eds.)
 1991 *A Time to Act* (Birmingham: Racial Justice, Black and Third World Theological Working Group).
Hearn, Jeff
 1998 *The Violences of Men* (London: Sage).

Hester, M., with L. Kelly and J. Radford
    1996   *Women, Violence and Male Power* (Buckingham: Open University Press).
Isherwood, Lisa, and Dorothea McEwan (eds.)
    1996   *An A–Z of Feminist Theology* (Sheffield: Sheffield Academic Press).
Jarvis, I.L.
    1972   *Victims of Groupthink* (Boston: Houghton Mifflin).
Living Letters: A Report of Visits to the Churches during the Ecumenical Decade—
    1997   *Churches in Solidarity with Women* (Geneva: World Council of Churches).
MacPherson, William
    1999   *The Stephen Lawrence Inquiry: Report of an Inquiry* (London: HMSO).
Miedzian, Myriam
    1992   *Boys Will be Boys: Breaking the Link between Masculinity and Violence* (London: Virago Press).
Mies, Maria
    1986   *Patriarchy and the Accumulation of Wealth on a World Scale* (London: Zed Books).
Painter, K.
    1991   *Wife Rape, Marriage and the Law* (Manchester: Manchester University Press).
Pawson, David J.
    1989   *Leadership is Male* (Crowborough, East Sussex: Highland Press).
Poling, J. Newton
    1991   *The Abuse of Power: A Theological Problem* (Nashville: Abingdon Press).
Ruether, Rosemary Radford
    1989   'The Western Religious Tradition and Violence against Women in the Home', in Brown and Bohn (1989): 31-41.
Sasson, Jean P.
    1997   *Princess: A True Story of Life behind the Veil in Saudi Arabia* (London: Bantam Books).
Schwager, Raymund
    1987   *Must There Be Scapegoats?* (San Francisco: Harper & Row).
Summers, Montagne (trans.)
    1928   *Heinrich Institoris: Malleus Maleficarum* (London: John Rodker).
Tatman, L.
    1996   'Sin', in Isherwood and McEwan (1996): 217-18.
Wink, Walter
    1992   *Engaging the Powers* (Minneapolis: Fortress Press).

Making Her Case and Reading It Too: Feminist Readings of the Story of the Woman Taken in Adultery

Elizabeth E. Green

The episode of the woman taken in adultery has not—unlike, for example, the healing of the woman with the flow of blood, or the various anointing scenes—figured largely in feminist readings of the Gospels. The so called 'adulterous woman' is ironically forgotten by Elisabeth Schüssler Fiorenza's influential work of remembrance, *In Memory of Her: A Feminist Theological Reconstruction of Christian Origins* (1983), and likewise fails to figure in Adele Reinhartz's feminist commentary on John (1995). According to Reinhartz, the pericope's peculiar textual history does not allow it to 'contribute to our understanding of Johannine rhetoric' (1995: 599 n. 33). The episode of the woman taken in adultery is also omitted, without further comment, from Sandra Schneider's study of women in the Fourth Gospel (1982), while Martin Scott, whose work on the Gospel of John aims to be sensitive to the claims of feminist scholarship, dismisses it as an accretion and, tellingly, unable to illuminate his own particular thesis (1992: 239). It would appear that the marginalization of this text by androcentric scholarship—on which even malestream exegetes such as Xavier Léon-Dufour (1992: 390-92) feel obliged to remark (and in some cases rectify)—has decreed a similar marginalization by feminist interpretation itself.

Rather than investigate the reasons for this omission—and ask whether, for example, the 'adulterous woman' breaks with the patterns that feminist scholars discern in the Fourth Gospel's treatment of women—we will turn our attention to the existing handful of feminist readings of our text. These well illustrate the multiplicity of hermeneutical strategies employed by feminist interpretation which, far from being mutually exclusive, ideally interact with one another in an ongoing and mutually enhancing conversation (Schüssler Fiorenza 1992:

21-40). The diversity of strategies used by feminist hermeneutics to produce multiple readings continues to be seen as one of its greatest assets which signifies its 'refusal of mastery' by offering 'not a new system of domination but a continuous critique of all such systems'.[1] In the feminist readings of the woman taken in adultery I shall suggest that the interpretative strategies brought into play, occasionally by the same author, are of four main types: historical reconstruction; women's experience; the literary paradigm; and the literary unit. I shall look at each of these in turn, discussing each strategy and the reading it produces.

1. *Historical Reconstruction*

One of the earliest reading strategies adopted by feminists consisted in bringing to light those female characters in biblical texts consigned to oblivion by androcentric scholarship and preaching. This strategy had three main goals. In the first place it aimed at restoring both women to history and history to women. History, and specifically *biblical* history, was no longer considered an all-male affair but women were considered to have taken part in, for example, the Jesus movement from the outset. By bringing the tools of historical-critical scholarship to bear on the passages involving female characters, women would not only be restored to their rightful place in history, but such reclaimed biblical images would enable women to claim their rightful place in present-day society. In other words, women of both Testaments would become viable partners in the consciousness-raising process typical of the early days of the women's movement. The 'women around Jesus', as one influential work was entitled (Moltmann-Wendel 1987), thus became signposts for contemporary women in their search for identity, mirrors in which they could see themselves, their hopes and struggles reflected.[2] In the preface to a collection of feminist re-readings of biblical texts by German scholars, for example, we read that 'in searching for the history of their foremothers in the faith, women are seeking for women with whom they can identify' (Schmidt 1994: 5). Lieve Troch theorizes about the use of biblical women in the method of conscientization and writes: 'For many women, having a better grasp of the [biblical] stories means having a better understanding of their own existence and self. Recovery

---

1. The Bible and Culture Collective (1995: 270); Castelli (1994: 97).
2. Moltmann-Wendel (1987: 2), while not mentioning this text, writes of the 'spontaneous way in which women can rediscover themselves in the Bible'.

of the lost self goes hand-in-hand with the discovery of resistant women in the past' (1994: 363).[3]

The second aim of this strategy, held in some tension with the first, recognized the fact that the histories of women in the second Testament were important insofar as they form part of the larger history of Jesus of Nazareth. This strategy thus sought to discover Jesus' own relationship to women, as reconstructed by historical research. Most particularly, it is asked: How did Jesus relate to women in a way that changed their lives? What was at stake, of course, was not so much the historical Jesus' attitude to women *tout court*, but how the Jesus witnessed to by the scriptural texts could even now relate to (and potentially transform) present-day women (and to a lesser extent men). An unresolved conflict can easily be detected in this feminist move. On the one hand, women are restored to history seemingly for their own sake; on the other, their history is restored insofar as it is part not only of God's eventual history with humankind but, as Daphne Hampson never tires of pointing out, of that particular revelation in history tied to Jesus of Nazareth (Hampson 1996).

This tension brings a third, more subversive aim into view: What if the relation between Jesus and women were not unilateral? What if women themselves actively contributed to this history? Could the pericopes in question now be read in order to throw light on women's contributions either to Jesus' own self-understanding or to his redemptive work? Such was the option taken primarily by systematic theologians such as Isabel Carter Heyward (1982), Mary Grey (1989), and Rita Nakashima Brock (1992).

One of the earliest feminist readings of the woman taken in adultery to adopt this strategy is found in Leonard Swidler's well-known and much controverted article, 'Jesus Was a Feminist' (1971) subsequently incorporated into his book *Biblical Affirmations of Woman* (1979). Although Swidler is aware of the peculiar nature of the Gospels as historical sources, he believes that 'with careful, painstaking work, we can learn much about Jesus' life, and teaching' (1979: 162).

The point of this exercise is to uncover the religious truth contained in the Gospel which functions as a guide to Christian living today. Thus, Swidler concludes his article: 'Jesus was a feminist and a very radical one. Can his followers attempt to be anything less—*De imita-*

---

3.   On conscientization and feminist hermeneutics, see Green (1997).

tione Christi?' (1971: 110). To determine the attitude of the historical Jesus to women, Swidler makes ample use of the criterion of discontinuity. In Swidler's reconstruction, Jesus' treatment of women is in radical contrast both to the attitude of contemporary Judaism as well as to the early Church's view of women. He writes:

> The fact that the overwhelming negative attitude toward women in Palestine did not come through the primitive Christian communal lens by itself underscores the clearly great religious importance Jesus attached to his positive attitude—his feminist attitude—toward women (1971: 104).

That Jesus' treatment of the woman taken in adultery contrasted both with the rigorous position on sexual offences adopted by the early Church and with its increasingly negative attitude towards women, probably accounts, according to Swidler and later feminist readings, for this pericope's nomadic textual history. Thus, Louise Schottroff, who adopts a modified version of this approach, writes: 'The fact that this story had difficulty being accepted into the canon is, from a feminist perspective, an indication that the story could not be harmonized with the interests of a church oriented toward dominance' (1995: 180).

While feminist readings on the whole gladly accept the scholarly consensus that this pericope 'preserve[s] a primitive piece of Jesus tradition' (O'Day 1992: 639), the reason for its marginalization is, as we shall see, construed in different ways.

How, then, does Swidler read the text? Swidler's interpretation focuses on the trap set by those scribes and Pharisees who, by bringing before Jesus a woman who 'had been caught in the act of adultery', want to see how he will respond. Swidler claims that according to most scholars the dilemma is whether Jesus will go along with the death penalty commanded by the law of Moses, thus pleasing the scribes but alienating the Roman authorities (who alone, on this view, can enforce capital punishment), or whether he will shirk his responsibility to the Mosaic law, please the Romans and alienate the scribes and Pharisees. On Swidler's reckoning, however, such a view of the dilemma is misplaced insofar as it does not come to terms with the fact that the trap (so to speak) is a woman. Swidler writes: 'It is also clear that the enemies of Jesus would not have thought of this case as presenting Jesus with some kind of trap if Jesus did not already have a reputation among them as a champion of women' (1979: 186). The question thus now becomes, on Swidler's reading: 'would Jesus retain his reputation as the great rabbi, the teacher of the Torah, or would he retain his reputation as the champion of women?' (1979: 186).

How does Jesus get off the spot? Rather than deal in the legal niceties and abstractions favoured by his opponents, Jesus shifts his attention to the people involved in the episode, 'both the woman herself and her accusers'. According to Swidler, who dwells only slightly on this point, Jesus appeals in different ways to their 'humanness, their mind, spirit and heart' (1979: 186). In other words, both the woman and the male accusers are treated as persons. Jesus' attitude towards women proves to be, in fact, 'personalism extended to women' (1979: 164). This nicely coincides with Swidler's definition of a feminist: 'a feminist is understood to be a person who is in favor of and promotes the equality of women with men, a person who advocates and practices treating women primarily as human persons' (1979: 11). According to this interpretation, then, Jesus transforms the woman from 'sex object' (1979: 185) to which the action of the scribes and Pharisees had reduced her, to acting human subject, able to respond to Jesus' invitation: 'Go, and do not sin again'.

In Swidler's reading, Jesus is presented as the 'perfect man' (Schüssler Fiorenza 1995: 42) or 'knight in shining armour' (Schottroff 1995: 14) who rescues the woman in distress. Yet, as Schüssler Fiorenza has convincingly shown, such a view is firmly inscribed within the sex/gender system which holds sway in the West and actually encourages women's continuing subservient relation to men: 'Stories about Jesus the liberator continue to function for religiously inculcating feminine romance attitudes and to legitimate kyriarchal relations of dominance and submission' (1995: 42).

Furthermore, Swidler's interpretation, as Judith Plaskow has pointed out, is guilty of anti-Judaism. It reproduces (and actually establishes) the antithesis which has beset feminist biblical studies: 'Judaism equals sexism, while Christianity equals feminism' (Plaskow 1994: 119).[4] Disregarding the fact that all the actors in this drama are Jews, and that Jesus is depicted 'simply as a Jewish man that treated women like people' (Plaskow 1994: 119), Swidler paints Jesus as liberating the woman from the sexist and death-dealing intentions of the Torah and its interpreters. 'The claim that "Jesus was a feminist"', concludes Plaskow,

4. For a discussion, see Schüssler Fiorenza (1995: 67-96).

'can be argued persuasively only on the basis of a negative view of Judaism' (1994: 119).

I shall now turn to Schottroff's more recent treatment of the woman taken in adultery which, while welding together various interpretative strategies, aims primarily to restore women to their rightful place in the social history of early Christianity. Along with Swidler, Schottroff employs the tools of historical-critical scholarship. These, however, have been sharpened and modified, on the one hand, by her feminist analysis of patriarchy understood as a hierarchical 'system of domination', and on the other hand by her theological option for a 'gospel of the poor' (1995: 22). Rather than recovering the Jesus of history, then, Schottroff is concerned with restoring women to history and specifically to early Christianity. This is because '[t]he visions of early Christianity are a source of strength for the struggle for justice, including the feminist struggle of women' (1995: 42). The text can become a source of strength, or in Schottroff's view, 'God's word', precisely because it witnesses to a God who, beginning with the last, opts for the poor and struggles with them for justice (1995: 45). A christocentric interpretation of the Second Testament such as Swidler's, which reads Jesus as the divine male hero, is thus ruled out as both 'anti-Judaistic and hostile to women' (1995: 36). Indeed, Schottroff is acutely conscious of the anti-Judaistic nature of much New Testament scholarship. She seeks to eradicate anti-Judaism in her own work by three main moves. First, rather than considering the Jesus movement a 'renewal movement within Judaism', she sees it as a 'Jewish liberation movement within the Pax Romana'. This not only shifts the focus from a Judaism which presumably needed renewing to a movement which struggled for the liberation of the Jewish people from the imperial power of Rome, but also enables her to distinguish between different types of patriarchy and their inscription in the New Testament. Secondly, rather than distinguishing between the concepts of Jewish and Gentile Christianity which Schottroff regards as anti-Judaistic and Eurocentric, she prefers to speak of 'messianic communities within the Jewish diaspora' (1995: 14). Finally, as I shall subsequently consider, Schottroff sets her reading firmly within the literary history of Israel.

Putting to one side for a moment the other interpretative strategies brought into play by Schottroff, let us turn to her reading of the social historical aspect of the pericope. For Schottroff, it is not so much Jesus who is caught in a trap, but the woman. The declaration of the scribes and Pharisees—'This woman has been caught in the act of adultery' (Jn 8.4)—leads Schottroff to consider the question of witnesses required by the law (Deut. 19.15; Num. 5.13), and the likelihood that these witnesses had been deliberately planted: 'We must conclude that the woman was trapped, a procedure that has been used for ages to convict women of adultery' (1995: 181). This text, then, centres on one of the ideological mainstays of patriarchy: male control of women's sexuality (Schüssler Fiorenza 1995: 38).

Adultery, considered an offence against the husband to whom the woman's sexuality legally belonged, thus strikes at the heart of the patriarchal social order. In the case under discussion, not only is the patriarchal law accepted by the narrator (v. 3) but, insofar as the woman was trapped and the man involved was not likewise brought to Jesus, we have a misuse of that law. '[W]e must assume that the text reflects a social praxis of getting rid of women by means of accusing them of adultery' (Schottroff 1995: 181).

Schottroff's interpretation of this episode allows us to glimpse a Jesus who, by breaking with the male bonding necessary for the maintenance of patriarchy, takes a stand against the patriarchal order. Schottroff construes Jesus as refusing to identify with the male collectivity that insistently demands the woman's death. He refuses to condemn the woman and to take part in the stoning. He thus 'refuses the role of a Jewish male who restores the honor of a people injured by a woman's adultery' (1995: 184). This interpretation, then, sees Jesus as deliberately undermining (vv. 6 and 8) one of the linchpins of patriarchy: male control of women's sexuality and reproduction. Theologically, Jesus' response to the reiterated request of the scribes and Pharisees: 'Let him who is without sin among you be the first to throw a stone at her' (Jn 8.7), has the effect of putting 'adultery on the level of all other trespasses against God's will' (1995: 185). Although this pericope continues to consider adultery a sin, it is no longer regarded as a capital crime. In other words, the woman's adultery is put on the same level as other male trespasses against God's will. By failing to comply with patriarchy's requirements voiced by his male opponents, Schottroff understands Jesus' behaviour as an instance (as we shall see in Section 3, below) of God's siding with a debased woman.

How, then, does Schottroff deal with the charge of anti-Judaism? In the first place, she points out that the legal position of an adulterous woman under Roman law was worse than in Jewish legislation. Roman law, in fact, contemplated the immediate murder without trial of the allegedly guilty woman. Furthermore, the scribes and Pharisees, she argues, should not be seen as representatives of all scribes and Pharisees; rather, they 'stand for all agents of this form of killing women' (1995: 182), representatives not so much of Judaism as of patriarchy. Finally, Jesus' stand against the stoning of the woman was not levelled exclusively at the Jewish form of patriarchy, but also at the patriarchal order upon which Rome itself was built. Schottroff concludes that readings that focus on Jesus' concern for the woman as a person (such as Swidler's, which I have considered) fail to grasp the basic injustice at the heart of the episode. In their own concern for patriarchal law and order, they are forced to mitigate Jesus' radical stance. While early Christianity (even without the benefit of twentieth-century feminist analysis) rightly perceived '[t]hat stoning an adulterous woman constitutes a patriarchal-legal injustice like the crucifixion of Jesus' (Schottroff 1995: 197), the text's history shows that the early Church was unwilling to draw the revolutionary consequences of Jesus' praxis.

We have seen that one of the aims of restoring women to biblical history is to provide contemporary (presumably Christian) women with conversation partners, women with whom they can identify. We might even surmise that the sparse attention paid to this episode by feminist scholarship is because the 'woman caught in adultery' does not commend herself particularly well as a role model for contemporary women. Two brief readings, however, do take this approach. While one owes its insights to the experience women readers bring to the text (and will thus be considered in Section 2, below), the other by Sharon Muhlenkort (1987) revolves around an imaginative reconstruction of the so-called adulterous woman's encounter with Jesus.

Muhlenkort's reading is an exercise in 'creative actualization' and thus belongs to the final step in the feminist hermeneutical process outlined by Schüssler Fiorenza and adopted by Schottroff. In this case it specifically 'seeks to retell biblical stories from a feminist perspective' (Schüssler Fiorenza 1984: 24).[5] This reading, originally a homily given by the author at the Franciscan School of Theology at Berkeley, suggests that the 'adultery' or sexual act in which the woman was engaged when she was caught had actually been taught to the woman by her father: 'This morning when I was on my way...he wanted to talk with

---

5.   See also Schottroff (1995: 63).

me…and he said he wanted to lie with me. I did what I always do. I did what I learned to do with my father' (Muhlenkort 1987: 13). According to this interpretation, the woman had been made into a 'sex object' long before the scribes and Pharisees got hold of her. Muhlenkort draws the radical conclusion implied by the sort of feminist analysis Schottroff uses: male control of female sexuality is epitomized by the father's sexual access to his daughter. The woman is thus painted as a victim of patriarchy.

The one-to-one encounter with Jesus after the woman's opponents have left the scene is described by Muhlenkort in a rather starry-eyed, romantic way:

> He said 'Woman'. And there was a softening in me, a softening that made me hope he might forgive me. And so I looked up at him—looking into his face. But when I saw his eyes I did not see forgiveness. When I looked at him and he looked at me, I knew that he saw more in me. He saw parts of me that I had never shown anyone. He saw a part of me that I never knew existed. He saw my hope. He saw my ability to love (1987: 13).

In Muhlenkort's creative interpretation of the story, Jesus becomes the catalyst for the woman's consciousness-raising process. By inviting the woman to 'avoid this sin', he enables the woman to recognize that her sin is not adultery, but her own compliance with the patriarchal order. In other words, this woman had introjected the patriarchal definition of woman (as sinful sex object) and had acted accordingly. While she had 'longed for them to throw the stones and to do what I deserved' (Muhlenkort 1987: 13), she was in fact siding with the scribes and Pharisees against herself. The encounter with Jesus, our divine hero who mirrors the woman's own goodness to her, changes her. By addressing her as 'woman' he makes a new self-identity possible, giving her 'the freedom to believe that I didn't have to let them do to me what they wanted'. On this re-reading, then, the woman taken in adultery becomes a role model for women to say no to patriarchy's definition of femaleness: 'We don't have to be what they want us to be any more!' (Muhlenkort 1987: 13).

2. *Women's Experience*

Feminist hermeneutics claim that the oft-touted objectivity of historical-critical methods actually hides the life experience and vested power interests of a select group of men (the masters). The 'new critical para-

digm' advocated by Schüssler Fiorenza thus calls upon biblical scholarship to make explicit its own bias: 'It should become methodologically
mandatory for all scholars to state explicitly their own presuppositions,
allegiances, and functions within a theological-political context' (1984:
62).

Schottroff likewise invites historical criticism to become more critical, 'less critical in relation to the texts of scripture and more critical
concerning today's institutions of domination and their use of the
Bible!' (1995: 49; cf. 57). For its own part, feminist interpretation,
along with feminist theology in general, makes methodological recourse
to what has been called, not unproblematically, 'women's experience'.[6]

This is usually mediated by a theoretical analysis of patriarchy (or, as
in Schüssler Fiorenza's case, kyriarchy) and the way it functions to
oppress, marginalize, discriminate or otherwise disinherit women. Such
an analysis makes us aware, as Schottroff's reading has shown, of the
patriarchal interests inscribed in the text as well as the text's eventual
ability to lead us out of patriarchy. Occasionally, however, women's
experience is brought to the text in a more direct, even corrective, fashion. Schottroff in fact criticizes Schüssler Fiorenza's hermeneutical process for being insufficiently aware of the social context in which interpretation takes place. Schottroff's aim, which builds upon the insights
of liberation theology, is that 'the process of understanding moves from
"life to the Bible"' (1995: 64), and then from the Bible back once more
to life. How, then, does Schottroff use women's experience to illumine
the pericope?

We have seen that Schottroff makes the bold claim that the text
'reflects a social praxis of getting rid of women by means of accusing
them of adultery' (1995: 181). As well as citing Jewish and Roman law
in support of this statement, Schottroff also draws our attention (with
the necessary methodological provisos [1995: 266 n.18]) to the stoning
of Soraya Manoutchehri which took place in Iran in 1990. The account
of the stoning—in which, of course, the woman's own voice is not
heard—brings into focus certain elements of importance for our own
story. In the first place, it is clear that stoning represents a particular and
extreme instance of the male bonding required by patriarchy. The sentence itself is, in fact, pronounced by the woman's father who receives
concrete signs of male solidarity: 'Some men patted him on the

6.   Hogan 1995; Pears 1995; Jones 1997.

shoulder with rough affection, others embraced him, children clung to his clothing. Strong arms took hold of him and lifted him up high' (Schottroff 1995: 183).

The subsequent stoning, which takes place in an atmosphere of mass hysteria, respects a strict hierarchical order: first of all the offended father, then the offended husband, followed by his sons, and finally the imam. The order in which the men leave the scene in the biblical episode, 'beginning with the eldest' (Jn 8.9), may reflect something of the same sort of practice. Next, the execution is carried out in the name of the God who thus legitimates the patriarchal order. With the Qur'an in one hand and a stone in the other, Sheikh Hassan declares: '"It is not I who throws this rock. It is God who guides my arm. He gives me his orders and I avenge our imam for the heinous crime which this woman has committed"' (Schottroff 1995: 183).

In John's account, it would seem that the scribes and Pharisees call upon Jesus to take up the same sort of role. We have seen, however, how Jesus resists such pressure and by so doing attacks their under-standing of God. God the Father is not the foundation of patriarchy but, 'in terms of the text, Jesus, the messenger of God, takes sides with the afflicted and debased woman' (Schottroff 1995: 183). Finally, in the Iranian episode, Soraya Manoutchehri had been buried up to her shoulders in a hole around which a circle had subsequently been drawn. That the woman was put 'in the middle' (Jn 8.3), in fact, indicates that the stoning was about to begin. Schottroff thus draws the conclusion: 'The role of Jesus is, accordingly, that of a Jewish male whose responsibility to God, to the scripture, and to the people is being evoked, at a moment when the woman already stares death in the face' (1995: 184).

Schottroff, as I have mentioned, believes that the text, interpreted through insights gained from 'women's experience' (in this case the stoning of the Iranian woman) needs to return to transform that experi-ence. She says: '*Creative appropriation* must be related to a social fem-inist praxis intent on liberation' (1995: 64, emphasis original). To what contemporary issue does the pericope of the woman caught in adultery speak? Schottroff deals with this question only fleetingly. She argues as follows: patriarchy has at different times and in different places con-sidered adultery a capital crime because it undermines the male control of female sexuality so crucial to patriarchy. In contemporary Western society the fear of accusations of adultery works far less well as a coercive means to ensure that control. This does not mean, however, that women have complete control over their bodies. Women's bodies are still subject to male control (and patriarchy is thus maintained), not by laws condemning adultery but, in Germany at least, by current laws regularizing abortion (Schottroff 1995: 185). 'Why', asks Schottroff, if Jesus did not condemn the woman taken in adultery, 'is it that modern society cannot let go of condemning abortion?' (1995: 202). Not, Schottroff is quick to add, that abortion and adultery do not generate guilt, but as this pericope indicates, 'Jesus separates guilt from the criminal law, and by speaking of guilt at the beginning of new life ['Go, and sin no more'] he empowers the woman to live with existing guilt and walk in new ways' (1995: 202).

Schottroff uses one aspect of 'women's experience' to illumine realistically (and painfully) the machinations of the scribes and Pharisees described in our text. Gay Redmond, by contrast, allows contemporary women's experience to help us understand and redefine what happened to the woman who was presumably caught in adultery. At the same time, the reading she presents allows (some) women to identify with the woman of our pericope. Redmond's reading is, in fact, the account of a 'subversive bible study in a Christian base community of women' (1993: 26). Redmond, true to liberation theological form, begins her account by outlining something of the context in which the Bible study took place—a home for unwed pregnant women in Honduras. These women, she explains, have been forced into prostitution by poverty. When the women become pregnant both they and their children are regarded as non-persons by the male-dominated society. Redmond 'hears some of these women into speech' around the episode of the woman caught in adultery. Three aspects of her account are important and they all hinge on the women's identification with the woman caught in adultery. Angelina, from her own experience of being sexually abused by the young men of the household in which she was working, implies that the woman in the pericope would neither feel nor actually be guilty of any crime. It was just something she had done in order to survive. In this resisting reading, the woman caught in adultery is seen as a victim of the poverty that patriarchy engenders. 'The woman in the temple should not be called an adulteress', claims Elvia, picking up this theme; she is simply a 'Jewish woman' (Redmond 1993: 28). The silence of the woman in our episode is also commented upon. When one woman asks, 'Why didn't the Jewish woman speak out and defend herself?', another is quick to point out that all the odds were stacked against her. Just as none of these poor Honduran women had spoken out at the mistreatment she had received, neither had the woman taken in adultery, as she, like them, knew that nobody, neither the religious leaders nor the crowd, would have listened to her. By reading the story of the woman caught in adultery from their own experience, these women now read their own lives in a new way. As Elvia comments: 'The Jewish woman has given me new eyes to see myself as a Honduran woman in the same situation' (Redmond 1993: 28). Specifically, this means that she wants to be dealt with in the same way as Jesus treated the woman in the story and that she too wants to have the same courage as the 'Jewish woman' to follow Jesus. Jesus is thus seen as transforming the individual reality of the woman by intervening in the patriarchal society of his day to stop the execution. Redmond concludes: 'It is from such base communities of poor and victimized women that the power of the gospel can be experienced by all women who gather together to celebrate the good news of liberation' (1993: 28).

The first two sections of this essay have concentrated on the social and historical aspects of the text. I shall now turn to a further strategy adopted by feminist readings of this pericope, what I have termed 'the literary paradigm'.

3. *The Literary Paradigm*

This strategy, while not—at least in the two examples I shall be citing—disinterested in the socio-historical aspects represented by the text, seeks to read the text in terms of its literary paradigm. In other words, it is interested in the way the female figure in the text has been characterized, the literary model on which she has been constructed and the ideological constraints at work in that model. This approach not only recognizes that the 'author's point of view determines the ideological framework of the story even when it seems to be altogether absent from it' (Fuchs 1985: 118), but also recognizes the specifically androcentric nature of that point of view. Athalya Brenner outlines this strategy in the following terms:

> The critic or reader should read a relevant passage closely; identify the type(s) of personality that it describes, define the literary model or convention it follows, and then pay careful attention to deviations, elaborations, and specific details which constitute departures from the basic structure (1985: 81).

If, according to this theory, the literary characterization operative within the text reveals how patriarchy has symbolically constructed woman, fissures within or departures from the paradigm may provide clues to a different vision which leads beyond patriarchy's confines. Schottroff, in fact, classifies the different instances of the literary paradigm (or 'narrative tradition') operative in our pericope in terms of their capacity to sustain or challenge patriarchy: As Schottroff says: 'One should accept on principle that in this narrative tradition, the reestablishing of patriarchal order may be the foremost concern; or else its focus is on its injustice and the critique of patriarchy itself' (1995: 201).

Before turning to this aspect of Schottroff's multifaceted interpretation, I shall consider the reading of Australian scholar Dorothy Lee (1996).

Dorothy Lee chooses to read the text in terms of the characterization of women as 'sinners'. In her study she cites two further instances of this literary paradigm in the Gospels: the woman who anoints Jesus' feet in Luke 7.36-50, and the meeting of the Samaritan woman with Jesus in John 4. We might just note that some scholars consider the story of the woman taken in adultery Lukan in style and that in some manuscripts it does in fact appear in the Third Gospel, immediately after the anointing scene. Reading the woman caught in adultery in parallel with these episodes allows Lee to discover 'striking' similarities between them. These similarities are due to the literary paradigm of the Hebrew scriptures which each story shares: the harlot as heroine described by Phyllis Bird (1989). It is unfortunate that Lee does not outline in greater detail the paradigm Bird detects in the portrayal of Tamar, Rahab and the two harlots brought before King Solomon, preferring instead to give us an account of its sociological background. Lee thus briefly traces how adultery (and consequently the woman taken in adultery) is construed by the law (as a capital crime), by the prophets (the adulteress as an image of Israel's apostasy) and by the writings (the adulteress as dangerous presence threatening patriarchy). Lee provides further background to the paradigm in a brief reference to the honour–shame culture in the ancient world analysed by Bruce Malina (1981). This view claims that the role of women was to preserve, by avoiding 'shame', the honour of male kinship. How, then, does Lee define the paradigm with which she is working?

The dynamic of the harlot-as-heroine paradigm hinges, claims Lee, on the antithesis it creates between the woman's 'moral courage, insight and strength', on the one hand, and her role as 'socially type-cast prostitute', on the other (1996: 2). The same antithesis is present in the characterizations of 'woman as sinner':

> Their literary power resides in the opposition of 'female sexual sinner' and 'paradigm of faith' in the context of an impoverished religious leadership. The implied reader's gendered expectations about sin and faith are thereby overturned and re-aligned (Lee 1996: 2).

According to Lee, the vision which takes us beyond patriarchy is intrinsic to the paradigm itself. How does this work in her reading of the woman taken in adultery? What unites this pericope with the other examples that she cites? To these questions I now turn.

In the first place (and as is to be expected), each woman in Lee's examples is characterized as a sinner. This signifies both the low social status of the woman due to her having irretrievably lost honour/shame as well as her low moral status as 'sexually unclean' (Lee 1996: 4). Furthermore, the adulteress by being dragged into the Temple area where Jesus was teaching has, like the woman who anoints Jesus in Simon the Pharisee's house, overstepped (however unwillingly) the social boundaries which confined women to the private sphere. Finally, the fact that the woman taken in adultery (together with the other examples cited) remains nameless, points to 'her position on the periphery of society, a position that the text sets out to overthrow' (Lee 1996: 7).

Having set up one term of the opposition (woman as sinner), the literary paradigm proceeds to define the other. In the second place, then, male religious leaders epitomize 'moralistic religious authority' (Lee 1996: 7) who as legalists arrogate to themselves the right to stand in judgment. Lee interprets the scribes' and Pharisees' move as an attempt to discredit Jesus as a teacher of the law. Their attempt backfires, however, as Jesus' response, 'Let him who is without sin among you be the first to throw a stone at her' (Jn 8.7), identifies *them* rather than the adulteress as the real sinners while the woman is acquitted. In the third place, then, Lee argues that 'each story contains a pronouncement of salvation bestowed on the harlot-adulteress' (1996: 9). In our pericope, Jesus' words to the woman in vv. 10-11 assure her of forgiveness, a forgiveness made possible as Jesus distances himself (the writing on the ground) from the demands of the religious leaders. Jesus' action, read in the light of 8.31-36, means that the woman is now freed from enslavement to sin.

Lee, therefore, believes that the literary paradigm serves to reverse the characterization of the woman as sinner that Jesus' reaction brings about. Thus, in the fourth place, the woman is seen (in opposition to the religious leaders) as 'perceptive and insightful' (1996: 10). This seems rather more difficult to uphold in our pericope as the adulteress is portrayed as completely passive without the sort of initiative displayed by the sinner in Luke or the Samaritan. However, Lee considers the woman's willingness to wait on Jesus' response after her accusers have departed as a sign of her perceptiveness. Moreover, 'Jesus' final words to the woman (v. 11b) presuppose her receptivity to faith and forgiveness' (1996: 12). In the fifth place, each episode is characterized, according to Lee, by an 'uncompromising christology that undergirds the central point of narrative reversal' (1996: 12). What happens is the following: while the woman is freed of her sinner status so that her former honour status can be restored, *Jesus takes on her own shameful status*: 'Jesus himself loses honour in terms of his world; he makes himself vulnerable to uncleanness, criticism and sexual scandal; his support of shameless women shames him in the male world' (1996: 12-13). Lee's reading thus agrees with Schottroff's insight that Jesus makes a deliberate break with the male bonding that patriarchy requires. She actually claims that Jesus renounces 'identification with righteous male authority' to assume that of the female 'sinner' (1996: 12). The characterization of the woman in our pericope as 'sinner', then, far from maintaining the patriarchal identification of women, sexuality and sin, actually functions to overturn the symbolic (and theological) order on which that identification is based. 'The woman's sexual sinfulness serves not for prurient interest or moralistic denunciation, but rather to deconstruct cultural values through inclusion, reversal and embodiment' (Lee 1996: 15). At the heart of such a deconstruction is the figure of Jesus, who as 'symbol of God' (Lee 1996: 15) engages in the crossing of boundaries which have been constructed in terms of gender.

Lee's interpretation in terms of the antithesis between the woman on the one hand and the scribes and Pharisees on the other is compelling, I believe, if we understand the text as answering these questions: What is sin? More importantly, who is a sinner? Is it the woman caught in adultery and dragged into the Temple before Jesus, or is it the scribes and Pharisees who would condemn her? Lee recognizes the crucial role the crime of adultery played in upholding patriarchal order ('the adulterous wife threatens patrilineage and patrimony…she is a dangerous presence within society…she touches a raw nerve at the heart of patriarchal

society' [1996:3]), and therefore underlines the social consequences of
the woman's adultery: her having lost honour/shame, her marginal
status. It would seem that here patriarchy is seen (and denounced) as an
expression of sin. Lee, however, does not understand the women's
opponents as representatives of patriarchy but of 'moralistic religious
authority'—that is, of sin understood in moralistic and individualistic
terms. While the woman is not condemned on that basis, her opponents
by leaving the Temple one by one silently pronounce their own condemnation. The text, in fact, makes no specific mention of the woman's
faith which would point to an understanding of her sin as a personal,
moral misdemeanour. It would seem, therefore, that the opposition in
the text is not so much between 'female sexual sinner' and 'paradigm of
faith' as between competing notions of sin, an opposition which is
certainly destabilized but (tantalizingly) never finally resolved. In other
words, the opponents in this pericope (the woman and the religious
authorities) are made to bear the antithesis already present in the
literary paradigm itself. If my reading of Lee's interpretation is correct,
two further comments are in order. By describing the scribes and
Pharisees as representatives of 'moralistic religious authority' rather
than of patriarchy, and by understanding their aim as discrediting Jesus
through his attitude towards the law, Lee leaves herself open to the
accusation of anti-Judaism. Furthermore, the antithesis works only, as
Lee is quick to point out, with 'an uncompromising christology' (1996:
12). Is Lee's Jesus only another version of the knight in shining armour
who, by rescuing a damsel in distress, continues to uphold patriarchal
gender arrangements? I think not. If this passage, read through the
literary paradigm of 'woman as sinner', would lead to us to a new,
more nuanced understanding of sin, it would also lead us to a new
understanding of Jesus as boundary crosser, one who in order to overturn the patriarchal social order, is prepared to become a victim of that
order:

> Jesus, the true prophet of this Gospel, uses his authority to step over the
> invisible but impassable boundaries between righteous and sinful, male
> and female, insider and outcast, clean and unclean. This exemplifies the
> revolutionary dynamic of Jesus' coming in Luke (see 1.46-55) (Lee
> 1996: 13).

Lee maintains that Jesus' boundary crossing which 'overturns hierarchies of sin and status, transgressing divisive barriers and restoring
honour to that which is marginalized' is the outworking of that supreme

boundary crossing, the incarnation. While our author fails to draw out the theological implications of this statement,[7] her reference to Mary in Luke's infancy narrative opens up further interpretative possibilities which are developed in Schottroff's reading.

According to Brenner, more than one literary paradigm may be used to characterize any female figure. It will come as no surprise, then, to discover that Schottroff catalogues our text, *together with that of the Samaritan woman and the woman who anoints Jesus in Luke*, as part of 'a broad Jewish narrative tradition that tells of the liberation of debased women as the exaltation of the lowly' (1995: 177). Schottroff cites 14 instances of this literary paradigm which covers Hannah, Tamar, Ruth, Mary and the haemorrhaging woman and focuses on 'one pattern of activity: the struggle for justice for women in a patriarchal society that inflicts gross injustice on women' (1995: 180). Not only does this paradigm make us aware of how patriarchy debases women but it also offers women and men 'options for action'. Schottroff briefly analyses this narrative tradition in terms of the way in which the woman is debased, how the woman helps herself, how men help her, the liberation achieved and whether or not the patriarchal order is sustained (1995: 177-79).

Recognizing the literary paradigm operative in the pericope of the woman taken in adultery enables Schottroff to add one more piece to her mosaic-like interpretation. The suffering of the woman taken in adultery which she has already described is thus in line with other 'debased women, whose side God takes; women who themselves struggle against degradation at whose side is a man as God's representative' (1995: 185). Just as the story of the woman taken in adultery imperfectly fitted the 'woman as sinner' paradigm chosen by Lee, so it fails to adhere perfectly to Schottroff's selected narrative tradition. The woman in fact does nothing, or can do nothing, to help herself. Schottroff chooses to read the episode of the woman caught in adultery alongside the Mary traditions, not only because of their common narrative tradition, but specifically (and perhaps surprisingly) because she believes that they 'both speak to adultery from different perspectives' (1995: 202).

While Schottroff accepts that the 'low estate' to which Mary refers in the Gospel of Luke could bear sexual overtones, she rejects the thesis that Mary's pregnancy was the result of some sort of extra-marital

7.   On the possibility of reading Jesus in terms of the practice of 'passing', see Green (1999) as well as Heyward's seminal work (1984).

relation. What the text makes plain, according to Schottroff, is that while Joseph *thought* Mary was an adulteress (Mt. 1.19), he was in actual fact mistaken (she is not disposed of). Schottroff believes that Mary becoming pregnant without male intervention is a miracle that overturns patriarchal logic according to which Mary's pregnancy must result from an adulterous liaison. The aim of the infancy narratives, then, is to challenge our presuppositions about procreation and male control of the female body and call into question the whole notion of fatherhood so crucial to patriarchy. Thus Schottroff states: 'Given the significance attributed to male procreation in patriarchy and to the role of the father as the pivotal bearer of power in heaven and earth, one cannot call this legend less than daring' (1995: 201).

Schottroff understands the stories of Mary and the woman taken in adultery as examples of the exaltation of women who have been debased by patriarchy. By treating the question of adultery in different ways (the woman is acquitted, Mary is vindicated—her pregnancy is the work of the Holy Spirit), they both call into question the very power-base of patriarchy: male control of women's sexuality. The liberatory power of these stories is not, however, confined to women. Just as Joseph came to believe that Mary was not guilty of adultery and as the scribes and Pharisees were forced to recognize the truth in Jesus' reply, so 'these texts can clear a space in the midst of patriarchy for a liberating praxis of women *and men*' (Schottroff 1995: 203; emphasis mine). I will now turn to the final interpretative strategy which specifically attends to those dynamics in the text which affect its male characters—the scribes and Pharisees.

4. *The Text as Literary Unit*

The strategies employed thus far have all used information external to the text to interpret the passage in hand. Thus, our first strategy augmented the text by enquiring after, for example, the role adultery plays in a patriarchal economy both now and then; the second strategy read the text through specific examples of contemporary women's experience; the third understood it in the light of literary paradigms originating in the Hebrew scriptures. The fourth strategy self-consciously excludes finding 'the interpretative key to John 7:53-8:11 in something outside the given story' (O'Day 1992: 636) and aims to interpret the text by examining its rhetorical shape. Indeed, Gail R. O'Day's study maintains that our pericope has been the object of several malestream misreadings precisely because it has not been interpreted on its own terms. By concentrating on the exchange between Jesus and the woman, the fear of antinomianism, or what Jesus wrote on the ground, interpreters have actually missed the point of the text. All of these misreadings have one thing in common: they presume the 'unlawful sexuality of the woman at the heart of the text' (O'Day 1992: 631). By reading the text on its own rhetorical terms, O'Day hopes to correct such misreadings.

What, then, is the shape of the text? O'Day divides the text into two main parts: the introduction in 7.53–8.2 and the central conflict in 8.3-11. This latter part, the story proper, consists of three scenes: vv. 3-6a in which a question is posed to Jesus by the scribes and Pharisees, and the twofold response offered by Jesus in vv. 6b-7 and 8-11. What commentators have failed to notice, opines O'Day, is precisely the double nature of Jesus' response, first to the scribes and Pharisees and then to the woman. Here we have, in fact, two parallel scenes in which each time Jesus bends down and writes on the ground (vv. 6b and 8), stands up to address his conversation partners (vv. 7b and 10), and speaks (vv. 7c and 11b). The structure of the story, therefore, is not bi-polar, concentrating—as in Augustine's interpretation—on the relation between *miseria et misericordia*, but rather triangular; Jesus is concerned not only with the woman but also with the scribes and Pharisees. By placing 7b and 11b in chiastic relation to each other as in the following diagram,

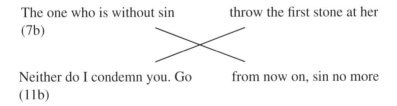

The one who is without sin (7b)   throw the first stone at her

Neither do I condemn you. Go (11b)   from now on, sin no more

the text reinforces its narrative strategy of depicting 'the woman and the scribes and Pharisees [as] social and human equals' (O'Day 1992: 637). This has two consequences, one for the woman and one for the scribes and Pharisees. The first part of the story depicts the woman, as Swidler had noticed, as 'an object on display, given no name, no voice, no identity' who is used to ensnare Jesus; she is 'not a subject but a point of law' (O'Day 1992: 632). By the end of the story, however, and thanks to Jesus' response, she has become a subject, an equal with the scribes and Pharisees. What is for the woman a gain in status must result in a loss of status for the scribes and Pharisees. Jesus in fact will not tolerate their treating either him or the woman as objects, pawns in their own game: 'By writing on the ground and not responding immediately or directly to the questions put to him, Jesus nullifies the presumed control of the scribes and Pharisees and *places them on the same level as the woman* (O'Day 1992: 637; emphasis mine).

Placed on the same level, that is, 'under the power of sin', both the woman and her opponents are invited to respond in the same way to Jesus' action. In other words, they are both invited 'to give up old ways and enter a new way of life' (O'Day 1992: 637). If the 'power of the old ways of life indicts both parties…the possibility of acquittal is also available for both parties' (O'Day 1992: 638). O'Day thus considers this text a story of forgiveness and empowerment which is offered to, and accepted by, both the woman and the scribes and Pharisees.

According to O'Day, commentators have concentrated on the encounter between Jesus and the woman in need of forgiveness, excluding the parallel position occupied by the scribes and Pharisees precisely because they were aware of the social implications of the story. By concentrating on the woman's (presumed) sinfulness, 'the larger questions of Jesus' relationship to the religious establishment and the challenge he presented to the status quo are lost' (O'Day 1992: 634). Commentators (and copyists) thus perceived that 'if the woman and the scribes and Pharisees are treated equally by Jesus, then social re-ordering is required' (O'Day 1992: 636). We might say that the history of interpretation has actually reproduced the dynamics of the text: by concentrating on the woman's sinful sexuality, it has continued to objectify women; by placing the woman in the centre of the interpretative temple it has insisted on her condemnation. The time has come, O'Day's reading suggests, for malestream interpreters to recognize their solidarity with the religious establishment represented by the scribes and Pharisees and hear Jesus' call to conversion. As Rosemary Ruether has persuasively argued, the new life to which we are called will follow different trajectories according to the different positions occupied by women and men in the patriarchal social and symbolic order (1983: 183-92). Thus, on this reading, male interpreters who have evinced 'no sense of scandal about the way the story testifies against a male-dominated status quo' (O'Day 1992: 640) should quietly quit the interpretative scene, perhaps beginning with the eldest. This text, then, speaks of the dismantling of patriarchy and the loss of status this will mean for men atop the powerful patriarchal pyramid. No wonder, therefore, that the text has been misplaced and misread.

5. *Conclusion*

In the pericope that I have been discussing, a woman is forcibly dragged into the Temple, a public sphere (as our text makes plain) of male theological debate. The woman remains silent and immobile until, after her accusers have departed, Jesus addresses her and orders her to leave the scene: 'Go!' In the story that I have been telling, the male narrator, transmitter and interpreter of this text—rather than following their forebears' example—have continued to occupy the same domain. Our feminist readers have, however, unlike the woman caught in adultery, refused to remain silent or quit the scene, preferring to occupy the public space of biblical interpretation. The space occupied by the Temple in our text has thus become something not dissimilar to the 'ecclesia of women' posited by Schüssler Fiorenza (1995: 24-31), a rhetorical site in which the multiple strategies of feminist hermeneutics engage each other in mutual conversation. The text which we have been reading together—albeit by no means at the centre of feminist interpretative interests—has, in fact, given rise to a rich, varied and fruitful conversation. Rather than rehearsing once more the principal elements of this 'polyglot discourse', I shall concentrate on the characters which have focused the attention of our different feminist interpreters: the woman, the scribes and Pharisees, and Jesus.[8]

According to Ilona Rashkow, 'readers effect characters who, in turn, affect readers' (1993:112). The character in our text that most eludes such effective reading is the woman herself. In different ways the readings of Schottroff, Lee, Muhlenkort and Redmond all concentrate on the woman, and specifically on the adultery of which she is accused. This, in turn, is considered emblematic of the cornerstone of patriarchy: male control of female sexuality. In all these readings the old adage of the women's movement is underlined: 'the personal is political'. Control of the woman's body thus means not only control of each woman's individual sexuality, but also (as Schottroff's liberationary paradigm

---

8.   While the narrator gets a brief mention in Schottroff (1995: 181), 'the people' (including the possible female elements) virtually disappear in our readings, overborne by the textual presence of the scribes and Pharisees.

suggests) of women as political body. Despite Muhlenkort's reading of the woman taken in adultery as a figure who authorizes (again, presumably Christian) women to withdraw allegiance to patriarchy, this character actually fails to affect our readers. In other words, the woman taken in adultery has been so flattened by this text that to date feminist readers have a hard time making her '[take] on an existence independent of the original story' (Bach 1993: 70). Thus, while Schottroff believes that this pericope empowers women (and men) in their struggle for justice, she has to admit that the one element of the narrative tradition important for the case she is making (how the woman helps herself) is missing from our text. Similarly, Lee's—at this point forced—reading of the text also shows that the woman caught in adultery is actually lacking in the faith, insight and perceptiveness integral to the literary paradigm of 'woman as sinner' she has chosen. The problem faced by feminist interpreters is undoubtedly the woman's silence and passivity. The fact that we are told nothing of the woman's reaction to her fate means that 'the narrator has eliminated a direct route of sympathy between the reader and the female character' (Bach 1993: 71). Schottroff tries to build that route drawing on the account of the stoning of the Iranian woman, yet even that account silences the woman. It is possible, then, that the inability of the text's portrayal of the woman taken in adultery to affect feminist readers has led to their inability to effect her and thus to the marginalization of this figure in feminist biblical scholarship. Can any meaning at all be found in her characterization? Schottroff here provides a clue to which I shall return shortly.

In some respects the scribes and Pharisees contend with Jesus for the centre scene in the readings we have been discussing. They are seen as setting a trap for Jesus (Swidler) or for the woman (Schottroff) and, according to both Swidler and O'Day, the story speaks as much to their fate as to the woman's. Indeed, without their initiative (however it is interpreted), we would have no story and none of the different antitheses discerned by our feminist readers. As O'Day forcibly argues, their presence is vital for grasping the social implications of the text, implications which do not escape other feminist readers using different strategies (Schottroff, Lee). As Muhlenkort's imaginative re-telling implies, they are only one element which indicates the patriarchal order running through the story, without which the pericope actually loses its meaning. However they are characterized, the scribes and Pharisees are considered as representing a patriarchal order which rests on the male control of women. That control is exercised symbolically by a religious tradition which identifies deity with fatherhood and sin with woman-hood and socially by legal sanctions (such as stoning). If, as I have suggested, women readers of this story have such a hard time effecting a female character that affects them, that is, with whom they can identify, could the Pharisees and the scribes provide the male reader with a useful role model? This is certainly the outcome of the readings I have been discussing. To resist that reading, O'Day maintains, malestream interpretation has deliberately ignored the fact that both the woman and her opponents are challenged as far as sin is concerned. Both Lee's and Schottroff's readings suggest that at the heart of the episode is precisely the redefining of sin. Men should thus quit proclaiming their sinlessness vis-à-vis women and admit, along with the scribes and Pharisees, their own sinful involvement in patriarchy. The story would invite them to the social re-ordering of which O'Day speaks, to the just relations envisaged by Schottroff. They are invited to set out on their own journey of conversion and follow Jesus in his breaking faith with patriarchy. Paradoxically, then, it would seem that the feminist readings I have been discussing assume more easily the role of the male reader. To resist this reading as a woman may mean to find oneself without a text.

If the scribes and Pharisees are the villains of the piece, Jesus is the king of the castle. O'Day's insistence on the triangularity of the text is appropriate; each character in fact mediates the relationship between the remaining two. There would be no encounter between Jesus and the woman without the scribes and Pharisees, no conflict between them and Jesus without the woman, no resolution of the Pharisee–adulteress opposition without Jesus. For if the scribes and Pharisees get the action rolling, Jesus resolves it. Only his intervention (or non-intervention) creates in the feminist reader's eye the vision of the downfall of patriarchy, the new life possibilities offered to both the woman and her opponents. Yet the figure of Jesus is fraught with problems for the feminist interpreter. When, as in Swidler's analysis, Jesus is set up as a Christian feminist for whom the presumed sexism of the scribes and Pharisees serves as a foil, the reading falls prey to anti-Judaism. When, as in Muhlenkort's (and Redmond's) reading, Jesus is presented as the perfect man who sparks off the woman's consciousness-raising process, patriarchy's sex/gender system is re-inscribed. The question is not so much 'can a male saviour save women?', but 'what on earth would women want a male saviour for?' The question, despite Schüssler

Fiorenza's opinion that feminist theology's concentration on the masculinity of Jesus is misplaced, won't just go away.[9] Schottroff has avoided the first problem by firmly situating the Jesus figure within the literary history of Israel. He thus becomes (we might say) one more instance of God's siding with the debased woman. Yet all the interpretations depend on what Lee terms 'an uncompromising christology' (1996: 12). Does this mean a Christology of the 'knight-rescuing-the-damsel-in-distress' type? I believe that our readings offer some clues to the contrary which might deconstruct the Christ figure of patriarchy.

Let us assume, even as the feminist readings suggest, that this is an androcentric text addressed to the male reader—a man-to-man heart-to-heart, so to speak. Let us even accept Swidler's view that Jesus is an example which men are called to imitate. What does Jesus do? He refuses to comply with the insistence of the scribes and Pharisees that the woman be stoned. He breaks faith with the male bonding crucial to patriarchy. He will not comply with the constraints of the male collectivity based on men's control of women's sexuality. He withdraws loyalty from the social and symbolic dictates of patriarchy and invites his fellows to do likewise. Such a stand is not, of course, without a certain cost. It means, as Lee underlines, relinquishing the honour, power and privileges that patriarchy affords to all men (and to some considerably more than others) in favour of women and other marginalized peoples. It means so identifying with the female victim that he is prepared to take on the cross and effect the crucifixion of patriarchy. On this reading, the crucified Christ, rather than ideologically scapegoating women (as Daly's well-known critique opines), actually shows forth the journey men must take to overcome patriarchy.

The figure of Jesus, then, 'overturns hierarchies of sin and status... restoring honour to that which is marginalized' (Lee 1996: 15). One of the dilemmas feminist theology faces, once the crucified Christ is male, is to make sense of female suffering. While, on the one hand, the suffering Jesus functions symbolically to confirm women and other disinherited peoples in their role of victim, on the other hand, the suffering of Jesus, as male, deprives female suffering of meaning. The feminist readings of our passage may lead us, however, to see in the woman caught in adultery an icon of the Christ. In other words, the boundary-crossing to which Lee refers is not only effected by Jesus. Schottroff in

---

9.   Schüssler Fiorenza 1995: 33-57; Green 1999.

fact writes: 'stoning an adulterous woman constitutes a patriarchal-legal injustice like the crucifixion of Jesus' (1995: 197). Furthermore, in the Passion narrative, Jesus, just like the woman taken in adultery, remains silent. If the crucifixion and the events leading up to it can be interpreted in the light of the plight of the woman caught in adultery with whom Jesus as victim of patriarchy identified (as our readings suggest), then the story of the woman taken in adultery, and particularly her silence, can be interpreted in light of the passion narrative. In other words, if Christ becomes symbolically female to redeem the victims of patriarchy, then the woman taken in adultery becomes an icon of the risen Christ. Schüssler Fiorenza would have none of that, but as I and others have argued, at present there is no place to stand outside the sex/ gender system.

BIBLIOGRAPHY

Bach, Alice
    1993   'Signs of the Flesh: Observations on Characterization in the Bible',
                Semeia 63: 61-79.
The Bible and Culture Collective
    1995   *The Post-Modern Bible* (eds. Elizabeth A. Castelli, Stephen D. Moore,
                Gary A. Phillips and Regina M. Schwartz; New Haven: Yale University
                Press).
Bird, Phyllis
    1989   'The Harlot as Heroine: Narrative Art and Social Presupposition in Three
                Old Testament Texts', *Semeia* 46: 119-39.
Brenner, Athalya
    1985   *The Israelite Woman: Social Role and Literary Type in Biblical Narrative*
                (The Biblical Seminar, 2; Sheffield: JSOT Press).
Brock, Rita N.
    1988   *Journeys by Heart* (New York: Crossroad).
Castelli, Elizabeth A.
    1994   'Heteroglossia, Hermeneutics and History', *Journal of Feminist Studies in
                Religion* 10: 73-98.
Daly, Mary
    1973   *Beyond God the Father* (Boston: Beacon Press).
Fuchs, Esther
    1985   'The Literary Characterization of Mothers and Sexual Politics in the
                Hebrew Bible', in Adela Yarbro Collins (ed.), *Feminist Perspectives on
                Biblical Scholarship* (Chico, CA: Scholars Press, 1985): 117-36.
Green, Elizabeth E.
    1995   'Extra nos? Il contesto femminista', *Protestantesimo* 51: 183-97.

1997   'Riflessioni femministe sulla testimonianza', *Gioventù Evangelica* 162: 10-16.

1999   'More Musings on Maleness', *FT* 20: 9-27.

Grey, Mary

1989   *Redeeming the Dream* (London: SPCK).

Hampson, Daphne

1996   *After Christianity* (London: SCM Press).

Heyward, Isabel Carter

1982   *The Redemption of God: A Theology of Mutual Relation* (Lanham, MD: University Press of America).

Hogan, Linda

1995   *From Women's Experience to Feminist Theology* (Sheffield: Sheffield Academic Press).

Jones, Serene

1996   'Women's Experience between a Rock and a Hard Place', in R.S. Chopp and S. Greeve Davaney (eds.), *Horizons in Feminist Theology* (Minneapolis: Fortress Press): 33-53.

Lee, Dorothy

1996   'Women as "Sinners" ', *Australian Biblical Review* 44: 1-15.

Léon-Dufour, Xavier

1992   *Lettura dell'evangelo secondo Giovanni* (Cinisello Balsamo: Paoline).

Malina, Bruce

1981   *The New Testament World: Insights from Cultural Anthropology* (London: SCM Press).

Moltmann-Wendel, Elisabeth

1987   *The Women around Jesus* (New York: Crossroad).

Muhlenkort, Sharon

1987   'The Story of the Used Woman', *Daughters of Sarah* 13: 13.

O'Day, Gail R.

1992   'John 7:53-8:11: A Study in Misreading', *JBL* 111: 631-40.

Pears, Angela

1995   'Women's Experience and Authority', *FT* 9: 109-119.

Plaskow, Judith

1994   'Anti-Judaism in Feminist Christian Interpretation', in Elisabeth Schüssler Fiorenza (ed.), *Searching the Scriptures*, I (London: SCM Press): 117-29.

Rashkow, Ilona

1993   'In our Image We Create Him, Male and Female we Create Them', *Semeia* 63: 105-113.

Redmond, Gay

1993   'Sin No More', *Daughters of Sarah* 19: 26-28.

Reinhartz, Adele

1995   'The Gospel of John', in Elisabeth Schüssler Fiorenza (ed.), *Searching the Scriptures*, II (London: SCM Press): 561-600.

Ruether, Rosemary Radford

1983   *Sexism and God-Talk* (London: SCM Press).

Schaberg, Jane
    1995   *The Illegitimacy of Jesus: A Feminist Theological Interpretation of the Infancy Narratives* (The Biblical Seminar, 28; Sheffield: Sheffield Academic Press).

Schmidt, Eva Renate
    1994   *Riletture bibliche al femminile* (Torino: Claudiana).

Schneiders, Sandra
    1982   'Women in the Fourth Gospel and the Role of Women in the Contemporary Church', *BTB* 12: 35-45.

Schottroff, Luise
    1995   *Lydia's Impatient Sisters: A Feminist Social History of Early Christianity* (London: SCM Press; Louisville, KY: Westminster/John Knox Press).

Schüssler Fiorenza, Elisabeth
    1983   *In Memory of Her: A Feminist Theological Reconstruction of Christian Origins* (London: SCM Press).
    1984   *Bread Not Stone: The Challenge of Biblical Feminist Interpretation* (Boston: Beacon Press).
    1992   *But She Said: Feminist Practices of Biblical Interpretation* (Boston: Beacon Press).
    1995   *Jesus, Miriam's Child, Sophia's Prophet: Critical Issues in Feminist Christology* (London: SCM Press).

Scott, Martin
    1992   *Sophia and the Johannine Jesus* (JSNTSup, 71; Sheffield: JSOT Press).

Swidler, Leonard
    1971   'Jesus Was a Feminist', *South East Asia Journal of Theology* 13: 102-110.
    1979   *Biblical Affirmations of Women* (Philadelphia: Westminster Press).

Troch, Lieve
    1994   'A Method of Conscientization: Feminist Bible Study in the Netherlands', in Elisabeth Schüssler Fiorenza (ed.), *Searching the Scriptures*, I (London: SCM Press): 351-66.

INDEXES

INDEX OF REFERENCES

OLD TESTAMENT

NEW TESTAMENT

INDEX OF AUTHORS

THE BIBLICAL SEMINAR